T0349998

Praise for *The Rise of Carry*

The Rise of Carry is an important and unusual book. The authors have a unique understanding of what has happened to our economy in the Fed moral hazard era and what makes the current period unlike any of the classic bubbles. The questions they raise are critical not just for investors but for all of society.

JEREMY GRANTHAM, cofounder of global asset management firm GMO

The authors present an amusing and entertaining analysis of the ubiquity of the carry trade in modern finance. Formally, this is an extension of the "speculative" component of the demand for money. Of greater interest for regulators and investors is the notion that all carry trades end in market dislocations.

HUGH SLOANE, cofounder of hedge fund Sloane Robinson

Carry trades aren't supposed to work. But, they are a prominent feature on the international financial landscape. This paradox and other mysteries of carry trades are unraveled in *The Rise of Carry*. Lee, Lee, and Coldiron have produced a thought-provoking, riveting read that shines much-needed light on an important, but neglected, topic.

PROF. STEVE H. HANKE, Professor of Applied Economics, Johns Hopkins University

The Rise of Carry poses a fundamental challenge to both conventional Keynesian and monetarist approaches to analyzing financial and economic cycles. With clear arguments and detailed supporting statistics, the authors show that the combination of "carry bubbles"—which create liquidity and inflate asset prices—and central bank socialization of losses in the wake of "carry crashes"—which do the reverse—requires a radically different analysis of the business cycle. The prevalence of "carry" in virtually all markets has resulted in the evolution of a global monetary system that is perched on a knife-edge between deflation and high inflation, unless a new monetary regime less friendly to "carry" can be introduced. This is essential reading for central bankers, investors, academics, and politicians.

JOHN GREENWOOD, Chief Economist, Invesco

The carry trade has long been a steamroller in front of which currency traders pick up small change. Coldiron, Lee, and Lee describe how this trade has expanded to many corners of the investment world with broad consequences for wealth inequality and financial stability.

RONALD KAHN, Managing Director,
Global Head of Scientific Equity Research, BlackRock

Do you want to look inside today's financial matrix? Do you want to understand why we have strayed so far from our capitalist roots and will inevitably have to face the consequences? *The Rise of Carry* provides the red pill to a system whose grotesque reality will be unmasked through the forces of populism. It isn't an easy read; truth rarely is.

HENRY MAXEY, Chief Investment Officer of asset management firm Ruffer

Carry trades involve picking up nickels in front of a steamroller. Investors who wish to avoid getting flattened should read this book.

EDWARD CHANCELLOR, author of *Devil Take the Hindmost: A History of Financial Speculation*

THE RISE OF CARRY

THE DANGEROUS CONSEQUENCES OF VOLATILITY SUPPRESSION AND THE NEW FINANCIAL ORDER OF DECAYING GROWTH AND RECURRING CRISIS

TIM LEE, JAMIE LEE, & KEVIN COLDIRON

New York Chicago San Francisco Athens London
Madrid Mexico City Milan New Delhi
Singapore Sydney Toronto

5 6 7 8 9 LBC 28 27 26 25 24

ISBN 978-1-260-45840-4
MHID 1-260-45840-7

e-ISBN 978-1-260-45841-1
e-MHID 1-260-45841-5

Contents

Figures and Tables

Preface and Acknowledgments

THE AUTHORS BEGAN WORK ON THIS BOOK ABOUT FIVE years ago. The original motivation was partly frustration with the inadequacy of standard explanations of how central banks' unconventional monetary policies had supposedly been working to support the economy since the global financial crisis. We recognized that the key was the suppression of financial volatility that the interventions of central banks and governments have engendered. This has become much more obvious over the years since we began to work on this book. But the full implications of the growing dominance of carry trades have yet to be understood.

From a purely financial perspective, the book contains a number of insights. Among the most important are the relationship between volatility selling and leverage and how these together make market dislocations inevitable; the consequence that the economic cycle is now a function of bubbles and busts in risk assets in the context of an overall tendency to deflation; and the manner in which these factors have combined with the centrality of US markets, particularly the S&P 500, to the global market structure, transforming the S&P 500 itself into a carry trade.

Beyond that, we recognized—and try to convey in the book—that at the most fundamental level carry, or volatility selling, is an aspect of the power structure in society as a whole. Central banks should be perceived as agents of this power structure. The conventional understanding of the forces that determine the financial markets and the economy is inaccurate, and accordingly has no hope of shedding any light on the next financial and economic crisis and its consequences.

In the book we explain in some detail the mechanics of carry, or volatility-selling, trades, but our purpose is to explain how these trades fit into and help create the bigger picture: a picture of decaying economic growth, recurring crisis, rising inequality, and fraying of the social fabric. Although some of the finance material may be difficult for non-specialist readers, it is simplified relative to the treatments in textbooks on derivatives or foreign exchange markets. The book is not intended to be an alternative to such textbooks, nor any kind of manual on options or currency trading. A detailed technical understanding is not necessary to grasp our basic conclusions.

We are indebted to Noah Schwartzberg and the team at McGraw-Hill Education for their help, support, and enthusiasm for and belief in this project. We have also benefited from advice and comments on the manuscript that have helped us improve the finished work. We would particularly like to thank Ivan Nurminsky, Caroline Lee, and Jae Sang Shim. We are grateful to Professor Steve Hanke, John Greenwood, Edward Chancellor, John Authers, Henry Maxey, Hugh Sloane, Jeremy Grantham, and Ron Kahn for kindly agreeing to read the manuscript and offer their comments or endorsement. We are especially thankful to Hilda Lee and Jody Brettkelly for their patience and encouragement.

Tim Lee
Jamie Lee
Kevin Coldiron

1 Introduction—The Nature of Carry

WHY HAVE STOCK MARKETS, OVER THE PAST 25 YEARS, EXPErienced huge rises and crashes? Why did the US stock market, in particular, quadruple over the years following the 2007–2009 global financial crisis even though US economic performance was at best so-so? Why do companies keep buying back their own shares rather than making real investments? Why do professional stock market investors and traders hang on every word that central bankers utter? Why does it seem that everyone wants to live in the big, overcrowded global cities, such as London and New York, even though new technology supposedly allows us to live and work almost anywhere? What explains the rise of populist political movements?

Needless to say, any attempt to answer all these questions thoroughly would require a much longer book than this. But the starting point to answering them requires a perspective through the narrow prism of financial markets. The behavior of financial markets today is not, as is commonly believed, some function of the economy or interest rates or the result of political developments. It is a manifestation of the rise of carry, or the suppression of financial volatility. The rise of carry can be understood as part of a much broader phenomenon, with implications for all aspects of human affairs, but its expression in financial markets alone has had profound consequences for the world.

What Do We Mean by "Carry" and "Carry Trades"?

Carry trades make money when "nothing happens." In other words, they are financial transactions that produce a regular stream of income or accounting profits, but they subject the owner to the risk of a sudden loss when a particular event occurs or when underlying asset values change substantially. The "carry" is the income stream or accounting profits the trader earns over the life of the transaction. In this sense carry trades are closely related to selling insurance, an activity that provides a steady premium income but exposes the seller to occasional large losses. The classic finance carry trade takes place in the foreign exchange market, when a trader borrows in a low interest rate currency and invests the proceeds in another, higher-yielding currency. If "nothing happens"—that is, the exchange rate does not change adversely or changes by less than the interest rate differential—the trade is profitable. However, when things do happen, when exchange rates or asset prices move against the carry trader, losses can mount suddenly and substantially.

A significant part of this book is devoted to explaining these trades, particularly in the currency and the stock markets. One conclusion is that the greater liquidity and breadth of financial instruments in the US markets, as well as the dollar's role as the global reserve currency, has placed the US markets, and specifically the S&P 500 index, at the center of the global carry trade. A further purpose of the book is to convey how carry has come to dominate the global business cycle, creating a pattern of long, steady, but unspectacular expansions punctuated by catastrophic crises. The growth of carry—the development of a "carry regime"—has had major implications for the distribution of income and wealth. In the view of the authors, these processes and mechanisms have not been recognized or understood properly, even by those economists who focus on the links between power and the distribution of wealth and income.

The Characteristics of Carry Trades

Carry trades matter because they have now spread far beyond their origins in currencies (and commodities) to every corner of the financial markets. Carry trades share particular risks, and those risks are becoming the core driving forces of global financial conditions. Since central banks react to these conditions, global monetary policy is increasingly driven by the effects of carry and, as we will demonstrate, contributes to its further growth in a self-reinforcing dynamic. We will ultimately explain how this process is transforming capital markets and wealth distribution. To begin to understand this process, we must first start with a simple explanation of the characteristics of carry.

In this book we define all carry trades to share certain critical features: leverage, liquidity provision, short exposure to volatility, and a "sawtooth" return pattern of small, steady profits punctuated by occasional large losses. These characteristics are very important, because as carry has grown in size, these very features have begun to define financial markets themselves.

Carry by our definition always involves leverage. This means that carry traders either explicitly use borrowed funds or else utilize some set of contracts that creates a potential risk of loss greater than the amount of capital initially employed in the trade. This makes carry traders, and the people that lend them money, especially sensitive to losses. In an attempt to avoid losses, which can potentially be unlimited, carry traders are often forced to close positions when prices move against them. This necessarily means selling assets that are falling in price (or buying assets that are rising in price). Thus, the dynamics of managing carry trade risks create fire-sale effects in which initial movements in prices are often substantially amplified.

The expansion of carry trades always increases liquidity; the reduction or closing of carry trades leads to liquidity contraction. "Liquidity" can be a slippery concept, and the word is typically used in two ways. From a trading perspective, liquidity refers to the ease of transacting. An asset that is liquid can be traded quickly and cheaply and in sizable amounts. When carry trading expands in a certain asset class, that asset becomes, or at least appears to become, more liquid. There is also a volume perspective; from this perspective, liquidity refers to the amount of money or money-like instruments in an economy. From this viewpoint, liquidity is related to the ease of obtaining credit and the availability of money in the economy, which is a fundamental driver of economic growth over the business cycle. The growth of carry thus means an easing of money and credit conditions and, since the availability of money and credit stimulates the economy, temporarily improved economic performance. By contrast, asset marketability, money, and credit conditions and the economy as a whole deteriorate suddenly and substantially during carry crashes.

Carry trades are "short volatility." This means they benefit from falling levels of variation in financial asset prices. More concretely, carry trades will provide a positive return above the risk-free rate as long as the volatility of the underlying asset, currency, or commodity price does not end up being higher than expected. Indeed, there exists a range of sophisticated carry trades that use financial derivatives to gain an income that depends directly on a relative lack of volatility of the underlying asset prices.

Carry trades can include everything from undertaking classic currency carry positions, writing insurance or selling credit default swaps, buying higher-yielding equities or junk debt on margin, taking out buy-to-rent mortgages to finance property investments, to writing put options on equities or equity indexes or buying exchange-traded funds that do so—but that is not all. Carry trades can also include dealings such as companies issuing debt to buy back their own equity or private equity leveraged buyouts, plus a whole gamut of more complex financial strategies and financial engineering. In all cases the carry trader is either explicitly or implicitly betting that changes in underlying capital values will not wipe out his or her income return; the carry trader is betting that underlying asset price volatility will be low or will decline.

The final feature of carry trades is their sawtooth return pattern. Profits typically accrue in a fairly smooth fashion, but they are punctuated by short periods of sharply negative returns—carry corrections or crashes. It could be argued that this pattern is not an independent characteristic but must follow naturally from carry's other features. While there is truth to this, we will show that the pattern of returns in itself is very important, as it attracts capital into carry from participants whose compensation is driven by short-term performance. Oftentimes these carry traders do not have the balance sheet strength to survive a crash, and their presence is a significant destabilizing force in global markets.

Central Banks' Role in Carry

Different forms of financial carry have always been central to modern financial systems. Banks do it. They take demand deposits on which they pay a low interest rate—because the deposits are liquid, they can be withdrawn at any time—and make longer-term loans at a higher interest rate. Insurance companies do it. They take premiums by assuming risks. Why is there anything wrong with this? In this traditional financial sense, as well as with liquidity provision, carry can be seen as being associated with risk pooling. Banks and insurance companies have the balance sheets to pool risk, and they perform an economic function in doing so. In the case of banks, the central bank stands behind them as an ultimate backstop, able to provide liquidity in the case of a run.

A problem arises, however, when traders or institutions that do not have the balance sheet to withstand a major crash nonetheless engage in carry. In theory, an appreciation for the risks of carry should keep those with weak or unsuitable balance sheets out of the market. This is where the trademark pattern of carry returns plays a role. If a carry crash has not occurred for a substantial period of time, carry trades appear very attractive. Competition for returns will tempt, or even force, some market participants into carry trades. Since expansion of carry trading is associated with increased liquidity, then as new entrants establish positions, financial markets will experience an excess of liquidity and credit. Then, during the inevitable carry crash, this liquidity and credit will contract quickly.

This dynamic, especially the sudden reduction in liquidity and credit, will have negative consequences for the real economy. As asset prices fall and liquidity contracts, central banks act to stabilize markets. Of course, stabilizing markets means reducing volatility, which acts to limit losses on carry trades. Thus, the full extent of carry losses is never felt, and this allows at least some carry traders, who should have been wiped out, to survive. Those that survive are almost always insiders with enough political and financial clout to either influence government policy or react very quickly to it.

There is an additional, less understood but very important, consequence of this practice that leads over time to a gradual increase in wealth inequality. Wealthy investors with strong balance sheets—those that in theory should be natural participants in carry trades because of their ability to withstand crashes—also benefit from central bank stabilizing actions because they do not end up experiencing the full extent of the carry crash. While their financial strength means that they could have survived the crash, central bank intervention nonetheless saves them money, helping them accumulate still greater resources in the recovery that follows. Meanwhile, smaller investors can get wiped out or suffer a catastrophic loss of wealth in the crash.

Thus the role of central banks is central to the growth of carry. Carry trades provide liquidity and credit to the real economy. Central banks in their role of lenders of last resort and, at least in the United States acting to maximize employment, underwrite some of the losses associated with carry. This encourages further growth of carry, and a self-reinforcing cycle develops.

Long term, this leads to three critical outcomes. First, it makes prospering in financial markets less about competence and more about insider status, as insiders with weak balance sheets are able to survive carry crashes thanks to central bank action. Second, it reinforces wealth inequality by truncating losses for already wealthy investors who do not necessarily need, but nevertheless benefit from, action to suppress volatility. Last, the distinction between economic recessions and financial market downturns becomes increasingly blurry. Recessions no longer cause severe asset price declines, or bear markets; they are a function of the asset price declines.

Very few people have grasped this. Investors, economists, financial commentators in the media, and policy makers continue to think that an economic recession must have purely economic causes or must be caused by proximate policy or regulatory failures, and they think that financial markets then reflect the recession. We argue that the reality is that the S&P 500 itself has become central to the carry regime in global financial markets; a stock market crash does not signal recession—it is the recession. The cycle of carry bubble and carry crash and the economic cycle have become the same thing.

Over time this gives rise to a ratchet process, through which carry trades become an ever-larger and more dominant force over the economy, and the necessary central bank and government intervention to halt and reverse consequent carry crashes and associated economic crises becomes correspondingly larger also. The financial structure, indeed the entire nature of stock markets and financial markets as a whole, evolves to become one that exists primarily to take advantage of carry trades and central bank or government intervention. Since carry always involves leverage, its continual growth leads to an accumulation of debt that makes this a fundamentally deflationary process—as long as it goes on—despite the enormous rise in asset prices that is a corollary of the carry bubbles. The rise in asset prices during the carry bubble phase acts to keep deflationary pressures at bay, and then the carry crash manifests as a "deflation shock." We define this ongoing evolution of the financial structure to be the "carry regime."

In the limit it becomes more obvious that this must fundamentally be a wealth-destroying process. The wealth that is made by the financial players (and businesses and individuals) who are implementing carry trades is not real wealth of the sort that derives from an economy's greater ability to produce better goods and services that the general population needs and desires. On the contrary, it causes financial asset prices to become hopelessly distorted, unhinged from the real economy, and therefore ends up misdirecting scarce capital into potentially unproductive uses. Over time, the economy will perform progressively more poorly, with income and wealth more and more concentrated in a few hands.

Nevertheless, it is also important to realize that the carry regime, as it progresses, fundamentally weakens the true power of central banks (and by extension governments). This may seem counterintuitive, but as with regulatory capture, central banks are themselves "captured" by carry. During the intensely deflationary carry crashes (such as occurred in 2008), they appear to have no option other than to increase moral hazard further, via even greater intervention and bailouts. In one of the various seemingly contradictory aspects of the carry regime, central bankers seem to have enormous power—their extraordinary power to create high-powered money, set short-term interest rates, and strongly influence financial markets with everything they say—but ultimately they themselves have little latitude to act. Central banks become merely the agents of carry. Their seeming immense power is, in reality, mostly illusory.

The ultimate, perhaps slightly unpalatable, conclusion from this book would be that in our present system, carry, volatility selling, leverage, profits, liquidity, and power are all very closely related, in the limit actually converging to the same thing. The economic system is developing toward one in which the "wealth," or market value, of any individual or individual entity is much more related to access (to the source of power) than it is to talent, merit, or more importantly the value of the individual or entity in terms of his, her, or its ability to contribute to increased living standards for society over time.

Today, the rise of carry is heading to some kind of zenith. No one can know what lies on the other side, but at the end of the book we make some general observations, at least with regard to the financial and macroeconomic arena. There is no hope of beginning to understand the future until the full importance of carry is understood.

2

Currency Carry Trades and Their Role in the Global Economy

Currency Carry Trades

THE MOST WIDELY UNDERSTOOD FORM OF CARRY TRADE is the currency carry trade. Indeed, in much financial commentary the term "carry trade" is synonymous with "currency carry trade." If a speculator were to implement a simple currency carry trade, he would borrow in a low interest rate currency and invest the funds borrowed in a high interest rate currency. He collects the difference in the two interest rates, or the interest rate spread, which is his income from the trade.

The risk is that the high interest rate currency depreciates in value against the low interest rate currency, and the capital loss on the currency depreciation ends up being greater than the income the speculator earns from the interest rate spread. This risk can be understood in terms of the volatility of the exchange rate. If the exchange rate for the currency that he invests in against that which he borrows in is volatile, the chance will be greater that a loss in value of the high interest rate currency in terms of the low interest rate currency outweighs his net interest gain.

The world of currency markets can be broken down into low interest rate currencies that tend to be "funding currencies"—that is, currencies that are attractive to borrow in to finance carry trades—and high interest rate currencies that are "recipient currencies"—that is, currencies that seem attractive to invest in to benefit from their high interest rates. Over the past 20 years or so, the most important funding currencies have been the US dollar, Japanese yen, Swiss franc, and euro. In recent years important recipient currencies have included the Brazilian real, Australian dollar, Turkish lira, and Chinese renminbi.

In a theoretical classical equilibrium model of the economy, currency carry trades should produce a zero return over time; their expected return should be zero, and therefore they should be an unattractive proposition. This is because, at equilibrium, the high interest rate for a high interest rate currency will reflect the expectation of a similarly high inflation rate over time. Conversely, a low interest rate currency would be expected to have a low inflation rate over time. Therefore, the expectation should be that the high interest rate currency will depreciate against the low interest rate currency at a rate in line with the inflation differential, and therefore in line with the interest rate differential, because this is required for the maintenance of the high interest rate country's trade competitiveness.

In theory, forward exchange rates should reflect this expectation for depreciation of the high interest rate currency; there will be no gains to be had from borrowing the low interest rate currency to invest in the high interest rate currency while hedging the currency risk in the forward market. If there were a gain to be had from an unhedged carry trade, then it could be achieved more simply by buying the high interest rate currency in the forward market. A positive return from this simple strategy would accrue if the high interest rate currency does not depreciate in line with the expectation priced into the forward exchange rate.

In practice, currency carry trades have often provided positive returns for long periods—as will be shown by an empirical study in Chapter 4. These extended periods of strong positive returns to carry often end in a carry crash—a crash that often takes the form of a financial crisis for the carry recipient, the country of the target currency. The carry trade capital flow into the recipient currency acts to support it, preventing the depreciation that would be predicted by the classical equilibrium model and very often causing the currency actually to appreciate. In the latter case the carry trader receives not only the interest rate pickup, or spread, on the currency carry trade but also the benefits from the currency appreciation, giving him a strong positive return from the trade—that is, until the carry crash.

Pure currency carry trades should, in theory, be unprofitable over time if markets are efficiently priced, but the trades can look very profitable if it is believed that central banks will try to slow or prevent currency adjustments that would otherwise occur. Central bank intervention potentially gives the carry trader the time and ability to exit the trade with much of his interest rate spread pickup intact. The presence of central banks in the foreign exchange markets potentially dampens currency volatility, therefore reducing the risk to the speculator implementing a currency carry trade.

The concept of a currency carry trade is fairly easy to understand in principle. In practice it is often difficult to define whether a particular transaction or financial structure actually constitutes a currency carry trade. If a hedge fund borrows a large sum in a low interest rate currency such as the US dollar or Japanese yen in order to finance a holding of a high interest rate bond such as a Brazilian real or Turkish lira bond, then this is obviously a currency carry trade; it has the classic elements of leverage and the intention to earn a (levered) positive income return from a currency mismatch. But what about the case, for example, of a Brazilian company, operating in a high interest rate currency (Brazilian real), which chooses to borrow in a low interest rate currency, such as US dollars, to finance an investment project that, if successful, could generate some revenues in US dollars and some in Brazilian real?

This second case is obviously less clear-cut. To the extent that the project could generate some US dollar revenues, it could be argued that financing in dollars does not constitute a currency carry trade; dollar earnings will be available to service US dollar debt. But what if the dollar earnings end up being disappointing or nonexistent? This example helps illustrate that currency carry trades cannot be identified precisely from data alone; the motivation of the speculator or investor is quite crucial to knowing in reality whether a particular transaction or financial structure is a carry trade or not.

The authors consider a currency carry trade to be any transaction or structure in which an investment in or holding of an asset in one currency with a relatively higher prospective yield is financed by borrowing in a different currency with a lower interest rate. This would encompass, for example, nonfinancial businesses in high interest rate emerging economies financing domestic investment by borrowing in dollars or other lower interest rate currencies. It would not include, though, all cases in which an investor in one country uses her savings to buy an asset in another country and currency to earn a higher yield (Japanese institutions and investors, for instance, have commonly done this). This latter case does have the characteristic of currency risk, which is common to all currency carry trades, but it does not involve leverage.

A very important theme we return to later in this book is that carry is closely associated with leverage, and therefore with credit, and with the flip side of credit—debt. At the macroeconomic level, the apparent disregard of currency risk, or perhaps simply willingness to assume currency risk, that is common to currency carry trades will tend to increase demand for credit in the economy for any given interest rate.

Consider the example of Turkey, a country that has had persistently high interest rates. Turkey has experienced periodic crises but also quite long periods of good economic growth and apparent stability. Imagine an entrepreneur in Turkey, during one of those periods of apparent relative economic stability, considering the viability of different investment projects. The rates of return on the different projects look unattractive when set against financing costs at high Turkish interest rates. But if the entrepreneur is used to borrowing in US dollars, at a lower interest rate, and is complacent about the inherent exchange rate risk, then magically the projects can appear viable.

In other words, in this example, complacency about exchange rate risk means that demand for credit within Turkey can be higher for any given Turkish interest rate. By the same token, the carry trade unwind, which will occur if exchange rate risk aversion increases dramatically, will cause overall credit demand to contract, and consequently money will be tighter at any given interest rate. It is usually assumed that, other things being equal, interest rate policy is the primary way that central banks influence aggregate credit demand. But this example suggests that, if carry strategies predominate in investment and financing, a central bank's policy toward the exchange rate—the extent to which the central bank is perceived to be prepared to suppress exchange rate volatility—can have an important influence on demand for credit in the economy.

In turn this creates—potentially large—imbalances in the economy. Turkey over the past decade has been a very good example of this. The carry trade into the Turkish lira (foreign investors and speculators buying Turkish debt because of its high yield and Turkish companies and individuals tending to borrow in dollars to finance domestic investments because dollar interest rates were so much lower than Turkish interest rates) meant huge inflows of capital into Turkey. It also meant a domestic credit boom and an associated real estate boom. The latter tended to draw even more capital into Turkey. The result was that the Turkish lira became very overvalued and Turkey's balance of payments deficit (that is, current account deficit) grew enormously, reaching close to 10 percent of GDP at its peak in 2011.

This situation can only be sustained for as long as the outstanding currency carry trade keeps expanding. The country requires constant new carry trade inflows to keep financing the deficit in the rest of the balance of payments in order to pay for net imports. Once carry trade inflows moderate, then the currency will fall unless the central bank intervenes in the foreign exchange markets and uses its own reserves to support it. At some point the central bank's foreign exchange reserves will be depleted. Therefore, ultimately the currency has to decline.

Once the currency of the carry recipient is falling, currency risk aversion increases; credit demand in the recipient economy weakens, and currency carry trades suddenly look unattractive. Then there is the likelihood of a carry crash; carry trade flows go into reverse, the currency collapses, and domestic debtors who borrowed in dollars or other foreign currency to finance domestic currency investments are left exposed or insolvent, as their domestic currency assets will now be worth much less than their foreign currency liabilities. In the case of Turkey, this all finally happened in 2018 when the Turkish lira crashed in July and August of that year.

The Dollar Carry Trade and the Circular Flow of Dollars

Over the recent decade the dominant funding currency for currency carry trades has been the US dollar. The US dollar–funded carry trade increased enormously following the 2007–2009 financial crisis principally because of the US Federal Reserve's commitment to very low interest rates and accommodative monetary policy, which to most appeared to remove the risk of a strong dollar. Dollar financing, for those around the world who could access it, therefore seemed to be a very cheap source of funds. In addition, the demonstrated willingness of the Fed to provide dollar financing via liquidity, or currency, swaps to other central banks (discussed in depth in Chapter 12) seemingly removed the risk to borrowers that dollar financing might become unavailable if and when financing had to be extended or rolled over.

For reasons already considered, it is impossible to quantify the outstanding dollar-funded carry trade exactly. But because the foreign (non-US) borrowing of dollars involves a cross-border flow, there are many different economic data series that are related to the carry trade, which when looked at together can give a strong clue to its development over time, if not its exact size. These include data for banks' foreign assets and foreign liabilities (picking up foreign borrowing that occurs via the banking sector), other available interbank data, balance of payments (capital flow), and foreign debt data.

In the case of the United States, which has to be the ultimate provider of dollar financing for dollar carry trades, a broad indicator for the carry trade is the net foreign assets of all US financial corporations, data for which are produced quarterly by the International Monetary Fund (IMF). This data series is for net foreign *assets*, not merely net foreign *lending*, and will therefore include equity holdings. To this degree, it will overstate the dollar carry trade, perhaps substantially.

On the other hand, there could be dollar carry trade transactions that are not included in this series because they do not involve claims of US financial corporations. An emerging economy business, for example, could finance a domestic investment by issuing a dollar corporate bond that is bought by a US investor that is not a financial corporation. This would be a dollar-funded carry trade under our definition, but it would not be included within the net foreign assets of US financial corporations. Furthermore, it is unlikely that most US hedge funds are included within "US financial corporations." A US hedge fund could borrow dollars from a US financial corporation (which would be a domestic loan and not a foreign asset for the US financial corporation) in order to finance the purchase of a high-yield (domestic currency) bond issued by a foreign entity. This would clearly be a currency carry trade but would probably not be picked up in the series for net foreign assets of US financial corporations. So this data series includes some things that are not dollar carry trade but excludes some things that are.

Another source of relevant data is data produced by the Bank for International Settlements (BIS) for the cross-border lending and borrowing of internationally active banks. We can look at global banks' net lending to countries that can be identified as significant recipients of carry trade flows. This is done in Figure 2.1 for a group of countries—by no means comprehensive—that have consistently been among those that have been recipients of dollar carry trade inflows. The data are in billions of US dollars.

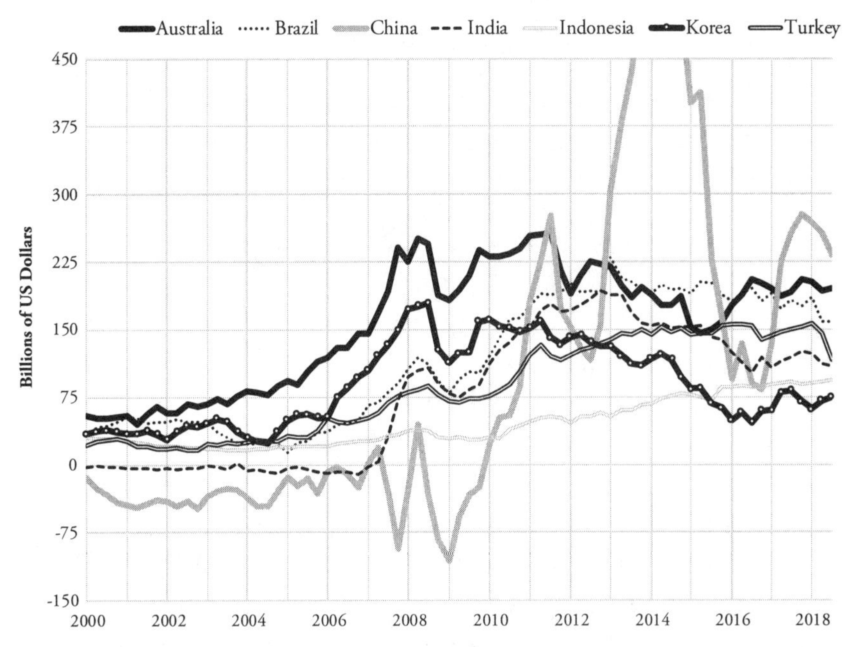

FIGURE 2.1 Global banks' net claims on significant dollar carry trade recipients
Source of data: Bank for International Settlements

Figure 2.2 shows the total for all the countries in Figure 2.1 and compares this total with the IMF series for the net foreign assets of US financial corporations. The two series are of different magnitudes and are therefore represented on the different axes of the chart. But it can be seen that the pattern of development of the two series is similar.

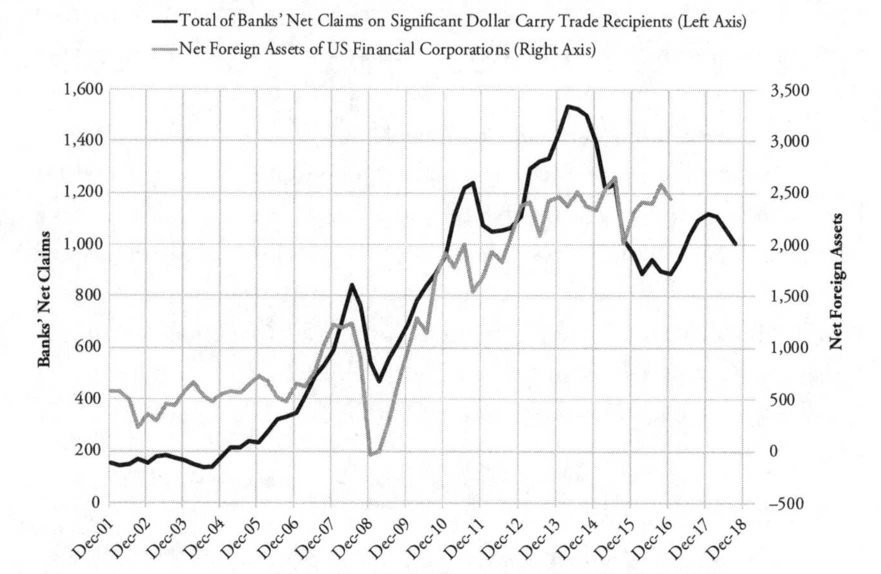

FIGURE 2.2 Indicators of the dollar-funded currency carry trade (US$ billion)
Source of data: Bank for International Settlements, International Monetary Fund

Both of these data series would exclude many dollar-funded carry trade transactions but also include much that would not be dollar carry trade. Global banks' net claims on, or net lending to, the countries shown in Figure 2.1, the total of which is shown in Figure 2.2, must obviously include a great deal that is not related to currency carry trades by any definition. Nevertheless, the two series have moved roughly together. This is circumstantial evidence that they are picking up the cycles—the expansions and the carry crashes—in the dollar carry trade.

These data do not, in themselves, allow us to estimate the size of the outstanding dollar-funded currency carry trade with any degree of accuracy. But other evidence, from balance of payments and foreign reserves data, suggests that the magnitude of the outstanding dollar-funded carry trade, to the extent that this is possible to know, is in the ballpark of the net foreign assets of US financial corporations shown in Figure 2.2. This would mean that the dollar-funded currency carry trade likely peaked at something close to US$1 trillion in 2007–2008 before collapsing to nearly nothing at the height of the global financial crisis in early 2009, only to explode in size again to reach a new peak toward US$3 trillion in mid-2014.

In a paper in October 2018, BIS economists studied how nonbank businesses in emerging market economies were engaging in dollar-funded carry trades, leaving themselves vulnerable to adverse exchange rate movements.[1] According to the BIS economists, the total outstanding stock of US dollar–denominated bonds issued by emerging economy nonbank businesses stood at US$3.7 trillion in 2018, more than double the level of 2010. Again, this is not a measure of the currency carry trade; not all of this debt would be funding for carry trades. But on the other hand, emerging economies do not account for the entire dollar-funded currency carry trade either—although Figure 2.1 suggests that emerging economies are a large part of it. What we can say is that these numbers are of the same order of magnitude as the guesstimates that can be derived from the net foreign assets of US financial corporations and other data.

The interesting thing about the dollar-funded currency carry trade is that the United States is not a natural carry trade funding country because it is a current account deficit economy. In simple terms this means that the United States spends more dollars than its income and thus needs to import capital from outside the country to fill the gap. Dollar carry trade flows involve the exact opposite—capital flowing from the US dollar to fund investment in other currencies.

It would be more natural for a country with a surplus of savings to be a funding currency for carry trades. Japan is one such country, and we will discuss its important historic role in global carry shortly. Japan saves more yen than it invests domestically. This excess savings is a natural funding source for carry trades. Carry traders can borrow from this pool of yen at

1. Valentina Bruno and Hyun Song Shin, "Currency Depreciation and Emerging Market Corporate Distress," BIS Working Papers, No. 753, October 2018.

low interest rates and invest in higher-yielding accounts or assets in other currencies.

The United States does not have a similar pool of surplus savings; in fact, it has a deficit. When carry trade funding activity takes place in dollars, it adds to the funds flowing out of the United States, thus increasing its overall balance of payments deficit. Carry trade activity therefore adds to the amount of net capital that needs to flow back into the country to plug the gap.

Foreigners must be willing to supply capital to the United States—in the form of either equity or debt. As capital flows into the United States, these foreign entities build up a stock of US dollar assets. Since carry trade flows add to the net amount of capital the United States needs to attract, they in effect add to the amount of US dollar assets that foreigners must be willing to hold. This leads to a critical point: the US dollar–funded carry trade has not grown in a vacuum. It has been made possible by a willingness of investors in other countries, notably central banks and sovereign wealth funds, to continually accumulate US dollar assets. The "circular flow of dollars" diagram in Figure 2.3 explains in simple terms how this works.

In Figure 2.3, "Government" refers to governments and central banks together, and "Emerging Markets" are a proxy for the group of countries

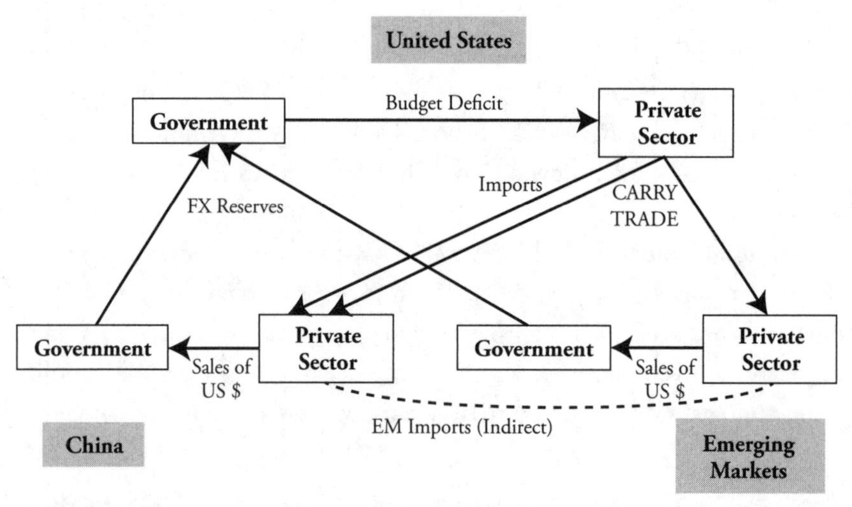

FIGURE 2.3 Circular flow of dollars

to which much of the dollar carry trade has flowed. The diagram is a very incomplete one; it simply illustrates an aspect of the circular flow of dollars, of which the dollar-funded carry trade is a part.

While the United States as a whole spends more than its income, the business sector has positive levels of net savings. In recent years this has been driven by a high level of retained profits relative to GDP. These net savings of private businesses provide a source for dollar-funded carry trades. This can happen in many ways. For example, companies can deposit money in US financial institutions, and these entities can directly invest in foreign currencies or lend the dollars to foreigners who in turn invest the money in higher-yielding currencies. US financial institutions (or US companies themselves) can also buy dollar debt instruments issued by foreign banks or foreign companies. In turn these dollars may be used to make dollar loans to banks and companies in other countries, including emerging economies such as Turkey and Brazil. In the diagram these transactions are signified by the arrow on the right-hand side of the diagram labeled "Carry Trade." These are the flows that lead to the accumulation of global bank net foreign assets quantified in Figure 2.2.

These are carry trade flows because ultimately they represent dollar borrowing, in countries such as Turkey, Brazil, and India, by individuals and entities that are not necessarily generating dollar income or acquiring dollar assets. The dollar funding might be used to buy imported goods, say from China—indicated in the diagram—or it might be used to finance domestic projects. In the latter case the dollars must be sold for domestic currency, because domestic currency is needed for paying for these domestic projects.

If the carry trade is expanding, the currencies of these dollar carry trade recipients will therefore tend to appreciate. The dollars borrowed are being sold to purchase domestic currency. To constrain currency appreciation (to defend their countries' trade competitiveness), their central banks may intervene to buy the borrowed dollars themselves, selling their domestic currencies in return. In the diagram this is represented in the bottom right-hand corner by the arrow between "Private Sector" and "Government" (sales of borrowed dollars to the central banks), and then the arrow from "Government" to the "(US) Government" (the investment of the dollars acquired by the central banks in US Treasuries). Similarly, the dollars acquired by the Chinese authorities also go into US Treasuries. The US government spends the proceeds of its Treasury bill and bond sales, representing its deficit, and the circle starts again.

Since currency carry trades involve credit creation, as the circular flow of dollars expands, global credit is growing. In the above exposition, emphasis is placed on the expansion of credit to the US government (that is, the increase in US government debt that finances the government deficit). But it is important to realize that the circular flow can expand from any point in the circle in a credit-driven fashion.

For example, in the case of Turkey, a US hedge fund might borrow from a domestic bank to finance a purchase of Turkish lira debt securities. This is a pure currency carry trade (given that Turkish interest rates are higher than US rates), and in this case it is associated with an increase in US domestic bank credit. The dollars are sold for lira to buy the debt. If we assume that the Turkish central bank is intervening in the foreign exchange market to prevent the lira rising in value, then the dollars may be acquired by the central bank. The central bank uses the dollars to add to its foreign reserve holdings of US Treasury bills and bonds. So the US Treasury then has the dollars, which finance the US government's deficit spending.

In terms of the US economy, the end result is that bank loans (and therefore money supply) and federal debt have risen; for the Turkish economy, corporate debt and the central bank balance sheet (and therefore money supply) have risen. The end result is the same as if the US government had borrowed from the US bank to finance its deficit, and the Turkish entity's debt had been bought by the Turkish central bank. The only difference in reality is that the interest rate carry—the higher yield on the Turkish entity's debt compared with the yield on US Treasuries (with its accompanying increased risk of a crash)—is being picked up by the hedge fund rather than the Turkish central bank.

But this counterfactual case in which there is no carry trade would be unlikely to happen. The Turkish central bank would be unlikely, in normal circumstances, to buy a Turkish corporate debt security. The US Treasury would not finance its deficit by borrowing directly from a bank. The existence of the currency carry trade—the hedge fund's willingness, in the example, to assume that the lira will not decline by as much as the interest rate differential over the life of the investment—encourages a greater increase in bank credit and money supply than would otherwise be likely to occur.

This is even more obvious in the perhaps more typical case of the Turkish company borrowing in dollars, an example already discussed earlier. In this case, if the Turkish company is borrowing dollars to finance a lira investment that will produce largely lira revenues, then it is the Turkish company that is effecting the carry trade. If the Turkish company's investment would be less viable if it had to be financed out of higher interest rate lira, then the Turkish company is the driving force in the circular flow of dollars. If it issues a dollar bond that is bought by a US hedge fund that, in turn, finances the purchase of the bond from a bank, or if it is bought by the bank itself, then there is, again, an increase in dollar credit and money. The "mispricing of risk"—the assumption that the lira will not depreciate in line with the interest rate differential—results in greater credit and money creation than would otherwise be the case.

The principle of covered interest parity states that there should be no arbitrage profit to be had from borrowing in the lower interest rate currency to invest in the higher rate currency while fully hedging the currency risk. For example, if the interest rate spread between Turkey and the United States is 10 percent, then the one-year forward exchange rate for the dollar versus the lira should be 10 percent higher. An investor can buy lira now and earn a 10 percent yield advantage, but if she wants to hedge perfectly the exchange rate risk, she must agree to sell the lira back into dollars at an exchange rate that exactly offsets the interest rate gain. In other words, there is an interest rate spread implied in the forward exchange rate that should exactly match the interest rates available in the interbank lending market. Furthermore, in theoretical equilibrium, the forward currency exchange rate for any time in the future should be the best expectation for the spot exchange rate at that time.

The growth of a currency carry trade means that, at least for those participating in the carry trade, there is an implicit expectation that the higher interest rate currency will not depreciate to the extent of the interest rate differential. So either the forward currency exchange rate for the carry recipient will be "too high" relative to the interest rate differential—if it reflects that expectation—or the carry traders' expectation for the future spot exchange rate must be above the actual forward rate in the market.

In two other important papers[2,3] by economists at the Bank for International Settlements, published, respectively, in October and November 2016, the BIS economists analyzed a failure of covered interest parity for various currency pairs in the years following the global financial crisis of 2008. They showed that the cost of borrowing dollars via foreign exchange swaps had become higher than for borrowing dollars in the interbank market and that this divergence had become greater as the dollar strengthened from 2014. (In the foreign exchange markets, this deviation has become known as the "cross-currency basis.") In the November 2016 paper, Professor Hyun Song Shin attributed this to banks facing constraints in their balance sheet capacity as the dollar strengthened—given the amount of dollar debt around the world—and therefore becoming less accommodating of currency hedging demands by nonbank institutions; the normal arbitrage between the interest rate implicit in foreign exchange swaps and the interbank interest rate became more difficult because banks were unwilling to execute or finance that arbitrage.

Professor Shin's paper and other work by the BIS highlighted the central and dominant role of the US dollar in the global financial system—the basis for the circular flow of dollars—while the observations about the balance sheet constraints faced by banks help explain the persistence of deviations from covered interest parity. But a further element in the failure of covered interest parity observed by the BIS could be that the implicit cost of carry trade funding in dollars was being forced up by the excessive growth of currency carry trades. This can tie in with the idea that the mispricing of risk implicit in carry trades causes credit creation to be greater than would be the case if the carry trades were not happening. Given that the dollar-funded carry trade—with the circular flow of dollars in the world economy—is dominant, greater demand for dollar funding as the carry trade expands

2. C. Borio, R. McCauley, P. McGuire, and V. Sushko, "The Failure of Covered Interest Parity: FX Hedging Demand and Costly Balance Sheets," BIS Working Papers, No. 590, October 2016.

3. Hyun Song Shin, "The Bank/Capital Markets Nexus Goes Global," November 2016.

might be expected to force the dollar interest rates implied in carry trades above what would be the normal equilibrium.

To return to the Turkey example, the growth of the dollar-lira carry trade following the financial crisis had (at least) two important effects. First, it expanded credit and money growth and, by extension, economic growth and inflation more than otherwise would have been the case given Turkey's high interest rates. This turned out to be very important, causing complacency and eventually leading to a Turkish currency and economic crisis in 2018. Second, it raised the cost of borrowing in dollars to lend in Turkey and thus pushed the implied interest rate differential below a normal equilibrium level.

A Brief (Modern) History of the Currency Carry Trade

We have used Turkey as an example in these hypothetical cases because the carry trade into Turkey was the most persistent of all the currency carry trades, in terms of recipients, over the post–financial crisis period. This is evident from Figure 2.1, earlier. We return to the example of Turkey again, in more detail, in the following chapter.

The Turkish carry trade has been principally dollar funded. But the currency carry trade is not, and has not been, only about the dollar-funded carry trade. Japan, following its financial bust after the Japanese real estate and stock market bubble burst at the beginning of the 1990s, was the first country to experience ultra-low, or near-zero, interest rates. In the earlier years of the rise of the currency carry trade, it was very much the yen-funded carry trade that was dominant.

The notion of a carry crash suggests collapsing values of high-yield bonds and currencies and soaring volatility. This much is true. But for currency carry trades, there are two sides to a currency exchange rate, and if a carry crash means a crash of carry recipient currencies, it is also likely to mean a "melt-up" in the value of the funding currency. The first true example of this was the melt-up of the yen that occurred in early October 1998, at the end of the Asia and Russia crisis and following the collapse of giant hedge fund Long-Term Capital Management (LTCM). Over October 7–8 of that year, the dollar collapsed against the yen by almost 15 percent, much of that melt-up of the yen exchange rate occurring during lunchtime hours in London (beginning of the day's trading in the United States), when the yen moved a number of "big figures" in just a few minutes. At the time this was unprecedented.

That carry crash was the culmination of a currency carry trade, directed principally at East Asian economies, which had built up from the early 1990s and had exploded in size during the mid-1990s. Much of these carry flows occurred via the domestic banking systems of the East Asian countries, and they also can be seen partially in the BIS data for the net claims of globally active banks.

Figure 2.4 shows the net claims of global banks on some of the key economies at the center of the 1990s currency carry trade and on some of the key economies at the center of the post-2009 carry trade. This allows a comparison between the currency carry trade then and more recently, but three considerations need to be taken into account. First, the big global banks are only

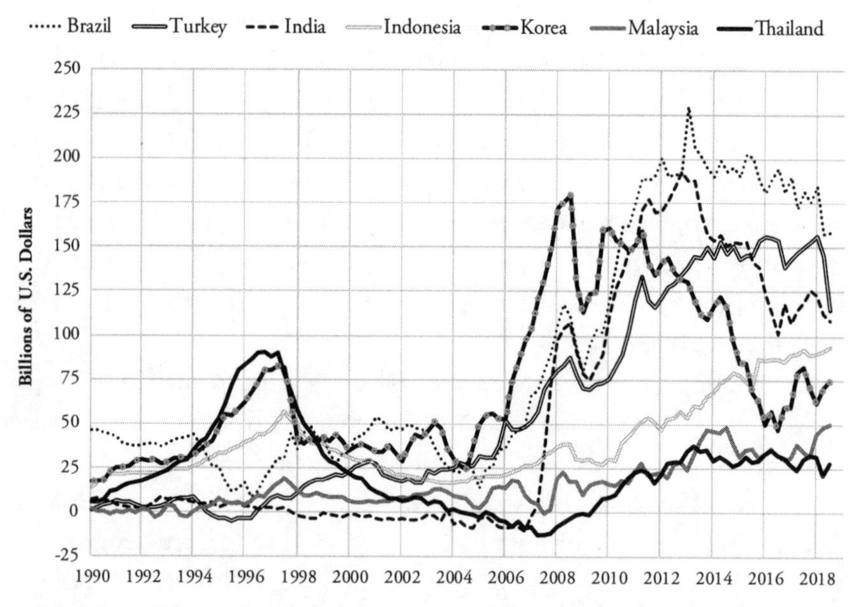

FIGURE 2.4 Global banks' net claims on various carry recipient countries
Source of data: Bank for International Settlements

part of the picture. The domestic banking sectors of the Asian countries were the important channels of carry trade inflows in the 1990s, but these inflows did not all originate from global banks outside Asia. Second, of course, the world economy now is substantially bigger in money terms than it was in the 1990s, and this chart shows nominal dollar amounts (in billions of US dollars). Third, in 1997, the economy of Thailand, for example, was very small, particularly compared with that of Brazil, Turkey, and India today.

So the Asian currency carry trade of the 1990s was big, and yen funding played a part in it. At its peak in 1996, Thailand's balance of payments current account deficit—the counterpart of the carry trade capital inflows—reached around 9 percent of GDP. To put this in context, as recently as the 1980s it had been a consensus among economists that a balance of payments current account deficit of 5 percent of GDP constituted a crisis level of deficit.

The Asian crisis began in Thailand in February 1997 when a Thai property developer defaulted and the Thai baht, which had been pegged to the US dollar, began to come under pressure. The Thai authorities took various measures to attempt to penalize foreign speculation against the Thai currency. But the reality was that once the carry flows had turned, there was no longer the capital inflow to finance Thailand's huge balance of payments current account deficit, and it was inevitable that the currency would collapse—a classic carry crash. The crisis then rolled through the other overly indebted Asian economies, with huge currency collapses suffered by Indonesia, South Korea, and Malaysia.

The Asian currency carry trade was not the only aspect of the 1990s carry bubble. It could be viewed as part of a broader carry bubble across many parts of the global debt and derivatives markets. For example, it also encompassed the debt of peripheral European economies that were anticipated to become part of the euro area. The fallout from that aspect of the 1990s bubble is still playing out today. Greenwich, Connecticut–based giant hedge fund LTCM pioneered the use of complex mathematical models to extract supernormal returns from highly levered carry, or volatility-selling, bets. The culmination of the carry crash in 1998 saw LTCM collapse, threatening—at least in the eyes of central banks—global financial markets as a whole.

In what must be considered a pivotal moment in the rise of carry, Federal Reserve chairman Alan Greenspan directly expressed his concerns about the sharp widening of credit spreads that marked the 1998 carry crash and implemented a surprise rapid easing of US monetary policy that featured three consecutive interest rate cuts within two months, over September to November 1998. The US economy at the time was very strong and in no way justified cuts in interest rates from what were already quite low levels. By doing this, the Fed, for the first time, made explicit that it viewed the stability of financial markets and, in particular, the level of credit spreads to be an express responsibility and priority of the central bank. That action has colored all market behavior since and laid the groundwork for successively bigger carry bubbles. The knowledge that the Fed and, by influence, other central banks stand behind them has made carry traders more confident in their levered bets on low financial volatility.

Yen funding played an important part in the 1990s carry bubble, as confirmed by the yen's spectacular surge in the foreign exchange markets as the bubble burst. But the heyday of the yen carry trade was still to come. In 2002, despite Japanese short-term interest rates at virtually zero, the yen had begun to appreciate in the foreign exchange markets again. The Japanese monetary authorities—the Bank of Japan (BOJ) and the Ministry of Finance (MOF)—were determined to prevent it appreciating too rapidly, because they feared damage to Japan's export competitiveness and the country's chance to regain a respectable economic growth rate. Over a period of just seven months up to March 2004, the BOJ/MOF accumulated well over US$250 billion in foreign reserves in the attempt to prevent the yen from appreciating. At the end of this period, the yen-dollar exchange rate was basically flatlining as the BOJ stood in the market and absorbed all the dollars that yen purchasers wished to sell.

The BOJ's "success" with its extreme interventions to prevent the yen appreciating, coupled with near-zero interest rates, made the yen an ideal carry funding currency, there being very little cost to borrow and very low volatility (thanks to BOJ extreme intervention), with seemingly no risk of appreciating. From 2004 the yen-funded carry trade took off again.

Also, unlike the United States, Japan was a "natural" carry trade funding country, with a large current account surplus. In 2003 the current account surplus was rising to over 3 percent of GDP, on its way to a peak equal to 5 percent of Japanese GDP by mid-2007. With a large current account surplus, by definition there had to be an equivalent capital outflow. Japanese banks played an important role in that outflow via their foreign lending and acquisition of foreign assets, which supplied financing for the yen-funded carry trade. So there was no global circular flow of yen to compare with the circular flow of dollars. Given that the yen is not the globally dominant currency, a global circular flow of yen would be unsustainable. But the yen carry trade was more than simply a recycling by Japanese banks of the Japanese current account surplus; the growth of the yen carry trade was a driving force, making the yen more and more undervalued and consequently helping the current account surplus to become bigger and bigger.

A paper produced by pi Economics in January 2006, titled "What Explains the Persistence of Global Imbalances?" put it this way:

> How can it be then that the yen has recently been trading at 20 year lows in real terms, not just on pi Economics' measures but on most measures of trade competitiveness? It defies the logic of economics, based on rationality, that the market would price the yen to generate an even bigger trade surplus in the future when the prospective path of net foreign assets is already unsustainable based on the current surplus. . . .
>
> The reason . . . is the growth of "carry trades." . . . Since March 2004 banks' gross foreign assets have now increased roughly Yen 30 trillion, the same magnitude as the huge rise from August 1996 to December 1997, the heyday of Long-Term Capital Management. It is worth mentioning that over the period since early 2004 the Korean Won has now appreciated by about 33% against the yen, and at this point is still rising sharply against the yen despite looking increasingly overvalued even against the dollar.

This was written in January 2006, but over the subsequent year the yen-funded carry trade became far larger in size. In a widely quoted paper in

January 2007, pi Economics estimated the size of the yen-funded carry trade to be "well in excess of US$1 trillion," an estimate that subsequently received support from others in the financial community. But even at that time, in January 2007, the yen carry trade was still growing rapidly before it finally reached its peak between June 2007 and October 2008. The exact month of the precise peak is difficult to pinpoint because different possible indicators peaked at different times. What is fairly clear is that June 2007 was something of an inflection point; there was little further increase in the outstanding yen-funded carry trade after that month. In what was certainly not a coincidence, the global financial crisis is normally dated to have begun in late July 2007. The role of the yen carry trade in the global credit bubble that preceded the crisis and the role of its unwinding in the subsequent global meltdown have been severely underestimated or ignored entirely by most subsequent analysis and commentary.

One of those indicators of the yen-funded carry trade, shown in Figure 2.5, is Japanese banks' net short-term foreign assets. This chart refers only

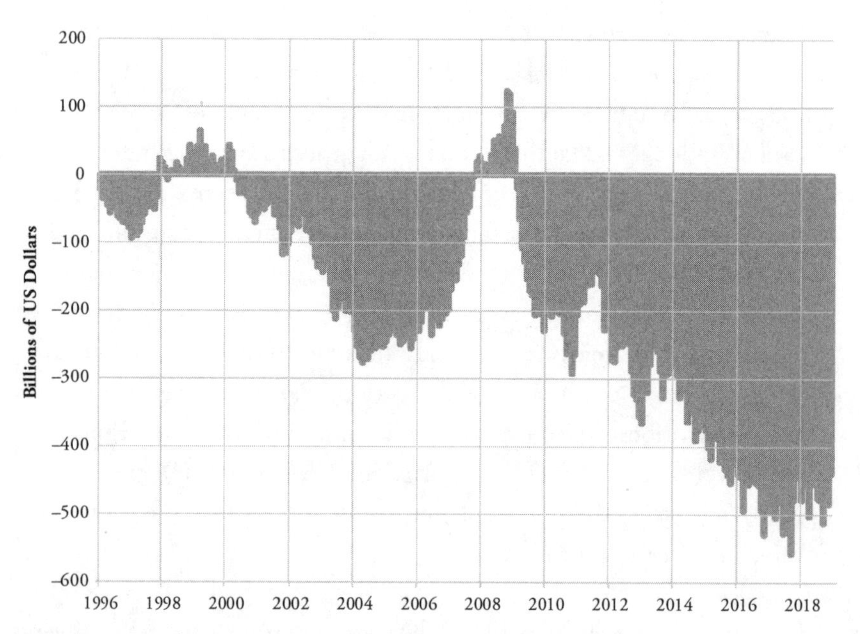

FIGURE 2.5 Japanese banks' net short-term foreign assets
Source of data: Bank of Japan

to short-term *net* foreign assets (that is, foreign assets minus liabilities), and the absolute level is not meaningful as a measure of the size of the yen-funded carry trade. But at the margin, the fluctuations in short-term net foreign assets can be considered as directional indicators for the expansion or contraction of the carry trade. The sharp increase during the global credit bubble, particularly in its latter stages, and then the even sharper contraction during the 2008–2009 global crisis are very clear in the chart.

If, as suggested here, the size of the yen-funded carry trade going into the 2007–2009 global financial crisis was on the order of US$1 trillion–1.5 trillion, then this would suggest that the outstanding yen carry trade was no greater than the outstanding dollar-funded carry trade at the time. This may be true, but the yen-funded carry trade was almost certainly more vulnerable, with yen funding markets being smaller and less liquid than dollar funding markets, and the Bank of Japan by that time being a less activist central bank than the US Federal Reserve. On the currency funding side, the contraction and collapse of the yen carry trade seems to have been a critical development over 2007–2008.

At the beginning of the global financial crisis, the total currency carry trade outstanding seems likely to have been on the order of US$3 trillion. The yen and the dollar were the dominant funding currencies, but there was also a Swiss franc–funded currency carry trade and a euro-funded trade. In May 2007 pi Economics estimated that the outstanding Swiss franc–funded carry trade may have been in the region of US$150 billion, although this was likely to have been an underestimate. Much of the Swiss franc carry trade at that time was accounted for not by hedge funds or financial speculators but by individuals and families in Eastern Europe who had taken out mortgages in Swiss francs because it was much cheaper than borrowing in their own currencies. At the end of 2006, Swiss franc borrowing by Hungarian residents from their domestic banks totaled about US$20 billion—this in what was a very small economy.

The collapse of the total currency carry trade began in earnest in July 2008, two months before the collapse of Lehman brothers. This is fairly clear from the charts shown in this chapter, such as Figure 2.2. But it is even clearer from simply looking at the key exchange rates themselves. Figure 2.1

suggests that the Australian dollar was probably the biggest carry trade recipient currency prior to the 2007–2009 global financial crisis. The Australian dollar began to plunge in July 2008, crashing from what had been a peak of over US$0.95 to around US$0.65 by October.

However, the big—and surprising at the time—difference between the carry collapse of 2008 and the earlier carry crash of 1998 was just how short-lived the 2008 crash would prove to be. For the Australian dollar, a short year later the currency was back over US$0.90, on its way to a new high of about US$1.10. The charts of indicators for the size of the currency carry trade, such as Figure 2.2, tell the same story. Terrifying though it seemed at the time, eventually the carry crash of 2008 was to turn out to be merely a "correction" in an unprecedented ongoing huge expansion of the outstanding carry trade.

Traditional macroeconomic indicators also highlight the differences—from a currency carry perspective—between the 1997–1998 Asian crisis and the 2007–2008 global crisis. Simple fair value (purchasing power parity) analysis suggests that during the Asian crisis the currencies of the crisis countries fell to severely undervalued levels, at which they remained for a long period of time. Strong supporting evidence for this comes from current account balances. At the end of 1996, Korea was running a large current account deficit of about 5 percent of GDP. By 1998, the country had a huge surplus, in the double digits as a percentage of GDP. The same applies to Thailand, the original crisis country, which went from a deficit of 9 percent in late 1996 to a surplus of 12 percent by the second half of 1998. The carry crash had taken these Asian countries from being very uncompetitive to being extremely competitive.

In contrast, the carry crash of 2008 did no such thing for the major carry recipient countries at that time. Simple fair value analysis suggests that recipient (or target) currencies such as the Australian dollar and Brazilian real fell to only mildly undervalued levels at the lows—despite the rapidity and severity of the declines—and remained at those undervalued levels for only a brief period of time before appreciating back up to severely overvalued levels again. Australia's current account deficit had been about 7 percent of GDP at the beginning of the global financial crisis. Following the Australian dollar crash, it did improve substantially, but never went into surplus and was back in wide deficit of 5–6 percent of GDP by the end of 2009 and early 2010. Brazil's current account had been in a deteriorating trend in which it remained with no significant interruption.

Carry traders were not deterred by 2008, at least not for very long. At its all-time peak in mid-2014, the outstanding currency carry trade seems likely to have reached between US$4 trillion and US$5 trillion in size, probably about 50 percent bigger than at the 2007–2008 peak. This is broadly consistent with banking data for recipient currencies, such as the data shown in Figure 2.1. As previously mentioned, the dollar-funded carry trade at this new peak seemed to be in the magnitude of US$3 trillion in size. Despite the Bank of Japan's adoption of quantitative easing policies and much talk in the financial markets about the yen carry trade, there was little evidence to suggest that the yen-funded carry trade had been resurrected back to its former heights. Instead, it seems likely that the European Central Bank's conversion to the central bank trend of zero interest rates and quantitative easing promoted the development of a euro-funded carry trade during 2013 and 2014. Certainly, there was substantial growth in the net foreign assets of German, Dutch, and Spanish banks over this period, which provides strong circumstantial evidence of a growing euro-funded carry trade.

So by mid-2014 the dollar-funded carry trade was dominant, but there was a significant euro-funded carry trade and probably a small yen-funded trade. What remained of the Swiss franc–funded carry trade blew up on January 15, 2015, taking a number of small financial institutions and currency traders with it, when the Swiss central bank announced that it would no longer cap the Swiss franc's exchange rate against the euro.

3
Carry, Leverage, and Credit

Carry Trades Are Levered Trades

A currency carry trade involves an implicit bet on the exchange rate for the borrowed currency in terms of the currency of investment remaining relatively stable. Even for the most attractive of currency carry trades, a large adverse move in the currency exchange rate can easily wipe out the interest rate spread. So the currency carry trade is, in essence, a bet on the exchange rate volatility being low, at least relative to what the market might expect. It can therefore be thought of as a "volatility-selling" trade—a bet on volatility declining or at least being low relative to market expectations.

A currency carry trade is also a levered trade. It involves investing in a financial instrument or asset in one currency financed out of borrowing in another. The outstanding position will therefore be much greater in size than any equity committed to the trade; in some purely financial currency carry trades, there may be no equity committed at all. In currency carry trades such as the Eastern European Swiss franc–funded carry trade, mentioned in the previous chapter, in which households in Hungary and Poland bought houses financed with Swiss franc mortgages, there clearly was significant equity committed. Sadly, as it turned out, those Hungarian and Polish families had, in many cases unknowingly, put at risk capital greater than the savings they had committed, being left with negative equity in their homes as the Swiss franc appreciated sharply against the Hungarian forint and Polish zloty.

Currency carry trades are only one type of carry trade. Carry trades can take many forms in the financial world. The most obvious example is perhaps writing insurance. The insurance company, or writer of an insurance policy, takes a premium, or income, for accepting the risk of having to pay out if the event that is being insured against occurs. In the financial markets a credit default swap is a form of insurance against default by a borrower. The buyer of the credit default swap (CDS) pays a premium to insure a bond (loan) against the risk of default. If the borrower does default on the bond, the CDS buyer is compensated by the seller of the CDS. (However, note that, unlike with a normal insurance contract, the buyer of the CDS does not actually have to own the bond or loan he is insuring against default.)

In the stock market a stockholder who wishes to protect himself from the risk of a large loss on the stock can buy a put option on the stock. He pays a premium for the put option, and it gives him the right to sell the stock at a fixed price, or strike price—in this case at or below the current price of the stock—up to a certain time in the future. The writer, or seller, of that put option therefore receives the premium, or income, in exchange for accepting the risk of a decline in the stock price below the level of the strike price of the option.

In this latter example the equivalence between the risk that the put option writer takes and the volatility of the underlying asset price (the stock price) is particularly obvious. If the stock price fluctuates enormously, the risk that it will at some point be below the strike price, therefore inflicting a loss on the writer of the put option, is much higher than if the stock price hardly ever changes.

A problem that is rarely appreciated is that when carry trades become prevalent in any financial market, it becomes virtually inevitable that they will crash. At an intuitive level the notion that carry trades tend to provide steady (income-based) returns until they crash can be understood from considering the example of the simple insurance contract. Say that an investor insures someone's very valuable home against the risk of it burning down. The homeowner pays the investor an insurance premium every six months. As long as the house is standing there safely, the investor collects her income from the insurance premium every six months without doing very much at all. But if one day there is a huge fire and the house does burn down, the investor will be subject to a big loss, when she will have to pay out on the contract for the full value of the house. Her return will be very steady until the point of catastrophic loss.

In this case, though, unless there is criminal activity involved, there should be no connection between the investor's writing of the insurance policy and the risk that the house will actually burn down; the two events should be independent of each other. That means the investor can spread the risk by writing insurance contracts on many different houses. But in financial markets, the more successful that certain types of carry trade are—the stronger the returns that they provide—the more capital will be attracted into those carry trades. This in itself will eventually create the conditions for the demise of the trade, at which point the catastrophic loss, or carry crash, occurs.

The conditions that create the inevitability of a carry crash, as more and more capital is attracted into a carry trade, include excessive leverage and what can be termed "imbalances." Carry trades are essentially aimed at extracting income, but a growing volume of carry trades will also tend to result in capital appreciation of the target asset. In turn the capital appreciation, because it is not based in fundamentals such as the long-term potential for earnings or economic growth, will result in imbalances—that is, it will encourage the creation of deficits between spending and income. An imbalance will come to require continuing growth of the outstanding carry trade for its financing. This situation is necessarily unstable and unsustainable. Once the carry trade begins to unravel, excessive leverage ensures that the unraveling occurs rapidly.

Credit Carry Trades and Mispricing of Risk

Carry trades can also be thought of as liquidity-providing trades. Depending on perspective, the carry trader can be seen as performing two functions:

one is the function of assuming risk, as insurers do; the other is providing market liquidity, as market makers in financial markets do. The currency carry trader is borrowing in one currency to provide funding in another currency for which interest rates are higher, essentially providing liquidity in that currency. As we show later in the book, selling volatility in the stock market is equivalent to "buying the dip"—being prepared to buy when others are forced to sell. This can be seen as akin to a market-making function, providing liquidity to the stock market.

Given that carry traders are performing these useful functions, they might reasonably expect to earn a positive return. Since the returns from carry tend to occur in a steady fashion, such as the insurance company collecting the premiums on its policies, the risk that has to be borne to earn these returns is the risk of sudden loss—that is, the carry crash. An obvious problem occurs if the period of positive returns from carry lasts "too long," meaning that excessive amounts of capital will tend to be attracted into the carry trade to earn those abnormal returns. If this happens, it means that the risks are being mispriced.

In the previous chapter we touched on the credit bubble leading up to the 2007–2009 global financial crisis in the context of currency carry trades. This is obviously not the usual perspective from which the financial crisis is perceived. The standard narrative sees the global financial crisis as having been the result of excessively levered banks that had mispriced the risks inherent in mortgage financing, particularly subprime mortgages. At the heart of the mortgage bubble was a giant credit carry trade; high-risk mortgages were being financed out of low-cost funds. The "innovation" that allowed risks to be seriously mispriced was the burgeoning market in credit derivatives, particularly collateralized debt obligations (CDOs) and credit default swaps. CDOs (and collateralized loan obligations) bundle together a collection of loans or mortgages or mortgage-backed securities and divide the collection into tranches. The owners of the highest-rated tranche get first claim on the stream of interest payments that accrue to the bundle of loans or securities, while the owners of the lowest-rated tranche get whatever is left—and are therefore most at risk from defaults on the underlying debts.

The lowest-rated tranches of CDOs are considered to be similar to equity. However, in the crisis they proved to be riskier than traditional equity. Risks inherent in different credits were assumed to be less correlated than they really were. Once the housing market in parts of the United States collapsed, the equity parts of mortgage-backed CDOs, or the residual claims left on banks' books, proved to be substantially worthless.

This was an example of how carry bubbles—which occur when carry trades have earned "too positive a return" for "too long"—always involve the mispricing of risk, which means the concentration of risk in the hands of speculators or entities that do not have sufficient balance sheets to bear those risks. This becomes apparent in the carry crash when those speculators or entities are faced with the potential to be completely wiped out. The fear of contagion spreading from these bankruptcies across the markets triggers central bank action to stabilize markets, reduce volatility, and ultimately truncate losses for some carry traders who would otherwise have been bankrupted. Thus central banks' "success" in the short term in terms of stabilizing markets encourages further growth in carry trading, which in turn builds up even greater risks for the long term.

Carry Trades and Credit Growth

If carry trades are always levered trades, it makes sense that in macroeconomic terms carry bubbles should be associated with credit bubbles. Credit is the flip side of debt—for every creditor there is a debtor—so it could be assumed that carry bubbles should also be associated with a buildup of debt. Broadly, this is true, but the relationship between carry and credit in a macroeconomic sense is much less clear-cut than the relationship between carry and leverage. Carry can involve leverage via the concentration of risk, which may not always be captured in macroeconomic statistics for nonfinancial-sector debt.

We can return to the insurance analogy. Imagine that a speculator, without much wealth to his name, is somehow able to write insurance on many different risks. As long as nothing goes too wrong, he collects the premiums. But if some kind of disaster causes many things to go wrong at once, he will be wiped out, and those he has insured will find that they are not fully insured for their losses and will have to liquidate assets. In this case the contingent liabilities involved in the accumulation of risk will probably not be fully accounted for in macroeconomic debt statistics.

In this example, there is an income transfer from those buying insurance to the insurer. The insurance can be considered an asset for the buyer of the insurance and a (contingent) liability for the writer. But certainly in the case of a tail risk event, no macro financial statistics will be able directly to capture the potential consequences.

In other words, a carry bubble can occur without an obvious credit bubble—obvious in the sense of being clearly visible in macroeconomic statistics—and this becomes more the case as financial market innovation creates ever-greater opportunities for carry trades and therefore for the concentration of risk.

But this is not to downplay the close connection between carry and credit. Because carry trades are levered trades and in aggregate leverage is likely to involve credit to a significant extent, we should expect that in general a large carry bubble should also manifest in a credit bubble.

This is particularly true for currency carry trades, and the relationship is surprisingly clear in available economic statistics. We can see the relationship in economic data for specific countries that have been large recipients of carry trade inflows over recent years.

First, it is useful to consider a hypothetical example. Imagine two countries, A and B, A being a low interest rate funding country and B being a high interest rate recipient country. If underlying credit demand in B is reasonable—that is, B is an economy that is growing quite well—then businesses in B may decide to borrow in the currency of A, assuming that they are confident of low volatility of the exchange rate. The cheaper funding costs in A then attract capital from A into B, possibly even strengthening B's currency, making further borrowing in A's currency look even more attractive—to those who assume that the currency trend will continue. Then, that apparent availability of cheap credit from A will strengthen B's economy further still, probably generating a cyclical boom, with asset price bubbles in real estate and financial assets. This increase in asset prices, particular for real estate, will in turn encourage more borrowing from local banks as well. This dynamic is likely to be even stronger, as rising inflation will make B's real interest rate appear lower as the boom develops.

The historic evidence suggests that this kind of carry bubble has worked better for countries that have had looser monetary conditions than for those that have had tighter financial conditions; that is, countries with looser monetary conditions have more easily attracted capital. In the years following the global financial crisis, for instance, it worked better for Turkey than it did for Brazil—and by "worked better" here, we mean it created a bigger domestic bubble-boom economy.

What it means for a carry recipient economy to have looser monetary conditions is that cyclical economic growth is strong and underlying inflation is high. For instance, high interest rate recipient country B in the example might have a 10 percent interest rate, but if the economy is growing and the underlying inflation rate is also 10 percent, then its real interest rate is zero. With real interest rates of zero, it will be very easy for a real estate bubble and other speculative investment activities to get going, even if they are financed in the domestic currency. So the country will attract carry capital flows—because of its relatively high nominal interest rates—but also experience strong domestic credit expansion as a boom develops. On the other hand, if real interest rates are actually high (nominal interest rates are even higher or underlying inflation is low), then there will be much less domestic credit expansion. Carry capital will be attracted by the high nominal interest rates, but these are less likely to be sustainable; with a weaker economy there will eventually be strong downward pressure on interest rates.

This all suggests that there should be a relationship between carry capital inflows and credit expansion within the carry recipient economy. Once domestic credit has weakened substantially, it will be difficult for carry capital inflows to be sustained. But to the extent that limited carry capital inflows do continue, interest rate spreads should be compressed quite quickly. At that stage, with little interest rate pickup remaining, there is likely to be a carry crash—a sudden withdrawal of carry capital.

Figure 2.1 showed a chart of the net claims of BIS reporting banks (covering much of the global banking system) on the most important carry recipient economies of recent years. To the extent that the data are indicative of the relative size of the carry flows for each country, they suggest that the most important carry recipient economies in recent times have included China, Australia, Brazil, Turkey, India, and Indonesia. Among these countries Australia has experienced particularly large and persistent inflows of carry capital and inflows that have correlated well with other available indicators of the global cycle in carry trades. Australia can be thought of as the bellwether of the global carry bubble from a currency carry perspective, and this has been reflected in the behavior of the Australian dollar, which was discussed in Chapter 2.

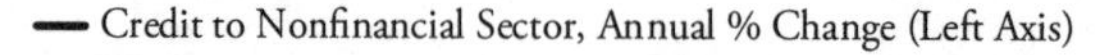

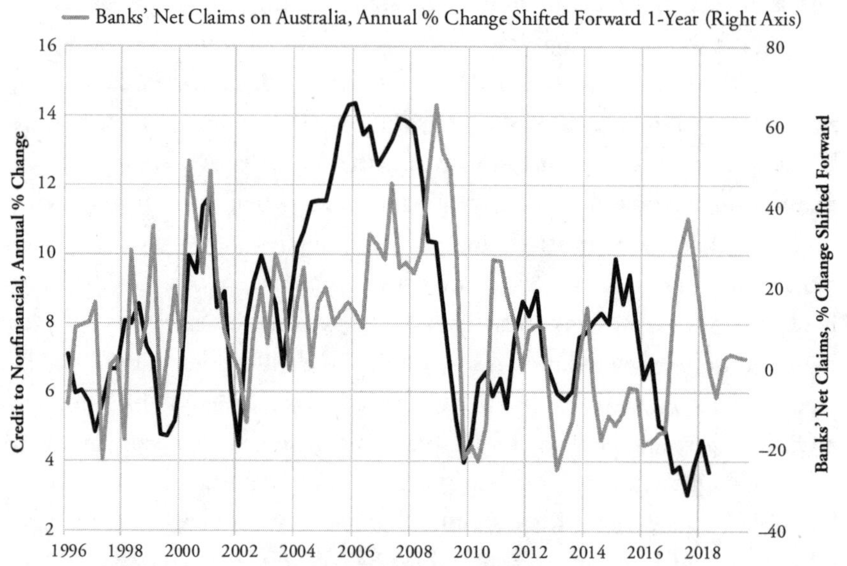

FIGURE 3.1 Australia's total credit and global banks' net claims shifted forward
Source of data: Bank for International Settlements

It is particularly interesting, therefore, to look at the relationship between carry capital inflows and credit growth for Australia. This is done in Figure 3.1 using data from the BIS. The underlying data used to represent carry flows are the data from Figure 2.1 for the net claims of BIS reporting banks on Australia. In Figure 3.1, though, we show the annual rate of change of the net claims on Australia, not the outstanding amount.

As discussed in the previous chapter, global banks' net claims on any given country are not a measure of the outstanding carry trade with regard to that country; at best the claims are a measure that overlaps with the outstanding carry trade. Nevertheless, there is fairly good reason to believe that directionally the movements of this indicator will correspond with the true carry trade. Using the rate of change of this proxy for the outstanding carry trade therefore should give a good guide to the carry trade *flow*, that is, the flow of capital that is attributable to carry trades being put on or taken off in net terms.

This carry trade measure is compared with total credit growth for Australia, also from BIS data. This is not merely bank credit; it is the growth of credit of all types to all people, businesses, government, and other nonfinancial entities resident in Australia. Credit that is the direct result of carry trades, including currency carry trades from overseas, is included in this credit measure, so there is overlap between the two series in the chart. However, we have found that in this type of comparison for individual carry recipient countries, there is a time lag between the carry trade flow measure and the total credit growth measure, captured in the chart by shifting the carry trade flow measure one year forward.

The lag represented in the chart by shifting the carry trade series forward is rather significant support for the theory that the carry trade has been a driving force in domestic credit expansion in Australia. The same applies to other carry recipient economies. Circumstantially, it also supports the idea that the BIS data for global banks' net claims are a reasonable proxy for the outstanding currency carry trade.

The chart shows three periods when there was potentially some divergence between credit growth and the carry trade for Australia. Perhaps "divergence" is the wrong word for the first case, from 2004 into 2008. Over this period the carry trade flow into the Australian dollar was strong, but credit growth was even stronger. This is a classic version of what we have already described in the hypothetical example of a carry-driven domestic credit boom. The carry bubble drives a domestic credit boom, which in turn makes the carry bubble even larger. The theory suggests that this should be accompanied by the interest rate spread remaining high, as booming domestic credit acts to draw in carry capital. The data show that this was the case; the 10-year interest rate spread between Australia and the United States was mostly in the range 1.0–1.5 percent over 2002–2005 but rose well above 1.5 percent in late 2007.

The second episode, from mid-2014 through 2015—a period when global carry was contracting—is less convincing. The interest rate spread continued falling through this period. The third period is the period of renewed carry bubble from late 2015. The carry trade inflow recovered sharply, but there was no concomitant recovery in domestic credit, which tended to weaken. The interest rate spread continued to narrow.

During the final period it appeared that capital was being pushed into Australia, not pulled in. Capital was, in effect, being thrown at Australia even though there was limited demand for it within Australia. This was consistent with the idea that the global carry bubble, at that stage, was being generated entirely from within the United States, keeping the dollar down and supporting the Australian dollar and other carry recipient currencies. The driver of the global carry bubble by that stage was simply volatility selling in US markets, a topic to which we return extensively later in the book.

The lesson here, though, is that a fully global carry bubble cannot really be sustainable for long based on only one pillar, even if that one pillar is volatility selling in the US financial markets, the most important of the world's financial markets. A giant and longer-lasting carry bubble needs to feed through into credit growth in different areas of the world; if there is a longer-lasting carry bubble, there will be a visible credit bubble.

Turkey's Carry Bubble and Bust

If Australia has been the bellwether of the global currency carry trade—in the sense that its cycles in capital flows and credit growth and the behavior of its currency have been good indicators of the waxing and waning of the long cycles in global carry—then Turkey has been the outrageous extreme. Turkey experienced the most persistent carry trade, persistent to the point of ridiculousness, as carry trade inflows continued through clear signs of extreme economic imbalances and acute political instability.

Figure 3.2 shows for Turkey what Figure 3.1 shows for Australia. The difference is that the lag used in the chart is only six months, rather than one year. The shorter lag and the surprisingly close correlation between the carry flow cycles and the credit cycles—at least until the period leading up to the 2018 currency crash—suggest that the carry trade fed into Turkish credit growth quite quickly, creating volatile cycles.

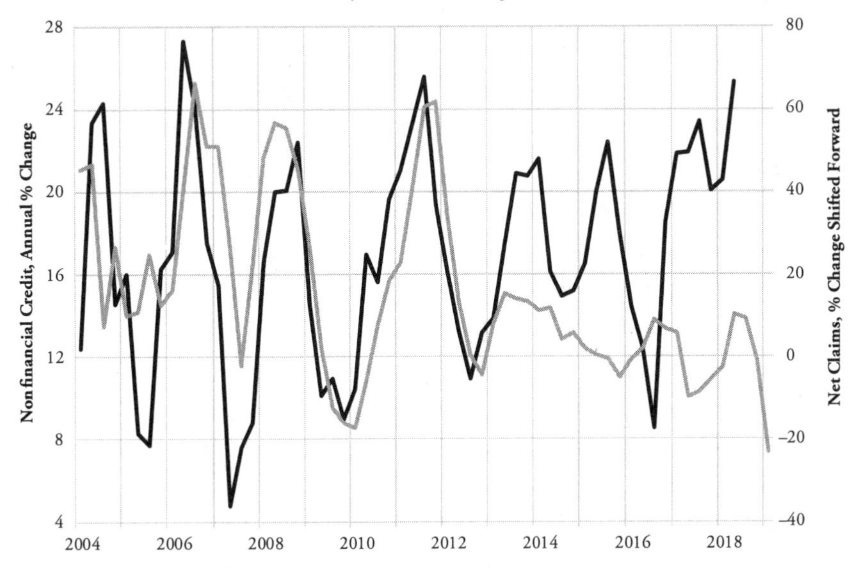

FIGURE 3.2 Turkey's total credit and global banks' net claims shifted forward
Source of data: Bank for International Settlements

A difference in behavior between the Turkish carry trade and the Australian carry trade was that the Turkish carry trade did not recover so strongly in 2016; on the contrary, the Turkish carry trade was in contraction at that time. This was despite the fact that Turkish domestic credit growth was firm over the period. The implication is that by that time there was, finally, a growing risk aversion to the Turkish carry trade in the light of political instability (including an attempted coup) and persistent severe economic imbalances.

In any prior period of economic history, Turkey, with its large foreign currency debt burden, persistent current account deficits financed by short-term capital, continuous rapid credit growth, a large real estate bubble, and high inflation, would have long since found itself in a crisis similar to the 1997–1998 Asian crisis. But year after year yield-seeking capital continued to flow into the country, and the economy consequently kept going—and the bubble kept growing. Turkey, more visibly than any other single part of the global economic picture, was testament to the power and size of the global bubble in carry that developed out of the 2007–2009 global financial crisis.

A lesson of Turkey's experience is how the global carry bubble masks the development of serious underlying economic problems, preventing analysts using standard macroeconomic metrics from foreseeing crisis until the moment it impacts. For instance, standard indicators of economic health such as the ratio of foreign debt to GDP are seriously distorted by the carry bubble. The carry bubble means huge flows of capital into the higher interest rate country—such as Turkey over many years up until about 2016—which tend to drive up the exchange rate for the currency, rendering the currency more and more overvalued. As already noted, the comparatively firm trend of the currency exchange rate only helps to attract more capital, because carry traders stand to benefit from both a large interest rate differential and, potentially, currency appreciation if the trend continues.

Sustained very high interest rates—which underpin the country's status as a carry recipient—must be associated with high inflation. For example, over the whole period from the end of 2002 until the beginning of the climax of the global financial crisis in August 2008, Turkey's consumer price index (IMF measure) increased by 83 percent. The US consumer price index rose by 20 percent over the same period. This is a big difference, and notwithstanding that sometimes rapidly growing developing economies can have higher rates of consumer price inflation without suffering loss of trade competitiveness, one would assume that such a big differential in inflation would be offset by at least some currency depreciation—in the context of the need to maintain trade competitiveness. Yet over the same period, Turkey's currency, the lira, appreciated, and not by a little—by about 35 percent, a substantial currency appreciation.

However one looks at this, it represents a huge loss of competitiveness. But it seemed sustainable for a time because persistent capital inflows driven by the carry trade encouraged domestic credit growth and supported the currency. Because of the credit bubble and high inflation, Turkey's GDP was growing rapidly. Translated into dollars the growth appeared even stronger because the lira was going up against the dollar as well.

At the end of 2002, annual GDP for Turkey was about US$240 billion. By the third quarter of 2008, when the lira was still close to its peak, GDP was over US$800 billion, a more than threefold increase in a few short years. Of course that level was not sustainable, and as the lira subsequently began to weaken sharply in the foreign exchange markets, the dollar value of GDP fell back. But the effect was to make Turkish macro statistics look much better than they really were in an underlying sense. The dollar value of GDP is the denominator in simple measures of debt sustainability, such as foreign debt as a ratio to GDP or current account deficit as a percentage of GDP. When the dollar value of GDP is so much higher, it makes these ratios look better—until the currency collapses in the carry crash, and then they suddenly look very much worse. But by then it is too late for any investor who has taken these kinds of indicators too seriously.

Turkey's balance of payments on current account deteriorated sharply over the 2002–2008 period, from being roughly in balance to being in large deficit by about 5.5 percent of GDP. But it would have been much worse without the exaggerated increase in dollar GDP, thereby storing up problems for later. Turkey's foreign debt ratios tell a similar story. The huge increase in dollar GDP made Turkey's external debt–to–GDP ratio look reasonably respectable in 2008, at under 40 percent of GDP, and much lower than the close–to–60 percent ratio that had been associated with the Turkish financial crises of 1994 and 2001. But, tellingly, a recalculation that substituted a fair value estimate for the Turkish lira rather than the actual exchange rate—thereby significantly reducing the measure of dollar GDP used to calculate the ratio—put the "underlying" ratio of foreign debt to GDP at over 70 percent in 2008, higher than the previous crisis levels. As the following years saw several bouts of severe lira weakness in the foreign exchange markets, the actual foreign debt ratio, measured at current exchange rates, inevitably moved toward the 60 percent level.

In 2018 the Turkish lira finally suffered the inevitable severe carry crash. Turkish corporates that had borrowed dollars excessively were left insolvent. The full story of Turkey will play out over many years. But it will stand as an admonishment to policy makers for ignoring the widespread consequences of the rise of carry, even more so for actively encouraging the rise and globalization of carry.

4

Dimensions of Carry and Its Profitability as an Investment Strategy

Growing Academic Interest in Currency Carry

CARRY STRATEGIES NOT ONLY HAVE GROWN IN SIZE, BUT have spread across the financial markets. The lessons of history can help us to understand what to expect in the future.

Academic researchers began documenting the existence of currency carry profits almost 40 years ago with studies showing that currencies with high interest rates tended to appreciate relative to those with low interest rates. This violates the theory of uncovered interest rate parity (UIP), which assumes currencies have the same expected returns. Under this assumption, a higher interest rate should be compensation for an expected depreciation of the exchange rate, making an investor indifferent between holding the high- or low-yielding currency. What these early studies showed, however, was that borrowing in a low interest rate currency such as the Swiss franc and investing the proceeds in a higher-rate currency such as the Australian dollar on average generated both an interest rate pickup (the carry) and also a capital gain.

This violation of UIP was dubbed a puzzle, and since puzzles to researchers are what profits are to traders, it triggered an eventual flood of work. For example, a 2014 paper by Daniel, Hodrick, and Lu documents at least 20 different explanations for carry trade profits put forward in the last decade alone.[1]

Most of these explanations in the academic work are risk-based stories. In other words, carry trade profit is not a free lunch but represents compensation for bearing certain types of financial risk. The specific risks include the possibility of large negative returns, with a tendency to lose money in "bad" states of the world in which volatility is high, liquidity is constrained, demand for safety increases, and other risky assets do poorly.

We agree with the broad thrust of this academic work. Carry trades are risky, and the nature of these risks is important. Empirical evidence confirms that currency carry returns do fit the expected pattern common to short volatility trades—an unusually large number of small positive returns[2] punctuated by occasional large losses that materialize at times of generalized financial stress (a carry crash).

A theme not often discussed in academic work, but critically important in our view, is the interrelationship between carry returns and subsequent government policy. Because the losses tend to occur during "bad" times, central banks often respond with stabilizing actions. This has the effect of truncating carry losses generally and, more granularly, concentrating those losses in the least sophisticated areas of the markets. This is a central topic of later chapters of this book.

Most academic research suggests currency carry returns are compensation for bearing risk that few others want to take. By underwriting, even if unintentionally, some of these risks, central banks have encouraged the growth of carry in and beyond the currency markets. Carry now represents the main driver of the global credit cycle and risk factor for the stability of financial

1. Kent D. Daniel, Robert J. Hodrick, and Zhongjin Lu, "The Carry Trade: Risks and Drawdowns," NBER Working Paper No. w20433, August 2014.

2. Compared with what would be expected if returns came from a normal distribution.

markets. Here we use the history of the currency carry trade as a lens to have a better understanding of the risks that are likely to be a feature of future financial crises.

Constructing a Carry Portfolio

There is no correct way to study the history of currency carry returns. Academic researchers started off using statistical analyses of exchange rates and, over time, migrated to examining returns to hypothetical portfolios that might be closer to actual practitioner experience. Since we are focused on the practical consequences of the growth of carry, our study of historical returns aims to be as realistic as possible while recognizing that no backtest can accurately replicate history. We therefore base our analysis on a backtest of a hypothetical currency carry portfolio built using simple but realistic rules that could easily be replicated in practice. Details of how we constructed our backtest are provided in the box ("Currency Carry Backtest") at the end of this chapter. Our backtest allows us to highlight the main features of the currency carry trade, features that other types of carry can be expected to share.

Our currency carry portfolio is constructed to be long-short. We can think of a strategy that borrows money in the short currencies and deposits money in the long currencies. The weighted average interest rate of the short currencies is the portfolio's funding cost, while the weighted average yield on the long currencies is the interest income. The spread between the two is the portfolio's carry.

A currency carry portfolio built this way that uses modest leverage—say, the equivalent of $1 long and $1 short for each $1 of capital—produces returns of only 2.0 percent per annum over our test period of 1986–2018. The volatility of this strategy is also modest at just under 5 percent per year, similar to a 5-year Treasury bond. The ratio of these two figures—what asset managers call the information ratio (IR)—is around 0.4.

This combination of a solid IR but low absolute returns presents asset managers with a conundrum. The risk-return trade-off appears good, but the strategy does not generate high enough levels of absolute returns. The "solution" is often to apply more leverage. This can generate higher absolute returns but, of course, comes with the trade-off of potentially much higher risk.

In order to provide a set of returns that we can compare with familiar asset classes, we chose a leverage level of 1,000 percent ($5 short and $5 long for every $1 of capital). This produces an annualized risk of around 15 percent, similar to what has been experienced for the S&P 500. While this level of leverage might seem high, it is certainly achievable in currency markets given typical collateral requirements for currency forwards.

Historically Solid Returns from Currency Carry

Figure 4.1 shows the cumulative value of $1 invested in this strategy over the 1986–2018 test period. The carry portfolio experiences two decades of strong results, a sharp drawdown during the global financial crisis, a bounce back in 2009, and flat returns thereafter. Table 4.1 confirms this by showing the annualized return to the strategy across these subperiods.

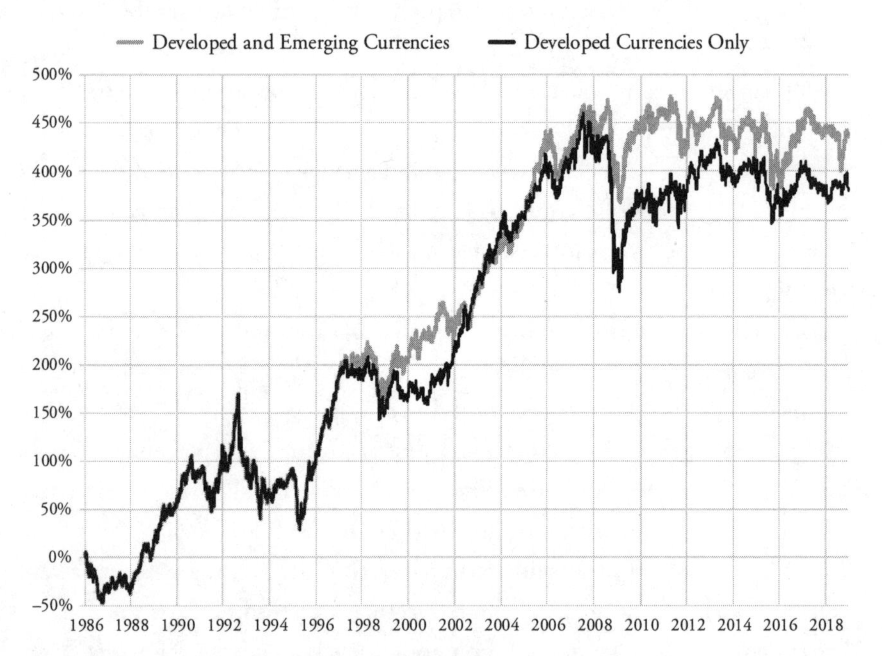

FIGURE 4.1 Cumulative returns to simulated currency carry strategy
Source of data: Datastream, Global Financial Data, authors' calculations (see box at end of this chapter for details of strategy parameters)

TABLE 4.1 Annualized Return and Standard Deviation (Risk) to Currency Carry Strategy

	Developing and Emerging		Developed Only	
	Return	Risk	Return	Risk
1986–2007	8.1%	16.8%	7.9%	16.7%
2008	–11.0%	12.2%	–23.1%	19.7%
2009	11.9%	8.8%	16.6%	13.9%
2010–2018	–0.3%	6.6%	0.1%	7.7%
Full Period	5.2%	14.4%	4.9%	14.9%

Source of data: Datastream, Global Financial Data, authors' calculations

In Figure 4.1, in the "Developed and Emerging Currencies" test, we include emerging market currencies as data become available and as trading volume as reported by the Bank for International Settlements reaches a certain threshold (see the box "Currency Carry Backtest" at the end of this chapter for details). These additional currencies should improve results by adding more opportunity to take long positions in high-yielding currencies. However, because emerging market currencies generally depreciated versus developed currencies during and after the global financial crisis, their inclusion in this period does not help. The strategy that merely trades developed currencies also does poorly in more recent years.

Given the solid returns earned by the currency carry strategy up through 2007, it is not surprising it would have attracted growing amounts of capital. Many practitioners are aware that currency carry strategies have a crash risk component. Therefore it is possible that the 2008 drawdown, while severe, was seen as an expected component of the strategy. Those who stuck with it and "bought the dip" were rewarded in 2009, and worries that the strategy was broken were likely assuaged. It is therefore not surprising that the scale of currency carry would have continued growing afterward. However, the later extended period of flat returns combined with a great deal more attention to the strategy might be making some practitioners reconsider currency carry's long-term viability.

Losses Occur During Bad Times

An underlying theme of this book is that carry strategies have grown in size, spreading from the currency markets to other asset classes. Because carry strategies are short volatility and because spikes in volatility happen during financial crises, losses from carry strategies will occur in large scale and at very inopportune times. This history of currency carry therefore gives us an opportunity to look in more detail at the pattern of returns that carry portfolios generate.

The standard deviation of the currency carry trade's daily returns is just under 1 percent each day, and the average daily returns were just above 2 basis points.[3] If returns followed a normal bell curve distribution we would expect around 21 percent of these returns to be small gains of about ½ percent or less. In fact, small gains happened much more often—just over one-third of the time.

On the other hand, losses greater than 3 percent should happen about once every 11 years, or 3 times during our sample. In fact, the portfolio had daily losses of 3 percent or more 77 times. While this is still relatively infrequent over a 33-year horizon, it is 25 times more likely than we would expect. Currency carry trade returns do not follow a normal distribution. Carry is more accurately thought of as following a sawtooth pattern with many small gains punctuated by occasional large losses.[4]

When exchange rates are stable, the carry strategy will by construction earn a profit. Like all short volatility portfolios, it makes money when "nothing happens." Conversely, periods of volatility tend to be bad for the strategy. Figure 4.2 demonstrates this visually. We calculate the monthly returns for the carry trade strategy and rank them from best to worst. Based on this ranking we group the returns in 10 equally sized buckets called deciles. Decile 1 contains the top 10 percent monthly returns and Decile 10 the worst.

Figure 4.2 shows the median carry trade return in each decile along with the median change in US stock market implied volatility proxied by the

---

3. Specifically, the developed market–only strategy had an average daily return of 0.022 percent and a daily standard deviation of 0.92 percent. The equivalent figures for the strategy that included emerging markets were 0.023 percent and 0.89 percent.

4. There are also more small losses than we would expect under a normal distribution and more frequent big gains. The small loss–big gain trade-off is not quite as pronounced as the small gain–big loss.

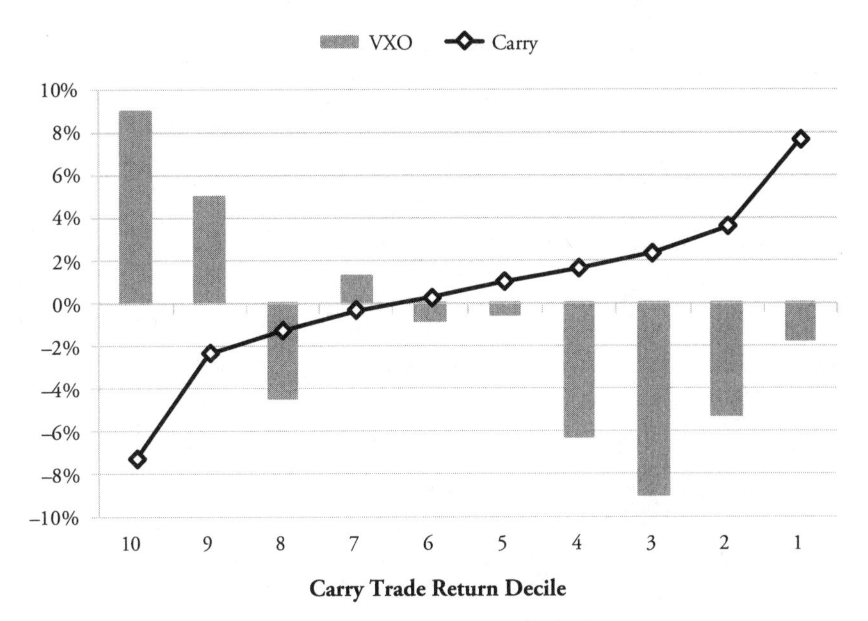

FIGURE 4.2 Median monthly return across carry trade deciles
Source of data: Datastream, Global Financial Data, CBOE, authors' calculations

CBOE's VXO index.[5] We use median returns instead of average returns to ensure that the results are not driven by a few exceptional events—such as the stock market crash in October 1987. The worst months for the carry trade strategy (Decile 10) are associated with jumps in stock market volatility. At the other end of the spectrum, profitable carry trade outcomes tend to be associated with a reduction in volatility.

There is a similar pattern with the S&P 500 itself. The worst months for the currency carry portfolio are also associated with negative returns for the stock market. On the other hand, when carry trade results are good (Deciles 1 through 5), the median monthly return to stocks ranges from 1.5 percent to over 3 percent.

5. The more popular VIX index only begins in 1989, so we chose to use the VXO index. Monthly changes in the two are correlated at a level of 0.96, and just using VIX from 1989 to 2018 leads to the same conclusion. The VIX index and stock market volatility in general are discussed in detail in Chapter 6.

It is also interesting to notice the kinked shape of the solid line in Figure 4.2, which links the median carry trade return across deciles. The median returns in the outer deciles are much greater in magnitude than the adjacent groups. This is another way of seeing that there are fat tails in the distribution of carry trade returns.

We also examined carry trade returns from the perspective of a risk manager. It is typical for managers of levered portfolios to be required to trim positions following losses of a certain magnitude. We chose 10 percent as a simple risk limit and identified each time the carry trade suffered a 10 percent decline from a previous high-water mark. Across our 33-year backtest, there were 42 separate episodes when the currency carry portfolio hit this drawdown trigger. In Figure 4.3 we graph the returns for the S&P 500 and changes to the VXO during those periods.

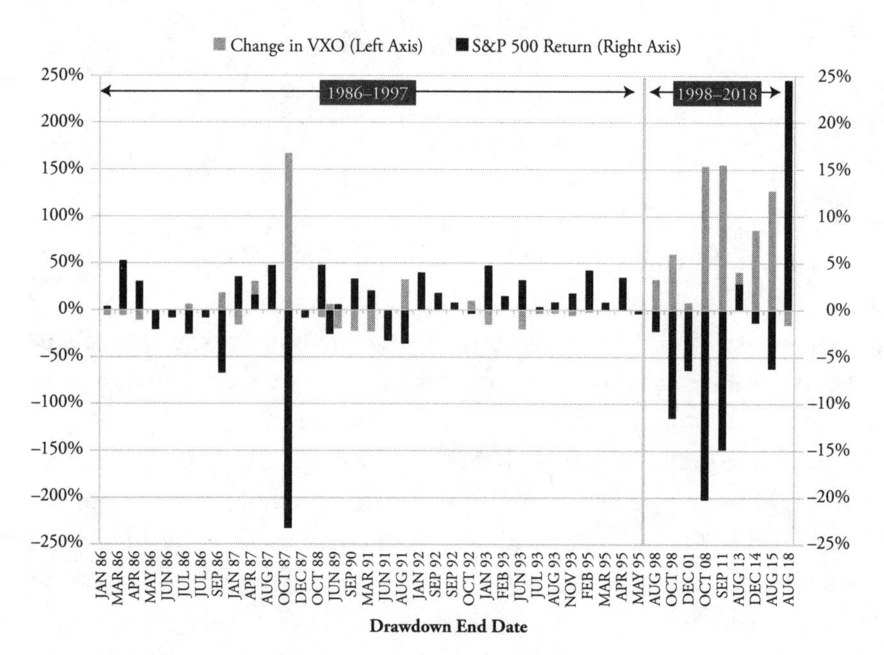

FIGURE 4.3 Implied volatility changes and stock returns during currency carry drawdowns
Source of data: Datastream, Global Financial Data, CBOE, authors' calculations

Two interesting features emerge—the pattern in drawdowns through time and the skewness in financial conditions during drawdowns. The horizontal axis notes the date a particular drawdown ended. The graph shows that during the strategy's first decade there were thirty-three 10 percent drawdowns. In the subsequent 23 years there were only nine. However, those recent drawdowns have been associated with much bigger spikes in stock market volatility and much worse returns.[6]

One possible explanation for this might be the inclusion of emerging markets in our backtest. We start off with 10 developed market currencies and add emerging market currencies as their data become available, finishing with 29 in our final portfolio. By increasing the number of positions in the portfolio, the strategy becomes more diverse, which could lead to fewer drawdowns. Second, since emerging market currencies often have higher yields, the carry strategy will tend to be long a basket of emerging currencies and short a basket of developed market currencies. Emerging currencies have a higher sensitivity to global stock markets, which could lead to more recent drawdowns being associated with big spikes in volatility and drops in the S&P 500.

However, the backtest that is restricted only to developed market currencies shows the exact same pattern. Most of the portfolio's drawdowns occur in the first decade, and the recent drawdowns are associated with large spikes in volatility and drops in the stock market. This helps us rule out the inclusion of emerging markets as driving the increasing association of carry returns and worsening financial conditions.

The graphs also depict a type of skewness in the relationship between carry trade losses and financial conditions. When currency carry losses are associated with S&P 500 losses and increases in volatility, these tend to be

---

6. The last drawdown is an exception. This is an unusual episode because the 10 percent fall was stretched out over 18 months, making it by far the longest drawdown period. Over this extended period the S&P 500 returns were very strong, and volatility was muted. A more granular look shows the carry strategy experiencing a 17-month period of slightly negative returns before dropping 7 percent in August 2018, when the Turkish lira fell by almost 40 percent. The lira was the carry strategy portfolio's largest long position at that time. The VXO measures of implied volatility did rise during this period—by about 5 percent—consistent with the carry trade drawing down when volatility increases. However, this was only a mild increase in volatility, and the S&P 500 rose by about 3 percent over the same time frame. Overall then, this was not a global "bad time" but more of an isolated episode of stress in one emerging market, albeit with some spillover effects to other emerging currencies such as Brazil and South Africa.

of much greater magnitude than when carry losses are associated with S&P 500 gains and decreases in volatility. We need to be cautious in making these comparisons because the bars depict periods that vary in length from 3 days to 168 days. However, if we take the risk management perspective, what can be said is that there is a meaningful chance that poor results in a carry portfolio will occur when other asset markets are also performing poorly, which means carry strategies amplify rather than reduce the risks of most financial portfolios.

The Currency Carry Trade Is Increasingly Correlated with Equity Carry

Carry drawdowns happen during bad times for financial markets; empirically do they also take place during bad times for the real economy? Here the evidence from data simply examined is not conclusive. Since measures of real economic activity such as GDP and industrial production growth are estimated at lower frequency, we examined the link between them and currency carry trade returns over longer horizons.[7] For instance, we calculated and ranked the worst nonoverlapping six-month periods for the carry trade portfolio and looked to see if there was a corresponding drop in real activity. There was no clear correlation.

Median industrial production growth over those periods was over 1 percent, very close to what would be expected had we chosen any six-month period at random. Merely focusing on extreme returns does not change the picture. In the ten worst six-month periods for the currency carry trade, industrial production growth was negative only twice. And carry trades do not necessarily do badly during recessions. There were three official recessions during our backtest period. The carry portfolio earned positive returns during the first two and lost 2.7 percent during the recession associated with the global financial crisis.

Of course, this is by no means a conclusive look at the empirical link between carry trade returns and the real economy. It could be that in certain

7. In both cases we used US GDP and industrial production as proxies for global real activity.

circumstances currency carry trade drawdowns trigger or precede a slowdown in the real economy. For instance, since carry trades have become a very important conduit for global credit creation, a carry drawdown might trigger a recession several quarters later when credit conditions tighten. This would require a more detailed study of the lead-lag relationship between carry and credit on a country-by-country basis. The previous chapter provided circumstantial evidence for such a lag, at least in the case of major carry recipient economies.

Later in the book, in Chapter 8, we argue that carry in broad terms is the driving force today in the business cycle. But financial markets have become increasingly complex, and carry trades—volatility-selling trades—can be implemented in all the various markets: stock markets, credit markets, commodities markets, even housing markets, as well as currency markets. The correlations between the various carry trades are not necessarily fixed over time; it is possible, for example, for carry trades in the commodities markets to be crashing even as the S&P 500 carry trade is expanding—at least for a period. There is no certainty that any one type of carry trade will be very clearly correlated with the economy, even as carry in the broadest sense now determines, or at the very least strongly influences, the business cycle. We explore this in much more depth later in the book.

Nevertheless and notwithstanding this theory, the evidence presented does show that when currency carry strategies perform poorly, stock market volatility tends to spike. To provide further confirmation of this, we looked at the correlation of the monthly currency carry trade returns with indexes of simple equity market carry strategies produced by the Chicago Board Options Exchange (CBOE).

The CBOE has created a variety of simple strategies[8] designed to exploit the fact that the volatility implied by options prices tends to be higher than the volatility actually experienced over the life of the option (a feature of the structure of volatility explained and examined in depth in Chapter 9). The two we examine here are carry strategies in that they involve selling options to earn a premium and are profitable when the volatility of the stock market

---

8. http://www.cboe.com/products/strategy-benchmark-indexes.

is lower than that implied in the options prices.[9] In other words, the strategies are short volatility. Figure 4.4 tracks the correlation of the currency carry strategy returns with the monthly changes in these various indexes measured over the trailing five years.

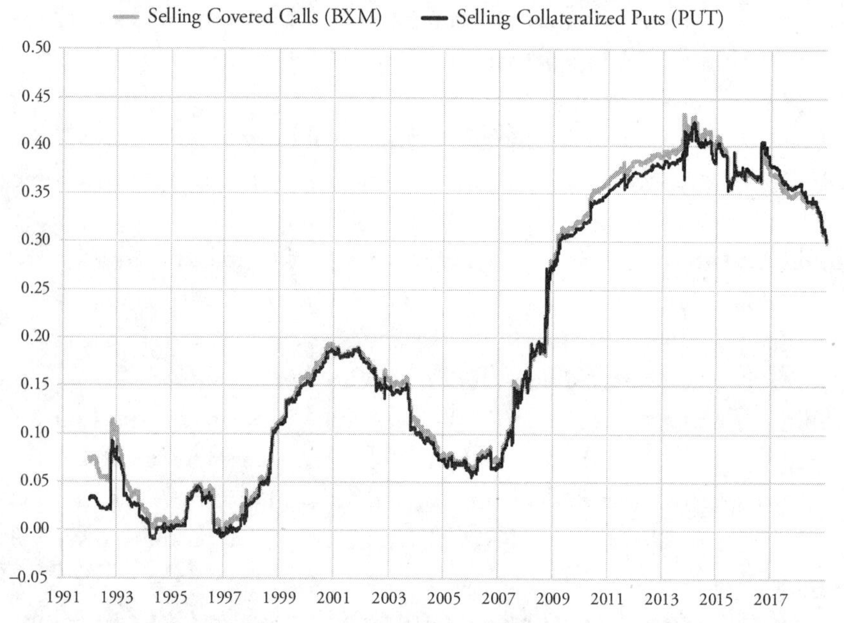

FIGURE 4.4 Correlation of currency carry trade returns with CBOE short volatility strategies
Source of data: Datastream, Global Financial Data, authors' calculations

The existence of the CBOE indexes is interesting in and of itself. The CBOE created its first short volatility index in 2002 and has continued to expand the range. It is clearly responding to an increased interest from practitioners to capture the volatility risk premium by providing historical data to estimate the potential rewards and risks of various strategies.

The chart in Figure 4.4 shows that there was not much correlation between currency and equity carry in the first decade of our backtest. This is

9. The BXM strategy buys an S&P 500 stock index portfolio and sells the near-term call option on the index. The PUT strategy sells S&P 500 put options against a collateralized money market account.

consistent with the pattern from the previous section where many of the 10 percent drawdown episodes from the period 1986–1995 were not associated with spikes in S&P 500 volatility.

The chart also shows the correlation trending upward through time. The correlation jumps in 2008 when the global financial crisis enters the calculation but remains elevated even after that period falls out of the window. The same pattern is present when looking at the currency carry trade with just developed market currencies, so once again this increasing correlation with equity volatility is not due to adding emerging markets to the carry portfolio.

Academic research supports the conclusion that US equity volatility has become an important driver of currency carry returns. In a 2012 working paper, economists Ricardo Caballero and Joseph Doyle constructed returns to an important strategy—which we discuss in detail later in the book—called a "VIX futures rolldown."[10] The VIX rolldown strategy historically earns profits from shorting S&P 500 volatility. They find that most of the returns from a currency carry portfolio can be explained by its effective exposure to this short S&P 500 volatility strategy. Since data are limited to the availability of futures contracts on the VIX and thus begin in 2004, their work cannot tell us if this link to S&P 500 volatility is a feature of the last two decades, as our data suggest, or has always been present.

Our view is that the empirical link between currency carry returns and US stock market volatility is a relatively recent phenomenon that represents the increasing integration of financial markets. The currency carry trade is constructed to be short volatility, but the volatility that directly impacts it should be that of foreign exchange rates. The empirical evidence is that as the S&P 500 becomes more central to financial markets, its volatility is important to all carry strategies, which means future carry unwinds will likely be correlated to a greater extent across asset classes. This is a very important point, which is central to the discussion later in this book.

10. Ricardo J. Caballero and Joseph B. Doyle, "Carry Trade and Systemic Risk: Why Are FX Options So Cheap?" Massachusetts Institute of Technology Department of Economics Working Paper 12-28, December 2012.

Currency Carry Returns Decrease as Interest Rate Differentials Narrow

The poorer results for currency carry over more recent years have coincided with a narrowing of the difference in global interest rates, particularly in developed markets. In Figure 4.5 we plot the spread between the highest and lowest one-month implied interest rates from our currency forward data. During the first decade of our sample, there was a substantial spread between interest rates in developed markets. In fact the spread in developed markets then was similar in scale to what we see more recently in emerging currencies.

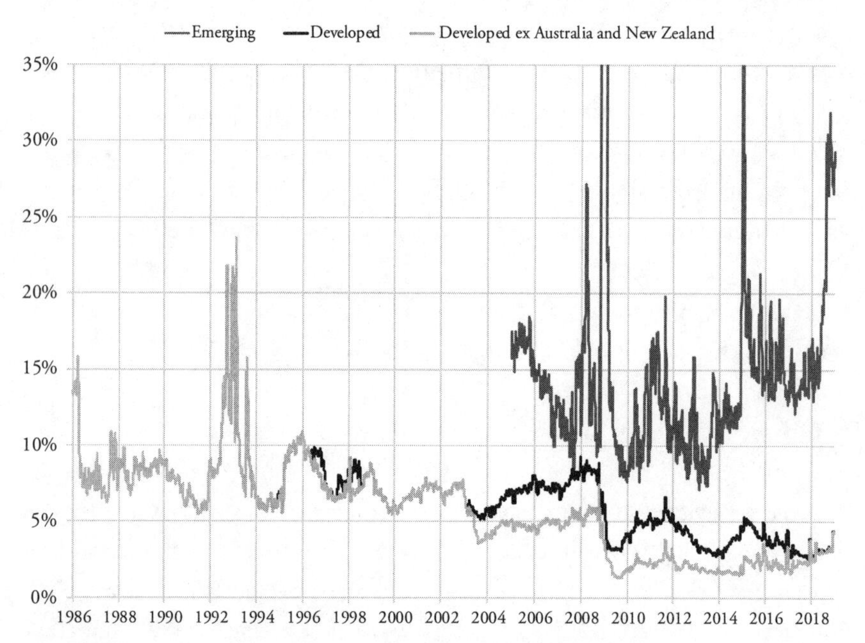

FIGURE 4.5 Spread between highest and lowest interest rates
Source of data: Datastream, Global Financial Data, authors' calculations

One reason for this is the inclusion of the Italian lira, which required higher interest rates because of a long history of high inflation. However, this is only part of the explanation. Italy had the highest interest rate among our developed country universe only 31 percent of the time from 1986 through 1998. New Zealand and Australia had the highest interest rate about half of the time, and the United Kingdom, also a country that had experienced very high inflation rates, had the maximum rate in about 8 percent of observations.

Australia and New Zealand have continued to have consistently higher interest rates than most other developed countries, at least up until 2018.[11] In fact, if these two countries are removed from the sample, we see that the spread between highest and lowest rates has been mostly below 3 percent since the crisis and at some points was even below 2 percent. The opportunity for profit in developed country currency carry has shrunk considerably over the last 40 years and is at an all-time low in recent years.

We can see this shrinking opportunity set directly by looking at the actual carry a backtest portfolio earns. The carry is simply the interest rate the portfolio earns on its long positions less the implied cost of borrowing on the short positions. In Figure 4.6 we present this for a portfolio that goes long $1 and short $1 for each dollar of capital. In contrast, our standard backtest employs five times this exposure, so the carry would be multiplied by five. But we choose this presentation to keep the units on a magnitude that is familiar and also more directly comparable to the preceding graph on the raw difference between maximum and minimum interest rates.

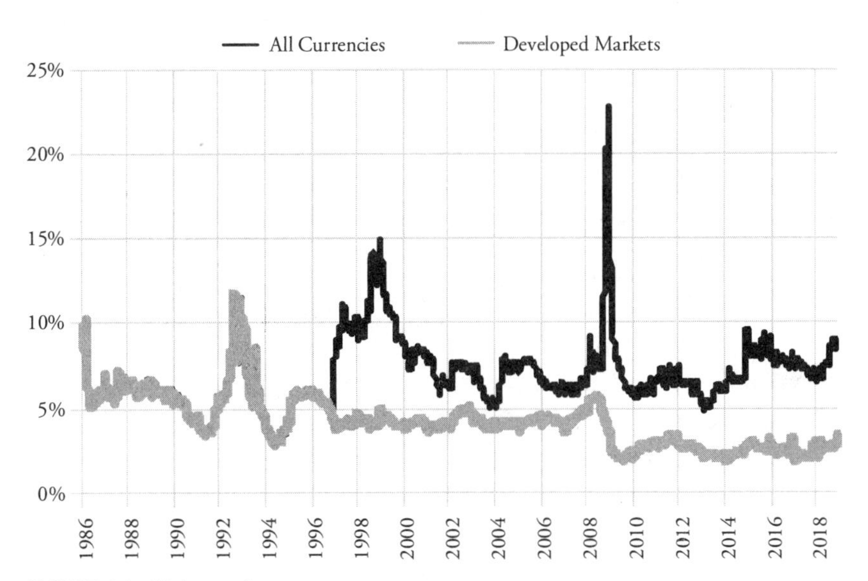

FIGURE 4.6 Unlevered carry on currency strategy

Source of data: Datastream, Global Financial Data, authors' calculations

---

11. Implied interest rates from New Zealand currency forwards have very closely tracked US interest rates since late 2016, sometimes being slightly higher and other times slightly lower.

As short-term interest rates collapsed after the global financial crisis, the carry on the developed currency portfolio ratcheted down and has stayed low ever since. Indeed, it is possible that this actually overestimates the carry because it assumes that some of the short positions—that is, borrowing—can be effected at negative rates. It is certainly possible that actual borrowing costs could be higher than those implied by our currency forward data. If we assumed that there was a lower bound at zero, then the carry in recent years would be as much as 1 percent smaller.

How have practitioners likely responded to this compression of spreads? One response is to continue to apply the carry trade using more leverage. Currency volatility over recent years is very similar to what it was during the first 20 years of our backtest, and correlations between currencies are somewhat higher. Increasing leverage in developed market carry trade portfolios would therefore increase risk, potentially by a lot, making carry-driven capital flows into currencies such as the Australian and New Zealand dollars even less stable than they were historically.

Another response to compressed spreads in developed markets is to apply the carry strategy more aggressively in emerging currencies. Figures 4.5 and 4.6 show that the raw spread among emerging currencies has not narrowed in the same way as in developed markets, and the carry on a portfolio that includes emerging markets has therefore not been compressed. In fact, the carry would be even wider had we not applied our liquidity filter to the universe (see the accompanying box, "Currency Carry Backtest"), which only allows currencies into our sample after they have achieved a certain trading volume threshold.

Nonetheless, the emerging currencies that pass our threshold are still far less liquid than developed currencies. According to the BIS data, the median daily turnover across developed currencies was around three times that of emerging currencies, and the total daily amount traded in developed currencies was five times as great. If a response to narrowing spreads is to allocate more currency carry trade risk to emerging currencies, then there is much more liquidity risk in carry portfolios now than in the past, and we can expect future unwinds to have sizable impacts on those exchange rates. This has already been apparent, for instance, in the dramatic crash of the Turkish lira in 2018.

Carry Portfolio Positions Are Consistent with BIS Data

In Chapters 2 and 3 we reviewed data from the BIS that implied that Australia, Brazil, China, India, Indonesia, and Turkey are the most important recipients of carry trade flows in recent years. This is a direct, albeit imprecise, estimate of carry flows based on bank balance sheets. The BIS data come as no surprise because these currencies consistently show up as significant long positions in our currency carry portfolio.

Table 4.2 shows the largest long positions, on average, across that portfolio over the final five years of the study. Altogether these countries represent about half of the long positions taken. More generally, for the final 10 years of the study, just under two-thirds of the net long positions are in emerging market currencies. In other words, a key outcome of currency carry is to channel borrowings in developed market currencies to emerging currencies.

TABLE 4.2 Average Size of Carry Portfolio's Biggest Long Positions, 2014–2018

Country	Average Long Position
Turkey	11.8%
Brazil	11.4%
Russia	10.9%
South Africa	9.6%
India	9.5%
Mexico	8.0%
Indonesia	7.2%
China	6.3%
New Zealand	5.4%
Malaysia	5.4%
Australia	4.2%

Source of data: Datastream, Global Financial Data, authors' calculations

In terms of developed markets, the Australian and New Zealand dollars stick out as consistent recipients of carry trade flows, which is also consistent with BIS economic data. Our backtest that only uses developed currencies allocates over half its long positions in the last decade to these two countries. Even in a global carry strategy that includes emerging currencies, these two countries retain their positions in the long portfolio.

Currency Carry History Lessons

As discussed in the previous chapters and explored further in subsequent chapters, carry trades are, by their nature, levered. Our backtest history tells us that purely as an investment strategy, currency carry needs to employ substantial leverage—total gross positions of 10 times capital—in order to generate absolute levels of returns that are competitive with conventional asset classes. Moreover, the narrowing of global interest rates since 2008 is likely to have increased pressure to apply more leverage to currency carry trades.

These observations are important because drawdowns in levered strategies have their own important dynamics. In particular, since the use of leverage means that even modest changes in position value can translate into a total loss of capital, risk controls will force trades to be closed when certain thresholds are hit. Risk controls can come from internal limits and can also be forced upon managers by lenders who require additional collateral to be posted to cover losses. In either case it is very easy for a "bank-run" dynamic to take place—losses lead to position reduction, forcing managers to trade into markets that are moving against them and, in the case of many emerging currencies, are illiquid. This activity triggers further losses, which require even more position reduction, and the cycle continues until moves in the exchange rate are so extreme that unlevered traders are induced to enter the market or central banks are forced to intervene to stabilize conditions. This idea of "ruin risk" is crucial to understanding carry and is also discussed in greater depth in later chapters of this book.

To the extent that currency carry trades are more levered now than in the past, we can expect future carry crashes to follow this script more violently. We should expect this to be felt most acutely in emerging markets, which are the main recipients of carry trade flows, along with Australia and New Zealand. A recent example confirming this was the crash of the Turkish lira in July–August 2018, examined at the end of the previous chapter.

Experience in Brazil over the past few years also broadly fits this pattern. Brazil has been a major carry trade recipient and therefore a prime candidate for the dynamic we have described. Its currency began turning against the dollar in late 2014, and this depreciation eventually turned into a collapse. The Brazilian real lost over 20 percent of its value against the dollar in just two months in early 2015 and fell again by over 25 percent during a similar window that summer. Since carry trades now play an important role in credit creation, we can expect carry crashes to trigger more severe downturns in the real economy than we have seen in the past. Again, Brazil and Turkey serve as warnings: Brazil's economy was in recession every quarter through 2015 and 2016, shrinking by 8 percent in total over those two years. Turkey's fate is likely to be similar.

In sum, it can be concluded that currency carry strategies involve lots of small gains, punctuated by occasional large losses. These drawdown periods, especially in the last two decades, have tended to coincide with bad times for financial markets. There is also evidence of a growing correlation between currency and equity market carry, suggesting that a single global volatility risk factor may be a driver of all forms of carry in the future. If this is true, future carry crashes may impact all asset classes at the same time. Later in this book we point to the nature of this single global volatility risk factor.

These crashes could be more severe than in the past because spread compression is likely to have increased the already substantial leverage employed in currency carry portfolios. We can expect emerging markets to be particularly sensitive to carry trade drawdowns. Our backtest portfolio—designed broadly to mimic the behavior of money managers—consistently channels borrowed capital from developed to emerging economies. Data from the BIS on bank balance sheets show that this is indeed happening on a large scale in the real world. However, these currencies are often far less liquid than their developed market counterparts and, as we have seen with Brazil and Turkey, could require very large depreciations to deal with carry trade unwinds.

Currency Carry Backtest

We start our testing with data from 1986 and end with data from 2018. This gives us 33 years of daily data and a portfolio with a minimum of 10 currencies. There is a significant amount of noise in the daily data. We clean the data with an algorithm similar to that used by Koijen, Moskowitz, Pedersen, and Vrugt in their excellent study of carry returns across asset classes.[12]

To be included in our test, we require daily spot and one-month forward exchange rate data. In addition, the currency must account for at least 0.2 percent of global foreign exchange turnover according to the BIS triennial foreign exchange turnover survey. When the last BIS survey was conducted in 2016, this cutoff represented around $10 billion in daily turnover. The 0.2 percent cutoff is a semi-arbitrary figure chosen to deal with two issues. First, we wanted the test portfolio to be a strategy that could be implemented in reasonable size in real markets. The cutoff helps eliminate illiquid currencies with high interest rates whose inclusion might make returns higher than could realistically be achieved in scale. At the same time we wanted to include—at least for several years—the currencies we believe are major recent recipients of carry trade flows. The cutoff level mostly impacts emerging markets in the last 20 years but also eliminates small European countries like Ireland, Portugal, and Finland in the early part of the sample. Other legacy European currencies like the French franc and Italian lira that meet our criteria are included in the sample. We recognize that this might bias returns to the upside in the years leading up to the formation of the euro. However, from our own experience in the currency markets in the 1980s and 1990s, we know these currencies were part of carry trade strategies.

The portfolios are equally balanced long and short, with leverage chosen as an independent parameter. Portfolio weights are based on the size of the currency's interest rate differential with the US dollar. For example, at a given point in time the portfolio position in the Japanese yen is:

$$Weight_{Yen} = Target\ Leverage * (Rank_{Yen} - \frac{\#\ of\ Currencies + 1}{2})$$

We re-rank the currencies and rebalance the portfolios daily, but add a two-day implementation lag to acknowledge that an actual rebalanc-

12. "Carry," *Journal of Financial Economics*, 2018, vol. 127, no. 2, 197–225.

ing process does not happen instantaneously. Trading costs are charged for each transaction. Trading costs vary by currency ranging from a low of 3 basis points for the Japanese yen to 2 percent for the Russian ruble. We recognize that this is a major simplification, as actual costs vary over time and also with trade size.

Most practitioners would use estimates of currency volatility and correlation to create portfolio weights that are risk adjusted. We chose not to do this because we did not want our results to be driven by a choice of how to estimate volatility and correlation and then combine them in an optimization framework.

The interest rate differentials are calculated by using the short-term interest rates implied by the 1-month forward exchange rates smoothed by taking a 20-day trailing average. Smoothing eliminates occasional sharp spikes in the data that practitioners would be unlikely to act on. Recently, a number of studies have documented the fact that implied interest rates from the forward foreign exchange markets do not match reported interest rates from the interbank market. This is a violation of covered interest parity and for a long time was thought to be unsustainable because it seemingly creates a risk-free arbitrage opportunity. However, since most currency carry strategies are executed through the forward market, we feel our approach still reflects the rates actually available to traders. We recognize this as another assumption that could drive a wedge between backtest and actual returns.

5
The Agents of Carry

The Nature of Institutional Liabilities

THE EVIDENCE, FROM FINANCIAL AND ECONOMIC STATIStics and financial market behavior, suggests that carry trades have become more pervasive in global financial markets. We make the case in this book that carry, broadly defined to include all types of volatility-selling trades, has, even more than this, become the dominant force in global financial markets and by extension the dominant determinant of the global economy. It is not possible to understand the business cycle, the behavior of the global economy, without understanding carry.

This book is mostly concerned with explaining the theoretical basis for the rise of carry, analyzing the empirical evidence, and divining the consequences. We pay somewhat less attention to the nuts and bolts—the institutions that are actually implementing carry trades. Nevertheless, virtually by definition, the growth of carry must be intimately linked to the growth of various types of financial institutions whose structure creates an incentive for them to engage in carry. Furthermore, we could posit that as carry has become the primary driving force in financial markets, financial institutions and other businesses have evolved—perhaps new businesses have emerged—primarily to take greater advantage of the rise of carry.

Which types of financial institutions are likely to be these agents of carry? As a first step, we can consider the nature of their liabilities, the structure of their compensation, and the amount of leverage they employ, these being important elements that create the incentive and ability to engage in carry trades.

We saw in the previous chapter that carry drawdowns happen during "bad times"—periods of turmoil for financial markets characterized by falling asset prices and rising volatility. All else being equal, this makes for a return profile that seems to be unattractive at first sight. Most of us prefer to invest in strategies that do well during bad times. Indeed, assets that play this safe haven role—such as German government bonds—have in recent times traded at negative yields. Investors have been willing to pay to hold them in part because they provide insurance against bad times.

The flip side of this is that carry traders ought to earn a premium for accepting a return profile that most people prefer to avoid.[1] Which institutions are best placed to earn this? Since carry drawdowns happen during bad times, a carry trader should ideally have liabilities that either are very long-lived or at least do not increase meaningfully during bad times.

Compensation Incentives to Carry and the Importance of Leverage

We have described carry trading as a strategy that makes money as long as "nothing happens." As shown in the previous chapter, currency carry trades deliver relatively steady returns punctuated by periods of sharp losses. Conversely, a short carry trade—that is, a long volatility trade—has the opposite profile of steady losses offset by occasional large gains.

Institutions that report returns over short time horizons have an incentive to gravitate toward carry strategies because they will be regularly reporting profits. It is much easier psychologically to have a trading book with carry-

1. Carry strategies should also earn a premium for providing liquidity. We discuss this in depth later in the book. We recognize that it is not clear whether the insurance and liquidity premiums for carry can be disentangled.

like attributes reporting frequent small gains and occasional large losses than having constantly to explain small losses with the promise of a big gain in the future.

These incentives are particularly strong if the firm actually collects cash compensation based on those reported profits. Further pressure toward carry happens if employee compensation takes a similar form. If traders or portfolio managers are paid cash bonuses based on quarterly or annual profit and loss—and that compensation is not returned if their book subsequently loses money—they will strongly prefer strategies with carry-like cash flows.

Leverage amplifies returns, and since carry strategies involve occasional severe drawdowns, applying leverage to them significantly increases the risk of ruin. Carry inevitably involves leverage to some degree. For those managing their own capital, that should mean levered carry strategies would seem unattractive. However, for professional managers that act as agents for others—and this represents the bulk of managed wealth—the calculus is different. Professional trading strategies that employ leverage are likely to gravitate to carry.

To understand why, it is useful to think about the mechanics of managing a negative carry strategy. By definition, these strategies lose money most of the time. When a levered strategy loses money, it has the effect of increasing "gross exposure"—the ratio of assets controlled divided by capital. Since gross exposure is used as a measure of risk by lenders, if it increases enough, a trader will be forced to scale back exposure toward what is considered an acceptable level. This reduces the amount of money that the negative carry trader can earn when profits eventually do materialize during a carry crash. In fact, if carry crashes occur at sufficiently long intervals, then levered negative carry traders may already have been forced to close their positions and so never get to realize the profits. Thus, the mechanics of managing a levered portfolio create a strong incentive toward being long carry. These features of carry are discussed in more depth in Chapter 9, on volatility and optionality.

Further, the ability to leverage is often needed to bring the absolute expected return from carry up to levels deemed attractive. Think of a carry strategy that might have been typical in the middle of this decade, which borrows in US dollars at 1 percent to invest in New Zealand dollar deposits at 4 percent. Without additional leverage this trade yields a 3 percent annual return if the exchange rate does not move. Professional money managers and institutional investors will typically have much higher return targets. Employing leverage allows the carry trader to produce a target return that is attractive in absolute terms. In short, many carry trades are not attractive without the use of high levels of leverage, and anyone employing leverage is unlikely to want to be short carry (long volatility) in the first place.

This fact leads to a pernicious feature of carry. Leverage increases the risk of ruin, and carry involves leverage. Carry drawdowns are therefore likely to involve the risk of some participants facing ruin. This means the aggregate growth of carry is likely to represent a systemic risk to the financial system. It is therefore no accident that the increased involvement of central banks as lenders of last resort has coincided with the growth of carry. They are intimately linked.

Hedge Funds Are Important Agents of Carry

How do hedge funds stack up against these three metrics? Are they likely to be agents of carry? They certainly do not have a liability profile that lends itself to carry. Hedge fund liabilities can be roughly categorized as owners' capital, investor capital, and short-term borrowings. Of these, the longest duration is owners' capital. While this can sometimes represent a large fraction of the owners' net worth, it is typically a small proportion of total liabilities.

Investor capital is much more significant and can usually be withdrawn at quarterly or annual intervals. There are controls in place, called gates, designed to prevent short-term runs by investors, but this tool proved largely ineffective during the financial crisis in 2008. The third category of liabilities, short-term borrowings, is put in place to amplify returns and can usually be called in by banks at very short notice. Therefore, hedge fund liabilities are largely short term in nature, and at least on this criterion, hedge funds do not seem a good vehicle to pursue carry strategies. In fact, we can go further and say that because of their short-term liabilities hedge funds are a dangerous vehicle to pursue carry, and we should note that if owners have much of their own money at stake, they will not want to. But as hedge funds have become more institutionalized, with owners mostly managing other people's money, carry is more likely to be pursued.

While their liability profile argues against carry, their compensation structure creates a strong incentive in the opposite direction. Each year hedge funds collect a share of the accounting gains as a profit share—historically this has been 20 percent. A strategy that has steady accounting gains for four years and then suffers a loss in year five will still yield four years' worth of profit share—payments that are not given back even if the losses in year five wipe out previous gains. Given this reporting and fee structure, it makes sense that hedge funds would gravitate toward strategies with carry-like payouts.

Moreover, the same incentives operate at the level of the individual trader or portfolio manager employed by a fund. A trader's bonus virtually always contains some component linked to the performance of the portfolio she controls. Indeed, traders are often attracted to hedge funds precisely because their individual results are the primary drivers of their compensation. Once cash bonuses are paid, they are not given back, even if subsequent results wipe out previous gains. It is no accident that this closely mirrors how the firm itself gets paid by its clients. Therefore, the firm as a whole and the individuals within it have an incentive to pursue carry-like strategies.

Our third criterion for evaluating the likelihood of an institution pursuing carry is the presence of leverage. Virtually all hedge funds employ leverage, although there are huge variations in the amounts of leverage used across firms. This again creates a bias for hedge funds to employ carry strategies.

It is important to add a couple of caveats. Having owned, managed, and worked with hedge funds as clients, the authors are aware that these descriptions are generalizations. Nonetheless, the combined effects of the use of leverage and the compensation model continue to produce the incentives for the aggregate hedge fund industry to be long carry.

The Implications of Hedge Fund Carry Trading

Twenty years ago hedge funds were tiny players in the financial markets. According to Hedge Fund Research (HFR), at the end of 1996 hedge fund firms were managing approximately US$120 billion. This meant they controlled less than one-quarter of one percent of the world's stock and bond markets. The industry is no longer tiny. HFR now estimates that by the end of 2018 hedge fund assets under management (AUM) were US$3.1 trillion, a 25-fold increase from 1996. By comparison global stock market capitalization has roughly tripled over that same period. Moreover, the influence of hedge funds is magnified by two additional factors: leverage and trading frequency.

The use of leverage means that hedge funds control far more securities than represented by their AUM. This was most dramatically illustrated in 1998 when Long Term Capital Management (LTCM), the gold standard for hedge funds at the time, collapsed spectacularly. Entering that year, LTCM managed just under US$5 billion, but with an estimated leverage of 25 to 1, it controlled securities worth US$125 billion.

Leverage not only multiplies the assets under a hedge fund's control; it also directly reduces its margin for error, in turn making the portfolio much less stable. Even a relatively small loss on a highly levered portfolio can trigger a margin call. To meet the margin call, positions must be liquidated, often in adverse market conditions, and a vicious circle of forced selling can be triggered. In other words, the US$125 billion of securities controlled by LTCM was vastly more unstable than that same amount under the control of a traditional investor. While LTCM's use of leverage was extreme, the same principles apply to any levered portfolio; both its influence on markets and its instability, particularly during bad times, are increased.

Trading frequency acts like leverage in that it also magnifies the market impact of the securities under a hedge fund's control. A portfolio of securities traded very actively hits the market frequently—impacting prices and liquidity. A hedge fund that turns its holdings over every month will end the year having owned 12 separate portfolios. In terms of its impact on prices, this fund could have 10 or 20 times the impact of a more traditional fund that looks to hold securities for multiple years.

This combination of leverage and frequent trading makes hedge funds even more influential than their headline AUM would suggest. If this headline AUM has grown by 25 times in the last two decades, then hedge fund influence on markets has increased by an even greater magnitude. Given structural incentives to be long carry, it is no surprise that the last two decades have also seen a similar increase in the scale and impact of carry on global markets.

Sovereign Wealth Funds Are Natural Candidates for Carry Strategies

Another type of institution that has experienced significant growth in scale and influence over the last two decades is sovereign wealth funds. According to the Sovereign Wealth Fund Institute, sovereign wealth funds have AUM of approximately US$7.5 trillion, as of the end of 2018, up from only US$508 billion at the end of 1996.

How likely is it that their growth has contributed to the increase in carry? In terms of liabilities, sovereign wealth funds are ideal vehicles for carry. They take many forms, but they typically share a feature of having ultralong-duration liabilities. For example, Norway's Government Pension Fund Global is the fund established to invest the country's oil revenues. Its 2017 annual report listed assets worth US$1.07 trillion. Ninety-seven percent of corresponding liabilities were classified as "owner's capital," essentially equity of very long duration. While it is true that Norway eventually plans to spend some of this money to replace oil revenue, these liabilities will not begin to come due for many years.

Since it faces no pressure to sell assets during bad times, the Norwegian fund is well placed to invest in carry strategies. Indeed, it commissioned three well-known finance academics to write a report about its management, and they explicitly cited the nature of the fund's liabilities as something that should drive its investment strategy. One of the strategies they suggested that fits this profile was foreign exchange carry.

In addition, sovereign wealth funds have the ability to use leverage where they believe it is appropriate. This means that if they identify carry trades that seem to be attractive, they have the ability to lever the trades up to generate an expected return consistent with long-term return objectives. Further, since their balance sheets are very strong, they have the ability to ride out short-term drawdowns in carry strategies, making it more likely that they can capture the full-cycle returns.

On the other hand, since they do not have outside shareholders and in many cases offer little or no disclosure on results (Norway being an exception), there is no pressure to pursue strategies that regularly generate positive returns. Nor are they compensated with profit shares in the manner of hedge funds. On this criterion sovereign wealth funds do not have incentive to pursue carry trades.

On balance it is likely that many sovereign wealth funds exploit their liability structure and ability to use leverage to employ carry. One could even argue that they are natural providers of insurance to the market and, because of their strong balance sheets, are much safer vehicles for carry to reside in than hedge funds.

Most endowments and foundations share with sovereign wealth funds a long-duration liability profile. They typically consider themselves to be permanent institutions and operate with a view toward spending only a limited portion of their fund's capital each year. That amount is usually governed by rules that are unchanging. This means that liabilities do not move up or down with financial cycles. In theory this could support carry strategies.

However, these funds have more oversight and public accountability than sovereign wealth funds. They are smaller in size, more diverse in mandate, and more conservative in investment style. In addition, many have restrictions on leverage—precisely because they want to limit the risk of permanent capital loss. On balance, these considerations matter more, and we do not view these institutions as important agents of carry. Once again, this is a generalization; undoubtedly some of the larger funds, particularly those with in-house investment staff, do engage in carry. However, we do not believe that they are an important structural source of the secular growth in carry strategies.

Global Investment Banks' Proprietary Trading Highlights the Power of the Compensation Incentive

Prior to the implementation of the Volcker Rule in 2014, which required banks to close most proprietary trading operations, investment banks[2] operated very large proprietary trading desks. Of course, there was a vast array of compensation arrangements, but the broad structure was an annual bonus linked to profit and loss with no "giveback" for subsequent losses. This created a huge incentive for these institutions to have aggregate trading exposures with carry-like features.

Interestingly, the liability profile of investment banks in particular was the exact opposite of the structure ideally suited for carry trading. Only a tiny sliver of their liabilities was equity. Even including long-term debt did not change the fact that most of the liabilities were short term in nature, meaning that bad times for carry strategies could easily compound through a run on liabilities.

As it turned out, 2008 was a terrible year for carry strategies and coincided with a run on investment bank liabilities, with the result being the well-documented global financial crisis. That these institutions still engaged in carry strategies despite having liabilities ill-suited to them speaks to the power of the compensation incentive in driving investment strategy.

Since 2014, the scale of investment bank proprietary trading has been reduced. Anecdotal evidence suggests that many proprietary trading groups have simply joined hedge funds. Others suggest that "prop" positions are still present but better hidden within other allowable parts of banks' books. These claims are not easily verified. Given the Volcker Rule and the increased regulatory focus on systemic risk, it seems unlikely that banks have been a meaningful source of carry growth in the last several years, and this is not likely to change.

---

2. We use the term "investment bank" in a loose sense since most sizable global investment banks were converted to bank holding companies (Goldman Sachs, Morgan Stanley), bought by banks (Merrill Lynch, Bear Stearns), or closed (Lehman). European "universal" banks such as UBS and Deutsche have always engaged in both commercial and investment banking operations.

Private Equity Leveraged Buyouts Are a Form of Carry Trade

Thus far we have looked at institutional involvement in carry trades through the lens of incentives. With private equity leveraged buyouts, we take a more direct approach. We consider the core economic features of carry—liquidity provision, leverage, and short volatility—and explain that these private equity funds have the same characteristics.

The term "carry trade" suggests a transaction with a relatively short time horizon. Indeed, in the currency strategy we evaluated in Chapter 4, we assumed daily transactions. However, this is only one example; a carry trade is defined by the nature of its risks, not the duration of the transaction. Classic carry trades use borrowed money to take positions in high-yielding assets with less liquidity. This is precisely what private equity funds that focus on leveraged buyouts do. They combine investor capital (equity) with debt to purchase a portfolio of companies with earnings yields above the real cost of debt. Of course, their goal eventually is to sell those companies at a higher price, and thus there is more focus on capital gain than in traditional currency carry trades. Still, the basic feature is a levered yield spread between the cost of debt and the return on the underlying asset being bought.

Indeed, some researchers argue that once private equity returns are adjusted for leverage, their results are no better than public market returns. This is hardly a settled debate, but if true, it would mean that owners of private equity firms are extracting significant fees from investors to create a portfolio of levered equity.[3] Why would investors pay so much for this "service" when they could construct a levered equity portfolio easily and cheaply on their own?

If investors did lever up a holding of public equities, their portfolio risk as measured by volatility of returns would increase. Investing in private equity

---

3. Specifically, small-capitalization value firms according to Stafford (2017). This is because buyout firms have historically focused on smaller firms with higher-than-average yields. More recently, as buyout funds have attracted growing amounts of capital they have been buying larger companies with yields (i.e., valuations) similar to public companies. Stafford, E., "Replicating Private Equity with Value Investing, Homemade Leverage, and Hold-to-Maturity Accounting," Harvard Business School Working Paper, May 2017.

funds has the opposite effect. Why? The reason is that private equity firms have significant discretion in valuing their investments, and this allows them to report returns that are much smoother than public equities even though they hold a portfolio that is more levered. Researchers at AQR Capital suggest that reported betas of private equity funds (essentially the correlation of private equity returns with public market returns), even after adjusting for potential smoothing, are less than 1.0.[4]

This means that on conventional risk measures like portfolio volatility, shifting from public to private equity reduces a portfolio's reported riskiness. Short-lived market corrections—such as the almost 10 percent decline in the S&P 500 in December 2018—might barely be reflected in a private equity portfolio's return. Even extreme drops such as happened during the global financial crisis are significantly smoothed. For instance, from October 2008 through March 2009, the S&P 500 fell by 31.6 percent. Over that same period, an index of private equity fund returns published by Cambridge Associates fell by only 18.8 percent. During the following two quarters, the S&P 500 rose sharply, earning a return of 32.4 percent, while the private equity index rose by 10.6 percent. Even though the private equity index contains companies that are less liquid and more levered, it seemed much less risky than public equities across the worst credit crisis since the Great Depression.

Of course, if the S&P 500 had not bounced back so much after March 2009, then private equity valuations would eventually have had to catch up—or rather, "catch down"—with the public markets. This smoothing of returns in the short term and waiting for a rebound in value resembles the strategy of betting on mean reversion that volatility sellers pursue, albeit in this case the mean reversion is over a period of many months rather than days. Economically, though, it is similar in exposure and risk to "buying the dip"—that is, to selling volatility, as explained in Chapters 6 and 9 of this book. Selling volatility is, of course, also a core characteristic of carry.

In the latter chapters of the book, we also talk about a further, political-societal feature of carry as being a strategy that primarily benefits insiders—

---

4. A. Ilmanen, S. Chandra, and N. McQuinn, "Demystifying Illiquid Assets: Expected Returns for Private Equity," AQR Whitepaper, February 2019.

the wealthy and politically connected. Private equity certainly ticks this box as well. Regular people cannot invest in private equity, only the very wealthy and institutions. Even among those with the capital to invest in private equity, only a few can have access to the most successful managers. The value extracted by private equity fees and the returns earned by private equity funds are mostly the preserve of insiders.[5]

Private equity buyouts are therefore carry trades, and the growth in the value of these deals follows a pattern similar to our estimates of the global carry trade. There was an explosion in the value of deals from 2005 to 2007, followed by a collapse during and after the global financial crisis and a strong recent resurgence. The buyout industry is cyclical, so point-to-point comparisons can be misleading. That said, the scale of capital being employed in these deals is now much greater than it was 20 years ago. For instance, according to Bain and Company, which produces a detailed overview of the industry each year, the last five years have been the strongest in the industry's history, and there were US$582 billion in global buyout deals in 2018 alone.[6] This is virtually the same size as the combined deals over the period 1995–2002. Private equity has been an important component in the rise of carry.

Corporations Are Engaging in Carry Strategies

This chapter has focused on financial institutions as potential agents of carry. In recent years evidence has also emerged that nonfinancial corporations are also crucially involved in carry. We discussed the role of nonfinancial corporations in the currency carry trade in Chapters 2 and 3.

A further source of evidence for this is a 2015 paper by BIS economists Valentina Bruno and Hyun Song Shin.[7] Bruno and Shin collected data on

5. Carry returns can accrue to "regular people" if the institutions investing in private equity are doing so on behalf of pensioners. This is certainly the case with some important private equity investors such as Canadian pension plans.

6. "Global Private Equity Report," Bain & Company, 2010 and 2019.

7. V. Bruno and H. S. Shin, "Global Dollar Credit and Carry Trades: A Firm Level Analysis," BIS Working Papers, No. 510, August 2015.

individual firms domiciled outside the United States and tracked the scale, timing, and use of their borrowing in US dollars. They observed that companies operating in emerging markets borrowed more dollars when they already had cash on their balance sheets. Since this existing cash could presumably be used to finance capital investment, Bruno and Shin suggested that the motivation for the additional US dollar borrowings might be to engage in purely financial carry trades.

They created a measure of the attractiveness of a domestic carry trade—the interest rate differential with the US dollar scaled by exchange rate volatility—and found that dollar bond issuance is indeed more prevalent when the carry trade looks attractive. Further, the money raised in these US dollar offerings is more likely to end up being held in cash. Borrowing dollars to hold in local currency deposits is a pure carry trade. There are exceptions, but Bruno and Shin concluded that there is a consistent pattern of emerging market companies engaging in carry-like behavior.

Similar results were found in a more granular study of Chinese companies by Huang, Panizza, and Portes in 2018.[8] They segmented firms according to measures of profitability and risk and found that riskier firms "try to boost profitability by engaging in speculative activities that mimic the behavior of financial institutions." These firms were more likely to issue dollar bonds when measures of carry trade returns were high, and they were more likely to on-lend these funds to other firms rather than use the money to fund capital projects. This carry trade activity increased substantially following new regulations in 2009 and 2010 that were intended to reduce lending by financial firms to "risky" economic sectors. With financial firms restricted in their ability to extend credit, nonfinancial corporations began acting as shadow banks, raising funds in US dollars and lending the money to other firms operating in their sector.

Since the global financial crisis, the large increase in corporate debt issuance—not merely foreign currency debt issuance—has been a well-remarked phenomenon. As a percentage of GDP, outstanding US nonfinancial corpo-

8. Y. Huang, U. Panizza, and R. Portes, "Corporate Foreign Bond Issuance and Interfirm Loans in China," National Bureau of Economic Research, April 2018.

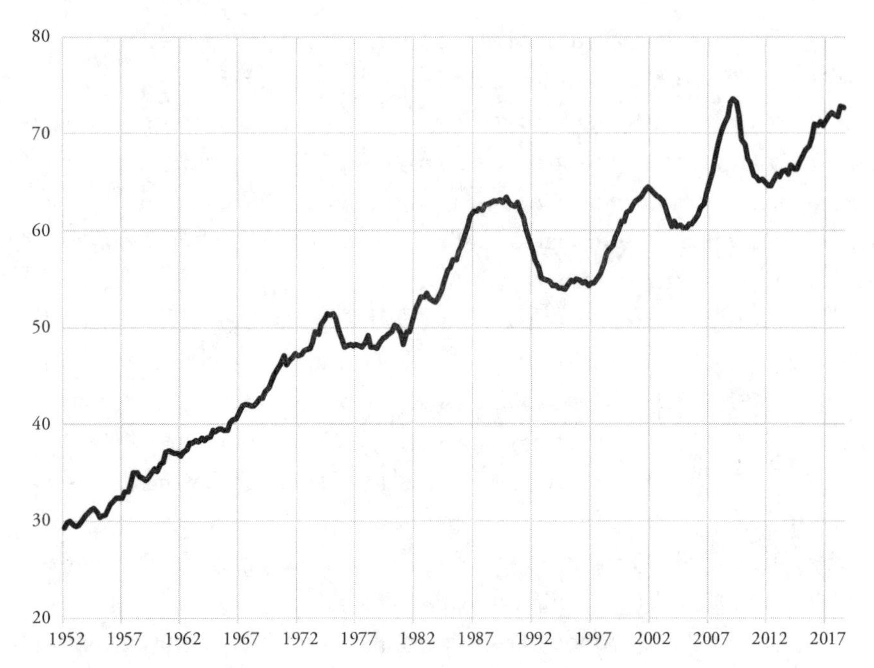

FIGURE 5.1 US nonfinancial business debt as a percentage of GDP
Source of data: Federal Reserve Board, US Bureau of Economic Analysis

rate debt is set to reach new heights (Figure 5.1), and this has occurred late in a long economic expansion, when GDP is potentially above its trend level.

A substantial part of this debt issuance has been to finance corporate share buybacks (Figure 5.2). The US nonfinancial corporate sector markedly increased its own leverage during the long post-crisis economic expansion. This can also be considered to be part of a giant carry trade. Profit share has been well above average. Most financial observers would say that high profit share is a very positive development. However, it does not sit easily with the low level of real interest rates over the post-crisis period. Economic theory would suggest that the return on capital and the cost of capital should tend toward equality—which would in turn imply that the long-run prospective return to investment and return on equity will be poor, given the very low level of real interest rates.

We would argue that profit share in the economy itself has become a function of carry. (We discuss this further in Chapter 8.) But whether or

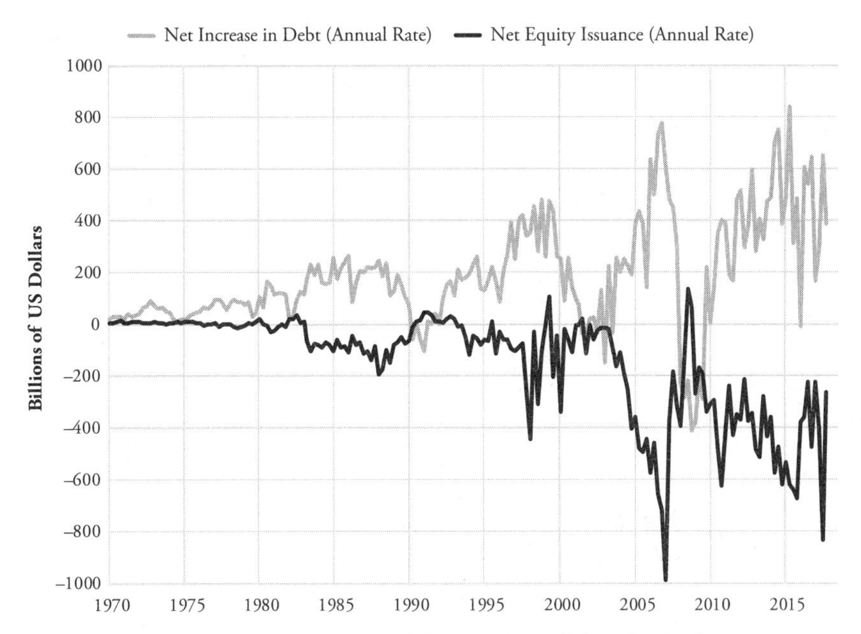

FIGURE 5.2 US nonfinancial corporate debt issuance and share buybacks
Source of data: Federal Reserve Board

not one accepts this, it seems evident that corporates taking advantage of very low interest rates on their own debt to finance higher-yielding financial investments—whether these businesses are non-US companies borrowing in dollars to buy higher-yielding domestic currency assets or US corporates borrowing at low interest rates to buy back their own equity—are themselves engaging in carry trades. It may even be plausible to argue that nonfinancial corporates have been the single most important economic sector driving carry trades in the post-crisis period.

The Transformation of Global Financial Markets

The global financial markets have been transformed in the last two decades. Hedge funds have evolved from tiny niche overseers of private wealth to giant institutional asset managers. Sovereign wealth funds have grown into a global force looking after long-duration pools of capital accumulated by government entities. Both types of institutions have incentives to engage in carry. Finally, there is evidence from corporate balance sheets that emerging market companies are using their access to international capital markets to engage in carry-like activities of their own, while the corporate sector broadly has been increasing leverage. Together the activity of these institutions and businesses has been an important driver of the structural growth in carry. Until and unless an ultimate carry crash changes their incentives, we expect this growth to continue.

There are other features of modern financial markets that we have not touched on here that can also be related to the growth of carry. High-frequency trading firms (HFTs) rely, as their name suggests, on rapid-fire trading controlled by computer algorithms and ultrafast access to exchanges. Much of the activity of HFTs amounts to market-making transactions; these are classic liquidity provision trades. In Chapter 9 we consider more rigorously the close relationship between buying the dip in stock markets, shorting volatility futures, selling options, and making markets (that is, profiting from the bid-ask spread), suggesting that in the limiting case these are all equivalent carry trades. We also introduce in the chapter following this the idea that the S&P 500 itself has become a carry trade. It might not be too much of a stretch to conclude that HFTs, with their extreme frequency of trading and with operations in the US equity markets at the center of the global carry trade, are an important part of the machinery of the carry regime. Their rise is perhaps another marker, in institutional terms, of the rise of carry.

As carry has become more pervasive in financial markets, and the structure of financial markets has evolved both to encourage and accommodate carry and to benefit from it, then it is reasonable to suspect that forms of financial activity that are manifestations of carry will grow in importance. But central to the rise of carry are the institutions that have been the most influential carry traders of all—the central banks. The central banks are the ultimate agents of carry, now with large balance sheets that themselves constitute a giant carry trade. We explore the crucial role of central banks in the rise of carry much further in the remaining chapters of the book.

6
The Fundamental Nature of the Carry Regime

IN THIS CHAPTER WE EXPLAIN SEVERAL IDEAS THAT ARE critical to understanding the full depth of carry's impact on global markets. First, we describe why some level of carry trading is both to be expected and to be desired. Carry traders provide liquidity and leverage to markets and are compensated for this service as well as for bearing the risk of carry crashes. We then explain why the epicenter of this activity is the US markets, particularly volatility trading in the S&P 500. We discuss how this has made S&P 500 volatility, as proxied by the VIX, the central risk factor in global markets. The chapter concludes by looking at central banks and demonstrating how their market activity has directly contributed to the expansion of global carry trading.

Is the Carry Regime a Natural Phenomenon or a Product of Central Bank Policies?

In the previous chapter we discussed who are likely to be the main players in the financial markets in terms of carry trade activity. The growth of these institutions—the main agents of carry—has been part of the creation of a "carry regime" in financial markets. The authors define a carry regime to be a structure of financial market pricing and a pattern of market behavior that, over time, rewards those implementing carry trades with outsized returns. Those outsized returns, if expressed as a total return index for a carry investment, will take the form of a usually steady ratcheting higher of the total return index—punctuated by severe carry crashes.

Here, and in more depth in Chapter 9, we will explore volatility selling—or volatility carry—in the US stock market, specifically the S&P 500. This is much less well understood than currency carry, but it has become central to the global carry regime, as implied by data we examined in Chapter 4. For the US stock market, the market structure that favors carry can be seen in the structure of volatility for the market: that is, in the relationships between the expected volatilities implicit in the prices of different options and the statistical volatilities realized in the behavior of the market. One interpretation is that the profits to carry traders that emerge from this market structure represent a return for their service as liquidity providers to the market. Our suggestion is that this is necessary because the marginal speculator is levered and therefore requires a "'liquidity backstop"; when the marginal speculator demands market liquidity, the carry trader is the supplier of that liquidity.

We further argue that the high level of expected return to carry that has been built into the structure of volatility for the S&P 500 is because carry traders in the deeper US markets—and the markets for derivatives and ETFs linked to the S&P 500 are the deepest equity risk markets in the world—have to be the marginal providers of liquidity not only to levered speculators in US markets but, to some extent at least, to levered speculators in all global markets. In other markets, which do not have the same market depth and range of instruments available, some hedging of risk will be hedging into the US market instruments. This places the S&P 500 at the center of the global carry regime and makes the S&P 500 itself the ultimate carry trade.

This may seem relatively benign at first sight. What could be wrong about financial markets pricing in the service of providing liquidity? In contrast, we have argued that the growth of the global currency carry trade has represented a mispricing of risk and misallocation of resources—and we put much of the blame on the central banks and their policies.

At first this seems inconsistent. For a long time it has been widely recognized that, to a substantial degree, the global financial markets have converged to a "market of one,"[1] either trading as "risk on" or "risk off." It is fairly clear in recent years that over most (not all) periods when currency carry "works," the S&P 500 carry trade will also work. This was indicated by the data presented in Chapter 4. The IMF data for the net foreign assets of US financial corporations—which we contended provide a rough guide to the development of the dollar-funded global currency carry trade—also show an obvious association between the S&P 500 and the currency carry trade, as indicated by Figure 6.1.

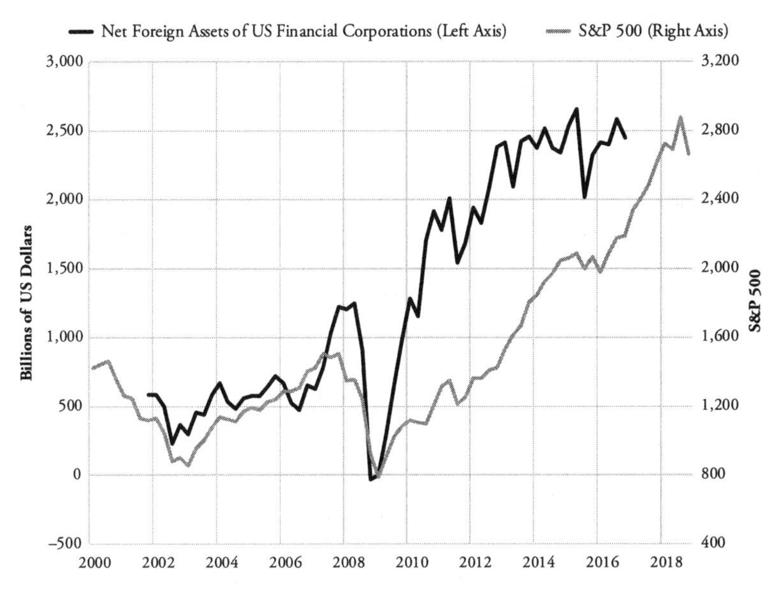

FIGURE 6.1 S&P 500 and net foreign assets of US financial corporations
Source of data: International Monetary Fund

1. This phrase was first coined during the 2003–2007 credit carry bubble by Henry McVey, at that time a strategist at Morgan Stanley.

Further, a parallel argument can be made that the currency carry trade is also about liquidity provision. Most (not all) carry recipient currencies are currencies of emerging economies. These economies are often fast growing but are more volatile; they are reliant on capital inflows but with debt that is more lowly rated than the debt of developed economies and with managed exchange rates and less policy flexibility than the major developed economies. In short, they are arguably analogous to the marginal levered speculator in a developed economy stock market; they are potential demanders of liquidity and will be demanders of liquidity in a crisis. So perhaps positive returns over time to currency carry trades, and the consequent growth of the global currency carry trade, are justified by the need for capital, or liquidity, of the carry recipient economies?

To some extent this may be true, but in the case of currency carry trades, the important influence that central banks (and the IMF) have had in encouraging the growth of carry trades, along with the instability that this has engendered, is quite obvious. Some of this history was summarized in Chapter 2. If there is a parallel between currency carry trades and stock market volatility carry trades—and it is clear both from the theoretical arguments and from the empirical data that there must be—then it seems that central bank policies may have been a malign influence on the latter too.

The authors believe that the answer to this conundrum is the following: carry is a naturally occurring phenomenon in financial markets. It can be understood at an even more fundamental level, beyond merely financial markets, which we will touch on later in this book. In its more limited form, carry can be a motor, or at least a lubricant, for progress. The problem occurs when carry comes to dominate over other market behaviors or forces, in which case it can begin to manifest in forms that could be considered rent-seeking or even corruption or infringement of liberties. In financial carry trades, on the one side are those who could ultimately be desperate for liquidity, and on the other side are those—the carry traders—who are the suppliers of that liquidity. This can be perceived as an economic relationship, but in a broader context it could also be understood as a power relationship.

The transformation of the natural force of carry into what looks more like exploitation would not occur in the theoretical free market economy of an economics textbook. But it could occur in more monopolistic forms of economic organization, those with reduced degrees of economic freedom. In particular, it seems it might be a tendency in a financial and economic system in which base money is created by a central authority with considerable discretion—the central bank—in which case, carry can rise to exploit the decision making of that authority, coming to dominate all other macrofinancial influences and ultimately "capturing" the central bank. Then the carry regime emerges as a carry bubble, or rather a sequence of ever-bigger bubbles and carry crashes, inflicting progressive damage on the economy and society as a whole.

So the answer to the question posed in the heading at the beginning of this section is "both." The natural phenomenon of carry is morally neutral or benign, but in its interaction with the authorities over the financial system—particularly the central banks—lies malign potential.

Volatility Selling in the S&P 500

To understand fully the carry regime, we need to understand further the relationships among carry, leverage/debt, and liquidity. In this chapter we explain this from the perspective of volatility trading in the stock market. In the following chapter we look at the issue from the perspective of monetary economics.

In the stock market, direct bets on volatility can be made in the options and futures markets. A stockholder who wishes to protect himself from the risk of a large loss on a stock—or the market as a whole—can buy a put option on the stock (or the market index). He pays a premium for this put option, which gives him the right to sell the stock (or market) at a fixed "strike" price—in this case below the current price of the stock—up to a certain time in the future. The writer, or seller, of that put option therefore receives the premium, or income, in exchange for accepting the risk of a decline in the stock price below the level of the strike price of the option.

The writer of the put option is implementing a simple volatility selling trade, or carry trade; she will receive an income that depends on the stock or market not falling heavily in price. If the stock, or market, remains relatively stable (that is, volatility is low), then her carry trade will be profitable. As is well known, the price of the put option will depend on how far the current price of the underlying stock or market index is from the strike price, the time left until expiration of the option, and, importantly, the expectation of future volatility of the stock price or market index—"implied volatility." Other things being equal, the higher the expected volatility, the more the option will cost and the greater will be the income to the writer of the option. However, if the underlying falls below the strike price of the option, she will have to pay out an amount of money that will be greater the further the underlying falls—that is, the more volatile the underlying is. In expectation, therefore, the writer of the option will make money if volatility is lower than expected; she is "selling volatility."

Volatility is the measurement of the extent to which prices can change, and it is a critical component of the cost of options. Future prices are distributed in a range around the current price, and volatility is a single number that sums up how wide that range is likely to be.

"Realized" or "historical" volatility is measured by looking backward—by looking at the distribution of price changes over some period in the past. But volatility itself is volatile. We can measure last month's volatility, but volatility will be different next month. Fortunately it seems to change somewhat slowly; it is "persistent." Last month's volatility, most of the time, is a pretty good guess at the distribution of tomorrow's price change, even though it might not be useful for thinking about daily price changes in a year's time. Therefore implied volatility, the market's expectation for future realized volatility, tends to move in line with realized volatility—albeit that implied volatility is normally higher than realized volatility by some margin.

In modern financial markets implied volatility can be sold directly. The simplest and most popular way to do this is through VIX futures or through exchange-traded notes (ETNs) that correspond to simple VIX futures strategies. The VIX is an index representing the implied volatility for the S&P 500 over the next 30 days, derived from the prices of options on the S&P 500 index.[2] VIX futures are monthly-expiring contracts that settle at the VIX.[3]

2. Strictly speaking, the VIX represents the volatility corresponding to the implied variance for the S&P 500 over the next 30 days.

3. The less widely followed VXO implied volatility index is based on prices of options on the S&P 100, which have a longer history; because of the longer data history, the VXO was used as the basis for the study of historical data in Chapter 4 rather than the VIX.

Most of the time VIX futures prices are higher than spot VIX, and longer-dated futures have higher prices than shorter-dated contracts. In other words, the VIX futures curve typically slopes upward. Figure 6.2 illustrates this by showing the average shape of the curve since the financial crisis. Shorting VIX futures when the curve has this shape has positive carry—it is a carry trade. If a trader shorts a longer-dated VIX future and the spot VIX does not change, then over time the trader will make money as the price of the contract falls toward the spot price at expiration. This is called the "roll yield"—the income that accrues to the carry trader as the price of the VIX future "rolls down" the curve toward the spot price. The trade is even more profitable if implied volatility falls and the spot VIX is lower at expiration than when the short futures trade was initiated. Thus, like the currency carry trade, the VIX carry trade has two components: the roll yield (analogous to the interest rate differential) and the change in the underlying asset price. In this case the underlying asset is volatility itself.

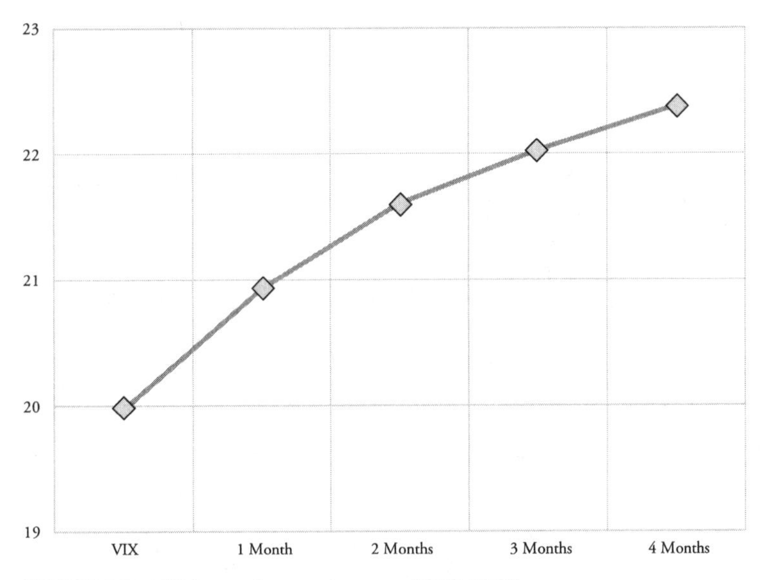

FIGURE 6.2 VIX forward curve, average, 2009–2018
Chart shows average of daily closing values for VIX spot, VIX 1 month forward, 2 months forward, etc., from the first trading day of 2009 to the last trading day of 2018, where forward points are interpolated from the futures curve and the average is calculated as the root mean square.
Source of data: CFE/Interactive Brokers, authors' calculations

By the same token, holding VIX futures long is expensive. Figure 6.3 shows the performance of the VXX ETN, an instrument that represents a continuously rolling portfolio of VIX futures with constant average time to expiry of one month, since late in the financial crisis. The scale for the chart is logarithmic.

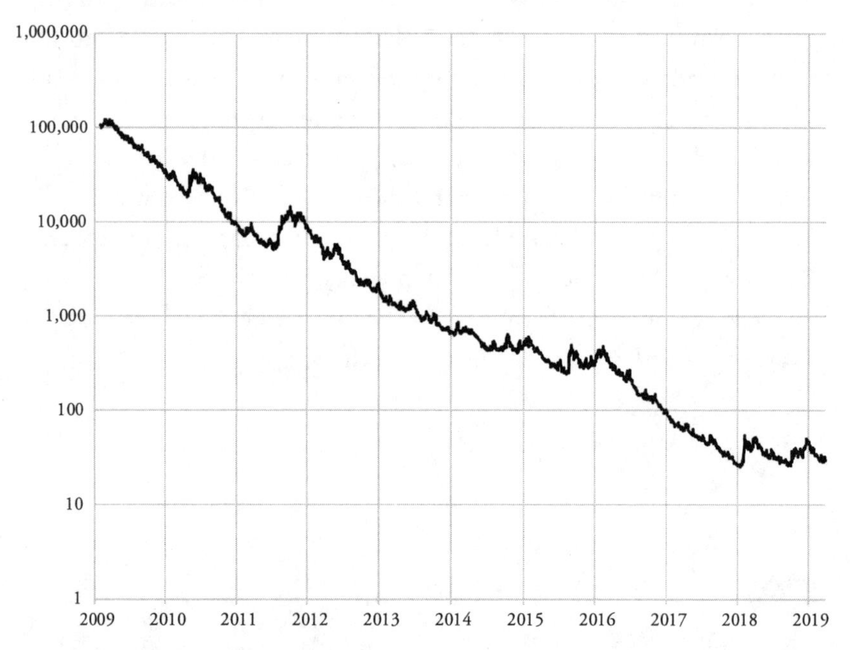

FIGURE 6.3 VXX/VXXB—cumulative total return
Chart covers the period from the inception of VXX on January 30, 2009 to March 29, 2019. Note that VXX was delisted and replaced with the otherwise identical instrument VXXB on January 30, 2019.
Source of data: Yahoo! Finance

Selling VIX futures—that is, shorting the line in Figure 6.3—has been steadily profitable at the cost of severe drawdowns during volatility spikes, such as those in May 2010, August 2011, August 2015, and February 2018, which each saw VXX rise between 80 and 180 percent. Why should this be the case? Specifically, why should VIX selling be profitable, and why should it be subject to such extreme drawdowns? That is, why does volatility matter?

Volatility, Optionality, and Leverage

Volatility matters because it gives the cost of, or payment for, optionality. Optionality is something implicitly traded in running certain kinds of dynamic investment strategies. The simplest example is running constant leverage. Given that the carry regime is fundamentally about leverage, this is an important concept.

For example, say an investor or speculator wants to be 200 percent levered long the S&P 500 at all times. Say he has $100 of equity and therefore a $200 total position. If the market immediately rallies 1 percent, his position goes to $202 and his equity goes to $102. Since $202 divided by $102 is less than 200 percent, he needs to buy $2 more in order to maintain constant 200 percent leverage. If instead the market falls 1 percent, his position goes to $198 and his equity goes to $98. In this case his position is now greater than 200 percent; he needs to sell $2 of stock in order to maintain his constant level of leverage.

Leverage changes in a similar manner for speculators who short the market. For example, suppose an investor with $100 of equity aims to have a 100 percent short position in the S&P 500. If the market falls by 2 percent, the investor makes $2 in profit and now has $102 of equity. However, his existing short position is only worth $98. To maintain a 100 percent short position, he needs to short-sell an additional $4. If instead the market moves against him and rises by 2 percent, his equity falls to $98 and his outstanding position rises to $102. In order to maintain a short position equal to his equity, he needs to reduce his short position by purchasing $4 in stock.

These examples demonstrate that if a speculator is levered or maintains a short position, he needs to buy when the asset price rises and sell when the asset price falls in order to rebalance and maintain a constant level of leverage. As shorthand, let us call this pattern of buying when prices rise (and selling when they fall) "trading with the market." On the other hand, if a speculator is underlevered—say, holding a 50 percent stock–50 percent cash portfolio—a similar example will show that he needs to sell when the price rises and buy when it falls, or "trade against the market," in order to rebalance his position and maintain a constant degree of underleverage.

A levered speculator, trading with the market, is buying optionality. She has the potential to make explosive profits if the market keeps moving in her favor, and she continues trading with it. In return for this potential, she will always find herself buying higher and selling lower around the fluctuations—the noise—in market movements, and every time she trades, there is a cost. It is easy to see that the total cost of trading with the market is related to the volatility of the asset price; the more the asset moves up and down, the more trades are required and the higher the cost. In expectation, the activity of trading with the market costs an amount directly proportional to volatility squared, or variance. (This is sometimes referred to as "volatility drag" or "variance drag.")

So optionality means trading with or against the market. Optionality is very important; its price, or its cost, is determined by volatility. It could be said that optionality *is* volatility, and volatility *is* optionality.[4]

What if the levered speculator chooses not to rebalance? If the market continues to move against her, her equity will approach zero; she will be ruined. This can happen even to a speculator who is attempting to rebalance, if market moves are sudden and very large—if the market crashes violently. In practice, as her equity falls below certain thresholds, her broker will require her to close positions or will forcibly close positions on her behalf. This is called getting "stopped out" of a position.

Getting stopped out, in this manner, of a levered long position means selling when the price falls; getting stopped out of a short position means buying when the price rises. Getting stopped out is always trading with the market. The expected value of the cost of trading with the market should be the same whether a speculator chooses to pay it explicitly by rebalancing or by accepting the risk of ruin.

In practice, the speculator's situation is further complicated by the fact that the point at which she can get stopped out changes, depending on overall financial conditions and her broker's own financial position. For example,

4. In options markets, optionality—the property of trading with or against the market—is referred to by the Greek letter gamma. We extend the arguments outlined here in more detail in Chapter 9.

in August 2007 speculators could lever a position in US high-yield credit as much as 10 times. One year later the maximum levered position was reduced to 4 times. Levered speculators in CDOs of asset-backed securities fared worse: in August 2007 a position in the highest-rated tranche of a CDO could be levered by 25 times; by August 2008 almost no leverage was available at all.[5]

Trading with the market, as a levered speculator is required to do, necessarily means demanding liquidity. A levered speculator will be willing to—or will have no choice but to—pay for that liquidity requirement. The profits of volatility selling can be seen, at least partially, as the payment for providing liquidity to levered speculators.

As chronicled in the previous chapter, hedge funds are levered market participants, and their influence has grown enormously in the last two decades. Therefore we should not be surprised that as their influence has increased, so has the cost associated with their liquidity demands, which forms part of the source of volatility carry trade returns. More generally, it is obvious that at higher levels of systemic leverage, much more market liquidity is needed. It seems likely that at higher levels of systemic leverage, the premium for supplying liquidity and leverage—that is, for selling volatility—is greater.

By 2018 total effective leverage in the global economy and markets very likely exceeded that at the 2007 peak.[6] Over the longer view, the past few decades of financialization have seen the world become more liquid and more levered than ever before. So much leverage demands liquidity; so much market liquidity incentivizes leverage. So the trade in volatility has become larger and more important than ever before. At the epicenter of that volatility market is the S&P 500 and the VIX.

---

5. Qiang Dai and Suresh Sundaresan, "Risk Management Framework for Hedge Funds: Role of Funding and Redemption Options on Leverage." 2010.

6. Available data on aggregate debt, including sovereign debt, suggest that the global debt-to-GDP ratio has continued to rise. However, as explained in Chapter 3, true leverage—including contingent and off-balance-sheet liabilities—is much harder, or impossible, to measure.

Leverage and Carry Crashes

One of the defining features of carry trades is that they always involve leverage. The instability of levered trades is the key reason that carry trades eventually crash. And since the S&P 500 is both the key driver of world markets and increasingly the epicenter of global carry, we can begin to see why stock market crash risk is very real.

Writing an option is a carry trade and as such involves leverage. Consider the potential exposure of the seller of an unhedged out-of-the-money put. When the put is sold, the option writer receives premium income that will be a fraction of the underlying notional amount—but the option writer, or seller, commits to purchasing that much larger notional amount should the market fall and the option expire in-the-money. Thus the option seller takes on a contingent liability much greater than the cash he receives; the seller's leverage has increased. The option buyer has purchased levered access to the price of the underlying asset—the notional her option gives her exposure to is far greater than the premium she has spent—and that access is being provided by the seller agreeing potentially to expand his balance sheet, contingent on market outcomes.

In every kind of short volatility trade, the return is collected by receiving the more certain amount and preparing to pay an uncertain amount. For instance, in the VIX roll-down trade described earlier, the carry trader sells long-dated implied volatility at a known price and will close out the trade by purchasing the spot VIX in the future at an uncertain price. Because the VIX cannot fall below zero but there is no limit to how high it can go, the volatility seller always has a larger potential downside than upside: the trade is levered. Selling volatility—whether writing options, shorting the VIX, or in other ways (some of which are detailed in Chapter 9)—always involves providing leverage and promising market liquidity.

The conception of carry trades as inherently levered helps us understand their key stylized characteristic—carry crashes. It is widely understood that carry trades have extremely skewed distributions of returns over medium-term horizons; this was discussed in depth, using empirical data, in Chapter 4. Their return paths have a sawtooth pattern, rising slowly and falling quickly—"up the stairs, down the elevator," "nickels in front of steamrollers," and so forth. The total return of the Australian dollar against the US dollar leading up to and during the 2007–2009 global financial crisis shows the classic carry pattern (Figure 6.4).

FIGURE 6.4 Australian dollar total return, 2006–2009
Chart shows the total return path of the Australian dollar for the years around the 2007 bubble peak, during which period it perfectly exemplified a carry trade.
Source of data: Bloomberg

The sawtooth pattern is explained by the effect of leverage. Simple models of prices suggest that they should look like "Brownian noise"—one day's returns should be independent from the next. But access to leverage breaks the independence of returns. As long as the carry traders collectively still have the ability and willingness to deploy further leverage, dips are a reason to buy, and so they are bought. Therefore, while leverage employed is rising, prices become mean reverting and continue to rise. But leverage cannot rise infinitely. When the supply of new leverage into the carry trade runs out, price declines lead to forced selling, in turn leading to further price declines. There is a deleveraging cascade. Liquidity for sellers evaporates. Price behavior briefly flips from mean reverting to momentum (downward), and volatility explodes.

Trades selling S&P 500 volatility show this pattern clearly over the last several years, with the largest carry crash or volatility spike in October 2008 and smaller such events in May 2010, August 2011, August 2015, and February 2018 (the latter spike now known as "Volmageddon," during which the VIX more than doubled in one day). During these spikes all forms of S&P 500 volatility selling fail simultaneously. Implied volatility soars, especially at the spot and nearest forwards, causing the VIX curve to invert; realized volatility explodes higher than even current implied; and the market falls without bouncing.

Since volatility *is* the cost of leverage and price of market liquidity, carry crashes are best understood as increases in the price of volatility on the carry asset. Where the volatility of a carry asset itself is tradable, it too must be a carry trade. It slowly falls and remains low in the leveraging phase, giving profits to sellers, before it bursts upward in the deleveraging. And, too, selling volatility in a carry asset must be profitable, since the carry asset is inherently levered and therefore the market for it contains levered speculators demanding liquidity. Conversely, the widespread application of leverage to selling volatility on an asset must turn the underlying itself into a carry trade. Heavy volatility selling in the S&P 500 turns the S&P 500 itself into a carry trade.

Most likely, more levered carry trades do not have lower expected returns; they simply have greater skew—more vicious crashes. If the skew risk—the crash risk—is severe enough, volatility can be "fairly priced" at any apparent expected return premium; the greater the apparent premium, the more leverage will be invited into shorting volatility and the more the skew risk will invisibly rise, as those who believe themselves liquidity suppliers must in extremis turn liquidity demanders. In a world such as today's, in which systemic leverage is extreme and the need for liquidity is paramount, the fact that many people and institutions are systematically short volatility does not necessarily mean that long-run returns to selling volatility will be low. It only necessarily means that volatility will be prone to extremely severe short squeezes.

Volatility Is the Value of Money

The depth of the US markets, and the range of financial instruments available in them, places the S&P 500 at the center of the global carry regime.

Derivatives and ETFs linked to the S&P 500 are the most liquid venues for equity risk in the world; the S&P 500 is highly correlated with most equity risk trades, and the S&P 500 is the world's most important benchmark. The S&P 500, through the derivative contracts tied to it, is therefore used to hedge positions and risk in a very wide variety of less liquid instruments—the S&P 500 is the world's hedge. In this way it absorbs the optionality demand, and therefore premium, from other less liquid instruments. Relatedly, while volatility indexes are available for a wide variety of other markets, none are as closely followed as the VIX. And while futures and options on some of these other volatility indexes also exist, those on the VIX are most liquid by far. Accordingly, the VIX, representing S&P 500 volatility, seems to be seen by both market participants and academics as the best available proxy for "global volatility"—the general level of risk, and overall price of optionality, across all financial markets.

It is all too plausible, then, that S&P 500 volatility actually is, in the limit, the single global volatility risk factor that we inferred must exist from the data presented in Chapter 4. Why is this significant? Because global volatility must be the most important and best-paying risk factor in the world.

Finance theory starts with the idea that a return must bear risk. Not all risks are equal. Obviously, it is only the painful risks, the risks people will pay to be free of—unpleasant uncertainty—that need provide a return. And some risks can be diversified away. These need have no return, because enough of these risks, offsetting, can be combined into a risk-free portfolio.

What is the painful risk that cannot be diversified away? The capital asset pricing model says, simply, market risk. More modern theory uses jargon like "stochastic discount factor" and "pricing kernel"—which means that the thing that matters most is what might be called "covariance with bad times."[7] The intuition can be summed up this way: the strategies or assets that suffer drawdowns at the worst possible times to draw down must have the richest long-run risk premiums. (In Chapter 4 we examined the empirical evidence that showed that carry trades tend to suffer the worst drawdowns in "bad times"—bad times for the financial markets and economy.) These worst pos-

7. John H. Cochrane, Asset Pricing (Revised Edition), Princeton University Press, 2005; Antti Ilmanen, *Expected Returns*, John Wiley & Sons, 2011.

sible times to draw down are the times when the dollars that are being lost at the margin are at their most valuable.

When is a dollar most valuable? Standard economic models focus on "consumption utility": the utility of that dollar in the real world. According to these models, an extra dollar is especially valuable when economies are shrinking; when commodity prices are rising; when a person is hungry and cold; when a person really *needs* that dollar—to feed himself, warm himself, shelter himself; when he needs that dollar to save his life. This is a reasonable perspective.

Let us offer instead an accurate perspective. Start by abstracting away hunger and cold; abstract away the real world. Assume, for example, that "the person" is a bank, or a shadow bank, or a hedge fund, or a corporation—an entity that does not feel any such things. Could such an entity ever *need* one more dollar to save its life as surely as if it were a person starving to death? It could if, and only if, it were levered. It could need one more dollar in the face of ruin risk. It could need one more dollar to answer the fatal margin call.

One more dollar has value even to a speculator who does not need it for himself. Because someone else, somewhere, does. So its value is the yield it can earn by lending it out to give that person or entity the leverage she needs, by trading with her to give her the liquidity she needs. A dollar is most valuable when it can earn the most. In a levered world, in a world dominated by carry and its risks, that time is when volatility is high and rising. *The marginal utility of a dollar is the price of volatility.*

In other words, if the VIX is rising, the value of money and the demand to hold it are also rising. And the demand for money ties the returns of all assets together. When it increases, investors prefer holding cash to holding risky assets, and asset prices rapidly adjust lower. This is why we see correlations spiking and diversification disappearing when volatility increases. There are few places other than cash to hide during a carry crash, particularly now that the carry regime is global. Conversely, if the VIX is falling—if volatility is being suppressed by carry trades—then the demand for money to hold is falling, and correlations between assets are also lower. Lower levels of volatility and correlation make portfolios of risky assets appear more stable, more money-like. Indeed, as we will discuss in the next chapter, one of the features of the expansion phase of the carry regime is that a range of assets can begin to be held as money substitutes because of their apparent stability. Of course, this stability is illusory, and when the risk of these assets is revealed in a carry crash, the demand to hold "true" money explodes.

If S&P 500 volatility has become "global volatility," then it represents generic liquidity risk—the risk that defines the value of money. This must be the best-paying risk in the world. At the same time, this absorption of the generic liquidity risk premium must convert the S&P 500 itself into an extreme carry trade, with high expected returns and terrifying skew. The chance of all-but-zero-probability events, such as flash crashes or October 1987s, rises, from all but zero, to something meaningful.

It also means that recessions and economic turbulence do not cause the S&P 500 to drop. Instead, now, they are caused by the S&P 500 dropping. The onset of the acute phase of the euro problem in 2011 can be interpreted in this manner; the widening of the generic liquidity risk premium blew up Italian and Spanish finances—or, probably more accurately, revealed their true state. (The manner in which market weakness in the second half of 2015 led global economic weakness, culminating in concerted monetary policy action to reverse this weakness at the beginning of 2016, can also be interpreted in the same way—with something a little similar to this cycle repeated in late 2018.) The widening of the generic liquidity risk premium is simply the VIX rising. A carry crash in US stocks, whenever it happens, has devastating effects on a liquidity-dependent and highly levered world economy, returning us to crisis.

But after that—it is the nature of carry trades to rise again.

Central Banks Are the Largest Volatility Sellers

Since selling volatility is providing leverage and providing liquidity, the most important volatility seller must by definition be the lender of last resort. With the advent of quantitative easing (QE), particularly in its open-ended form, QE3, which was announced in September 2012, the Federal Reserve became very active in providing liquidity and leverage—which is to say, effectively selling volatility in staggering amounts. QE3 saw the Fed's balance sheet balloon in size, from US$2.9 trillion in late 2012 to US$4.5 trillion by late 2014. If the Fed is seen as the greatest volatility seller, then the claim that volatility selling is extremely important to the stock market is closely related to the quite conventional claim that the Fed is extremely important to the stock market. This idea may help in understanding the well-known chart (see Figure 6.5).

FIGURE 6.5 S&P 500 and Fed holdings of long-duration securities
Chart shows the S&P 500 on the left axis and total Fed assets with maturity of greater than 5 years on the right axis (in billions of dollars), with the four major phases of Fed long duration purchases, as well as the interludes between them, marked. It covers the period from September 2008 to September 2014.
Source of data: Yahoo! Finance, Federal Reserve Board

The chart highlights an extremely important point, taking us on to the content of the following chapter (on the monetary ramifications of the carry regime.)

Figure 6.5, and similar charts showing different versions of basically the same relationship, such as the Fed's total balance sheet size and the stock market, or the monetary base and the stock market, have been very popular among financial market observers and commentators. In recent years the heroes of the financial markets have included those analysts and asset managers who, on the Fed's announcement of QE3, proclaimed that the stock market was bound to soar. That is indeed what happened, as the chart shows. The arguments of those who called the stock market right in the wake of QE3 were uniformly that the stock market would inevitably rise because the Fed would be pumping money into the financial system—on a large scale—some of which must be bound to flow into equities.

We would suggest that the true explanation of why the S&P 500 rose so strongly in the wake of extreme quantitative easing is subtly different. The idea that the stock market rose so much over 2013–2014 purely because the Fed pumped so much money into the economy is not credible. If the markets were really inflated by the Fed's extreme money creation, then prices of commodities, goods and services, and wages would have risen eventually also. Instead, commodity prices were broadly weak over the period, and the gold price, often considered an indicator of monetary inflation, was markedly weak. Rather than inflation, there were persistent fears of the risk of deflation. To believe that Federal Reserve money creation can drive up equity prices, but not drive up other prices, is to believe that the Fed can create real wealth. And it seems implausible that the Fed could create real wealth, at least not on a permanent basis—basic economics or simple common sense tells us this.

The true reason that the US stock market rose is that the S&P 500 has become a carry trade and the Fed's QE policy represented a massive selling of volatility. The Fed became possibly the biggest carry trader of all: its balance sheet is a huge carry trade with large holdings of yielding securities, such as Treasury securities and mortgage-backed securities, financed by very low-cost liabilities including zero-interest cost cash currency in circulation.

The Fed's increasing carry trade will eventually depress the returns to be earned from carry as a whole. As explained, carry trades should be expected to provide an outsized return because of the small chance of extreme loss and because by their nature they are liquidity-providing trades, which must command a premium. The central bank becoming a large carry trader must cause the forward-looking expected return to carry to eventually decline, because it represents an increase in the supply of capital to the carry trade. However, in the short term, as that extra supply is put to work in the markets, the realized return to carry increases. The carry regime then emerges as a series of carry bubbles and carry busts—successively larger bubbles and busts as central bank intervention increases progressively in each cycle—more than merely an equilibrium process arising from the world's need for liquidity.

In Chapter 2, when discussing currency carry trades, we emphasized the involvement of central banks in the process, which creates a form of moral hazard. The intervention of central banks in currency markets along with the knowledge that the central banks will be prepared to intervene in the event of large currency exchange rate movements makes currency carry trades more attractive. The idea that all carry trades are aspects of the same broad phenomenon, and that therefore there must be an equivalence between currency carry trades and stock market volatility-selling trades, would suggest that volatility selling by the central bank must create moral hazard. In other words, it would seem to suggest that quantitative easing and the resulting size of the central bank balance sheet could serve as a quantitative measure of moral hazard.

There is also a very direct link between Fed volatility selling and the currency carry trade, which we discuss in more depth in Chapter 12. At times when the global currency carry trade has contracted sharply, particularly at the time of the Lehman crisis in late 2008, the Fed has made dollar funding available via liquidity swaps. Fed liquidity swaps with other central banks—dollar lending to them—is equivalent to intervention in the foreign exchange markets. Imagine a dollar borrower in Europe who is unable to roll over his dollar funding, which finances a higher-yielding domestic currency investment, during the carry crash. (This happened in Eastern Europe, in particular, but also in the Eurozone during 2008.) The Fed lends dollars to the European Central Bank or appropriate national central bank, which then on-lends the dollars to the distressed borrower (via a domestic bank). The effect of this is that the dollar borrower, who has in place a carry trade, is not forced to liquidate his position; he is relieved from the pressure of the margin call that afflicts levered traders during a carry crash. In the absence of the central bank intervention, he would be forced to buy dollars in the foreign exchange market to repay his dollar funding, an act that would put further downward pressure on the domestic currency exchange rate with the dollar. The central banks' action in extending the liquidity swap is analytically equivalent, from a monetary economics perspective, to central bank intervention in the foreign exchange markets.

There is a clear inverse relationship between measures of the outstanding dollar carry trade and outstanding Fed liquidity swaps. When the carry trade contracts, the Fed's extension of liquidity swaps replaces the contracting private currency carry trade. In other words, the Fed is a carry trader, stepping in as other carry traders are forced to liquidate. In this case, the Fed's expansion of its balance sheet via liquidity swaps is a clear carry trade. We return to this topic in Chapter 12.

These different kinds of Fed interventions all fit together: the notions of the Fed as a seller of volatility, as a carry trader, and as a creator of moral hazard are different ways of viewing the same phenomenon. The Fed acting as a carry trader limits the scale of the carry crash and thereby provides the impetus for an even greater carry bubble to follow.

As the Federal Reserve expanded its balance sheet through successive rounds of QE, it earned record profits on its enormous balance sheet, to the approval of some observers but the concern of others. The Fed sent nearly US$100 billion in profits to the Treasury for 2015, for instance. In carry bubbles, carry traders earn supernormal profits. Those who were concerned feared that the Fed's supernormal profits might one day turn to huge losses, fears that began to look justified during 2018. Given that extended periods of strong returns to carry are followed by carry crashes, this should be expected if we accept that the Fed is indeed a giant carry trader itself.

7
The Monetary Ramifications of the Carry Regime

Carry Regimes

Carry trades produce superior returns when volatility of the relevant asset market prices remains low or falls lower. When this occurs for an extended period, capital is attracted into carry trades on the expectation that they will continue to produce superior results. Over time capital employed in carry trades increases and eventually can become large enough that market behavior itself becomes dominated by carry trades. This is what we call a "carry regime."

We have introduced the question of whether carry regimes are a natural outcome of a free market economic system or whether they are a function of policies implemented by central banks and other government institutions. Our answer is that carry is a naturally occurring phenomenon, but the specific carry regime that has developed in global financial markets over at least the past two decades is the result of the "supercharging" of this natural phenomenon by central banks, particularly the US Federal Reserve.

However, this cannot be the entire story. Could it be possible for a similar carry regime to that which has existed over the past two decades—or something with the same economic consequences—to emerge even if no central banks existed? Is the current carry regime a permanent state of affairs, or will it only exist for as long as central banks exist? We return to these questions later in the book, but introduce them now because they help us think about the monetary consequences of the carry regime, particularly the nature of carry crashes.

As explained in previous chapters, carry crashes are an inevitable and necessary part of the carry regime. But if the carry regime depends on the existence of central banks and an ultimate carry crash destroys the central banking system, then the crash could end the regime. Otherwise, because each carry crash brings forth more central bank intervention, the result tends to be even bigger carry bubbles followed by even bigger carry crashes. This would tend to suggest that the carry regime is unstable and must ultimately destroy itself.

The paradox is that although today's global carry regime could be viewed as a product of central bank policies and therefore a manifestation of the enormous power of central banks, the monetary effects of the carry regime actually severely weaken the power of central banks. The US Federal Reserve was legislated into existence in the early twentieth century in an attempt to end repeated financial crises. Could impotence in the face of repeated carry crashes lead its authority to be legislated away in the twenty-first century?

We argue in Chapter 10 that it is possible to imagine an anti-carry regime. The fact that this is possible means that the carry regime—at least in its present form—is not something that can be taken for granted, something that always must exist. It could end, and if it were to end, the demise of central banking might be inextricably tied up with that eventuality.

Money in a Carry Regime

Why do the monetary effects of the carry regime actually weaken the power of central banks? To answer this we must first understand something about the nature of money, the power over the supply of which is the source of the power of central banks.

Money is defined as being a means of payment, or assets that are readily and easily convertible into a means of payment without being subject to possible capital losses. Generally, the most acceptable means of payment is cash. A savings deposit in a bank can easily be converted into cash at a one-to-one rate without risk of capital loss and therefore is considered to be money. Money market funds, for example, are included in broader measures of money, but potentially there is somewhat less ease in converting a money market fund into a direct means of payment than there is a bank savings deposit. Also, although money market funds are generally assumed to have little risk of capital loss, the financial crisis of 2008 indicated this may not necessarily always be so.

Because some classes of monetary asset—balances in checking accounts, for instance—are clearly closer to the pure definition of money than others, there are different statistical measures of money supply. The narrowest measure, M1, includes the forms of money that can be used to pay for things directly—cash and checking account balances—while broader measures, such as M3, include those forms of money such as longer-term time deposits that, from the point of view of the holder, are available to pay for things but not immediately.

Money is created by the banking system. When a bank makes a loan, it credits the account of the borrower with the funds, which is creating money. When the borrower uses the credited funds to pay for something, the money created will end up in the hands of someone else. The money created is in the system. But from the traditional perspective, the central bank is in ultimate control of this process. An individual bank's ability to continue to lend, and therefore to create money, is constrained by its holdings of liquid balances, and specifically its clearing balances or reserve accounts held at the central bank. If a bank lends too much, then as that money created leaves the bank (because, in general, no one borrows money for long without intending to use it), the bank will lose its clearing balances at the central bank. Its balance at the central bank will be debited to settle the checks and payments that have been drawn on its customers' accounts. The bank can borrow in the interbank market to fund this. But for the system as a whole, the central bank has ultimate control; only the central bank can increase the total of reserve balances held with it.

The central bank can boost the total of the reserve balances—basically the purest form of liquidity, the "high-powered money" that the banks hold—by lending to banks (against collateral) or buying assets from banks or from the rest of the private sector. If the central bank buys assets from companies or individuals—as part of quantitative easing, for instance—then that boosts banks' reserve holdings and also increases the money supply directly. If the central bank buys a bond from a business that is not a bank, then it will make a payment to that business, which means not only that the business will acquire a deposit in a bank but also that the bank will then have a claim on the central bank. If the central bank makes the payment for the bond by check, for example, once the check is paid into a bank account, that bank will own the check, and in settlement of the check the central bank will credit the bank's reserve deposit held with it.

The central bank can therefore control the most high-powered form of liquidity in the economy—the banks' reserve balances—and through that control in theory the central bank has strong influence over the total amount of money in the economy. Banks cannot lend and create money, or at least are much more limited in their ability to do so, if they have insufficient reserves at the central bank (high-powered liquidity). Or at least that is the traditional monetary theory.

In traditional monetary theory, short-term interest rates are the outcome of the demand for credit in the economy—the extent to which businesses and individuals desire to borrow money—and the central bank's policy with regard to the provision of liquidity. If the central bank is attempting to restrict the supply of money in the economy in the wake of strong demand for credit, then the short-term interest rate will be high. The central bank will be relatively restrictive in its provision of high-powered liquidity (reserves), and this restriction of supply, set against strong bank demand for liquidity deriving from strong demand for credit, will force short-term interest rates upward.

If inflation is high, longer-term interest rates will naturally be high also. To be an effective constraint, shorter-term interest rates will need to be at least as high as long-term interest rates (that is, the yield curve will be flat or downward sloping). If short-term interest rates are lower than long-term interest rates, then the demand for credit at the short-term interest rate will still tend to be firm; inflation and growth will keep the demand for credit strong. If short-term interest rates are much lower than long-term rates, then the central bank is not being restrictive; in this case it must be supplying the liquidity (reserves) that the banks are demanding at a relatively favorable rate.

This is the theory. But the theory depends on a number of, always unstated, assumptions. What if domestic interest rates are less relevant to borrowers because they can borrow overseas, in another currency or currencies, at very low interest rates, and they have reason to be unconcerned about the currency exchange rate risk or the risk of being unable to refinance their borrowing? This is the case of currency carry trades, discussed in depth in Chapters 2 to 4. Furthermore, what if central banks can control, or at least strongly influence, the traditional supply of money but there are other financial assets, over which they have no or much more limited control, which nevertheless function effectively as money?

The concept of Divisia money is a measure of money derived as a weighted average, in which different monetary assets are accorded a weighting based on their degree of "moneyness," the appropriate weights usually being derived from the structure of interest rates. Cash, which pays no interest, would have the highest weight in the aggregate and assets such as money market funds a much lower weight. Measures of Divisia money calculated for the United States in the post–global financial crisis period tended to show the growth rate of money on this basis to be low.

However, it can be argued that what really distinguishes the purer forms of money from less money-like substitutes or nonmonetary assets is the latter's price volatility with respect to cash. The definition of money includes the concept of assets that can be converted into a means of payment at some time in the future. For example, say that someone is saving up to buy a car, which she will need in a few months' time. If some of her savings are in the shares of one high-risk company, the share price of which swings around wildly, she can hardly count on the proceeds from selling those shares when it comes to buying the car. In the case of a deposit in the bank, however, she can be pretty certain of what she will have when the time comes to buy the car. But what if she has shares in an exchange-traded fund (ETF), the price of which is not at all volatile and which she feels extremely confident will not fall in price? She may view that ETF holding as being as money-good as a bank deposit.

This suggests that in a carry regime, in which the volatility of asset prices is suppressed and eventually becomes very low, a greater range of financial assets will begin to appear more money-like; they will come to seem as good as money. As the carry regime broadens, encompassing more financial assets—bringing down their yields and reducing their price volatility—then the effective supply of money, in terms of what the holders of the assets perceive to be money, will be growing. One way to describe this is to say that "moneyness" is growing, even though the supply of money under the traditional measures of money may not be.

In turn this would say that the central bank is losing direct control over the effective supply of money—the amount of moneyness. The central bank has influence only over the traditional money supply because it only has direct control over the traditional banking system. The types of financial assets that may seem to become more money-like as the carry regime broadens will normally be assets that are liabilities not of banks but of nonbank institutions, such as other financial corporations or even other nonfinancial businesses.

In other words, a carry regime makes nonmonetary assets come to seem less risky, reducing yields (interest rates) on those assets and making them appear more money-like. The effective supply of money therefore seems to grow. Whether this occurs directly as the result of perceptions that the central bank is guaranteeing the nominal values of non-monetary assets, or whether it is more a process that is driven by the markets that the central bank is dragged into, forcing it to seem to guarantee asset values to avoid the risk of crisis, it must be the case that the central bank is the vehicle through which this process occurs.

Ultimately, it has to be the case that the degree of moneyness of an asset will be crucially dependent on the degree to which the central bank—or possibly the government—supports, or underwrites, the asset. Without that implicit, or even explicit, support, it would be difficult for investors, or the public as a whole, to accept that various formerly nonmonetary assets were now as good as money. In 2008, at the height of the financial crisis, the US government introduced a temporary guarantee for money market funds. In Europe, at the height of the euro area crisis, the European Central Bank announced its "whatever it takes" approach, interpreted as a statement of preparedness to guarantee the values of peripheral European government debt. These and all the other post–crisis and "experimental" monetary policy measures could be argued to have increased the moneyness of a whole range of financial assets.

A central bank's implicit guarantee for an asset arguably both increases the liquidity of the asset—because of the central bank's supposed willingness to buy it—and reduces the risk of capital loss for the holder, thereby bringing the asset closer to being a form of money. The central bank's implicit guarantee essentially makes the asset a contingent liability of the central bank, and this is ultimately what gives the asset its moneyness. The paradox is that the central bank is only able to do this because its power to create money is a great power, but the use of this power in this way actually serves to undermine its power. Its control over the total extent of moneyness is weakened. This becomes most evident in the carry crash—when moneyness evaporates and what had seemed to be financial assets as good as money suddenly revert to being risky nonmonetary assets again.

The Deflationary Nature of the Carry Regime

Another paradox is that although the growth of carry increases moneyness—increases the effective supply of money, considered in terms of perceptions of money—over the longer run the carry regime as a whole is associated with deflationary pressures and not inflationary pressures. This is a paradox because carry increases moneyness, and traditionally greater money supply relative to money demand is associated with rising prices and inflation.

As central banks, during and following the 2007–2009 financial crisis, implemented more and more experimental monetary policies, many "hard money" adherents ("gold bugs") confidently predicted very high inflation or even hyperinflation. For a time the price of gold was rising very rapidly. But very high inflation never appeared—with the exception of asset price inflation, such as inflation of equity prices and property prices in certain areas. What gold bugs did not understand was that these policies guaranteed, or more correctly seemed to guarantee, the values of nonmonetary financial assets, which hugely extended the carry regime. Over the long run the carry regime is fundamentally deflationary and not inflationary.

The carry regime in itself is fundamentally deflationary over the long run, primarily because it exists in an economic environment of very high, and burdensome, debt levels. This must be true almost by definition. The carry regime is about high and increasing systemic leverage, and this is associated with increasing debt. Carry uses leverage to provide liquidity, and through a process of yield spread compression and reduced asset price volatility, carry extends moneyness to nonmonetary assets—which in the first instance will be debt instruments. The carry regime depends on debt and alters the nature of debt, at least temporarily, making it more money-like.

A burdensome level of debt must be deflationary in and of itself. Other things being equal, if debt levels are too high relative to incomes, then the demand for credit will be lower. There will be a natural unwillingness to take on more debt. If demand for credit is lower, for any given level of interest rates the growth of the money supply will be lower, because as previously explained, money is created through a process that involves the extension of bank credit.

The carry regime therefore results in more subdued growth in the demand for credit over the very long term; it directly negatively impacts the long-term growth of the economy. This, of course, does not really apply during the extremes of the carry bubble phase. The carry bubble is associated with strong speculative demand for credit, meaning credit keeps growing well in excess of its weak longer-term trend until the point of the carry crash. It is this bubble in carry that counteracts the longer-term pressure to deflation resulting from excessive debt.

The carry regime results in a very suboptimal allocation of resources in the economy. The carry regime results in a suppression of interest rate spreads that rests on an assumption that central banks—and other governmental or multilateral institutions such as the IMF—will not allow excessive exchange rate volatility or asset price volatility in general and will effectively stand behind debt. This means that credit risk is mispriced from a free market perspective. It implies that there is an understanding that debt is at least partly socialized; the costs of default or failure will be at least partly shared across the economy, potentially the global economy, as a whole.

This mispricing of credit risk in turn will mean that unprofitable investments may have a longer life than genuinely justified and that there will be too much consumption relative to investment (because interest rates for consumer-related debt will be lower than justified). A 2017 research paper by the Economics Department of the Organisation for Economic Co-operation and Development (OECD), investigating causes of the productivity slowdown in OECD economies, noted that "there are reasons to suspect that non-viable firms may be increasingly kept alive by the legacy of the financial crisis, with bank forbearance, prolonged monetary stimulus and the persistence of crisis-induced small- and medium-sized enterprise-support policy initiatives emerging as possible culprits."[1]

Globally, central bank interventions together with excessive government involvement in economies (the "socialization" of debt and risk) have resulted in economies with too little savings, too much debt-financed consumption, and low prospective returns on real investment. Contrary to the popular Keynesian view, the global problem has not been too much savings but, in general, too little savings and too much debt. Some economies—most obviously China's—have had too much savings, but much of that savings ends up being wasted in unproductive investments. The global problem is that too little savings and misallocated resources mean that trend economic growth is very low. This further causes interest rates to be very low. It also means that debt burdens are barely sustainable, or clearly unsustainable in some cases.

It is worthwhile to note, however, that although the extreme carry regime will result in lower economic growth over time, an extended carry bubble within the regime can give a shorter-term boost to measured GDP. Given the way that GDP is measured, once a long-term misallocation of resources is "locked in"—once there is too much consumption and too much of the

1. Müge Adalet McGowan, Dan Andrews, and Valentine Millot, "The Walking Dead? Zombie Firms and Productivity Performance in OECD Countries," OECD Economics Department Working Papers, No. 1372.

economy devoted to the production of consumer goods and services, too much property speculation, and too many skyscraper apartment blocks being built—then the further extension of carry can give a boost to GDP, pushing the economy further in the same direction. There may be too many cars being produced, relative to some long-term equilibrium, but if car financing costs become even more attractive as debt yield spreads are compressed even further, then some people may be persuaded to borrow to buy another car. There may be too many apartment blocks being constructed, but if yield spread compression pushes mortgage rates even lower and leads to property financing terms becoming even more generous, would-be landlords or speculators may be tempted to borrow to buy another apartment. This process can raise measured GDP in the short run even as it reduces long-term trend economic growth further.

The result is then a "vanishing point," as trend economic growth and interest rates fall progressively lower, eventually to zero. GDP today occurs at the expense of GDP in the future. It should be noted that this is completely contrary to a conventional economic perspective. A conventional economist would believe that GDP growth begets more GDP growth—as new jobs and new demand are created—and that there is no such thing as some sort of limiting point to GDP growth. But what needs to be understood is that the carry regime is taking us farther away from the type of market economy that is assumed by conventional economic analysis. In fact, put in conventional terms, it is taking us away from a market economy in which risks are borne by individuals and individual businesses and institutions and priced in the market, to an economy in which risks are socialized, or perceived to be socialized.

In the carry regime, with high debt burdens, very limited economic growth, and very low prospective returns to real investment, it is easy for deflationary forces to take hold. With deflation, the demand to hold money tends to be high. If someone has $10,000 in the bank and prices of goods and services are not rising, he likely will be comfortable keeping that $10,000 in the bank. On the other hand, if prices are rising 100 percent a year and accelerating rapidly, he will want to get that $10,000 into something that retains its value better as quickly as possible. In an extreme inflation the demand to hold money is very weak, while in a deflation the demand to hold money is strong.

This means that in a carry regime, which is associated with long-term pressure toward deflation, the demand to hold money will have a tendency to be strong over time (even as the demand for "true money" is weak during the carry bubbles). People and businesses will, in general, wish to hold quite a high proportion of their assets in the form of money and will also be comfortable holding money in high proportion to their incomes. From an economist's point of view, this is the same as saying that the velocity of circulation of money will be low and declining; a greater proportion of the money stock will be held as a form in which to hold savings.

However, the chart in Figure 7.1 shows that as the US economy and financial system have developed into a carry regime over the past 20 to 30 years, the demand for money—in the traditional sense—has not been strong. As a proportion of total financial assets, US households have held comparatively little money (cash currency and bank deposits). In particular, during the intense carry bubble periods of the 1990s, 2003–2007, and 2009 onward, money held by households as a proportion of total financial assets declined markedly.

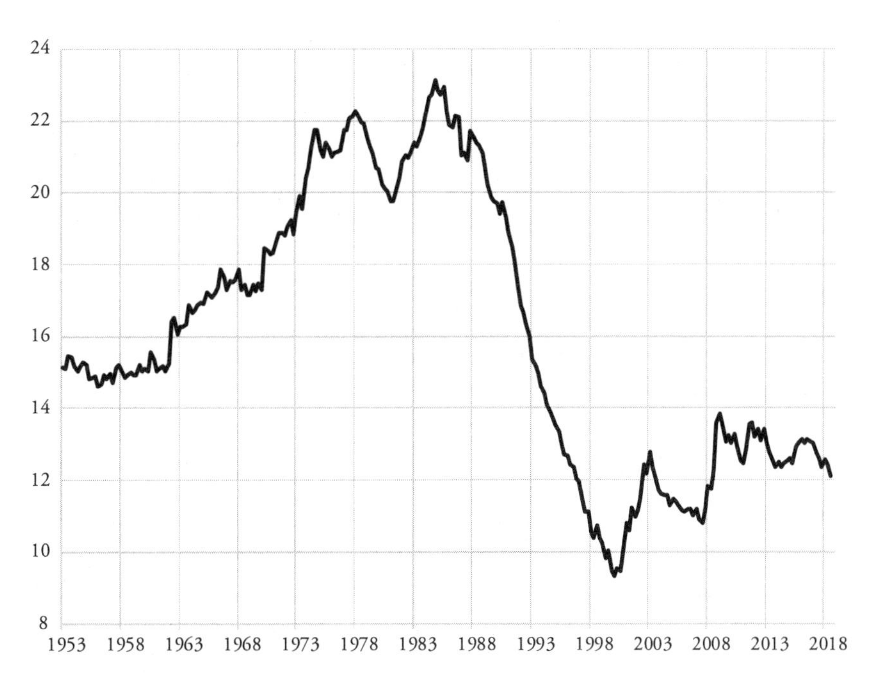

FIGURE 7.1 US household holdings of money as a percentage of total financial assets
Source of data: Federal Reserve Board

How have US households held their assets instead? The answer is in other financial assets, including bonds and debt instruments of various types, equities, and mutual funds including both bond and equity mutual funds (Figure 7.2).

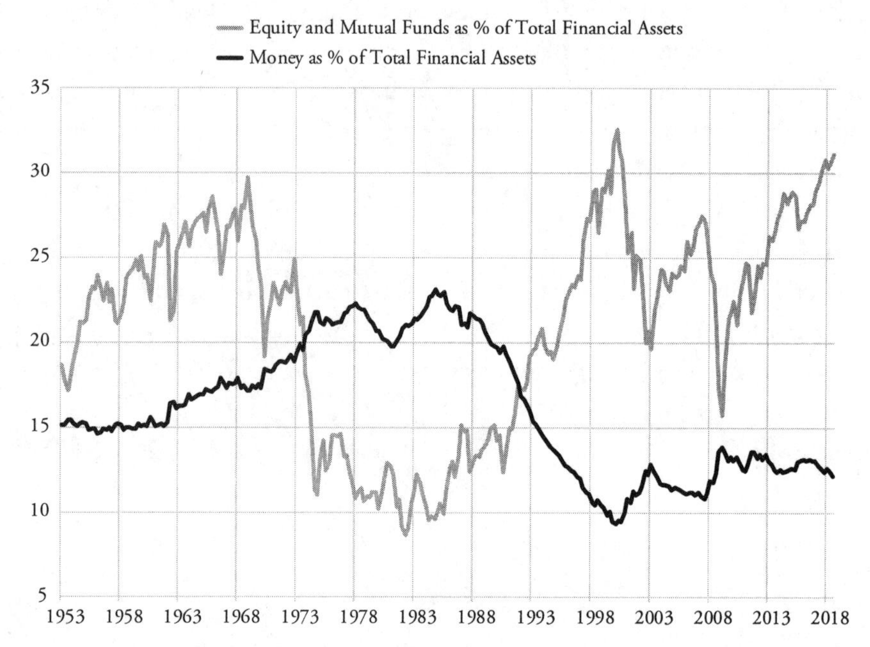

FIGURE 7.2 Percentage of US household assets in equities and mutual funds compared with money
Source of data: Federal Reserve Board

If the financial or economic regime is deflationary, or at least one of low inflation, why would households be so keen to economize on their holdings of money and instead want to put so much into equities and mutual funds? The conventional explanation is that they want some return, and money does not offer much return, particularly today. But the reality is that in a potentially deflationary world the return that money offers (in real terms) is better than it has often been in the past, in far more inflationary times. Equities and mutual funds are risky and over any given period may ultimately not provide any return—and that should be expected to be particularly likely in a deflationary period.

The true answer is that households are not perceiving equities and mutual funds to be particularly risky. They increasingly have perceived financial assets other than money, including equities, to be the responsibility of the central bank or government, in a similar way to money. If the stock market goes down by a large amount, the Federal Reserve will do whatever is necessary to rescue it. And after all, it can print money. This is what they believe.

The earlier chart (Figure 7.1) showed household holdings of money as a percentage of total household financial assets. Figure 7.3 shows money as a percentage of GDP. Looked at in this way, deposits have recaptured most of the loss that took place during the 1990s. Given the tendency to debt deflation, this is reasonable, but it still falls short of what might have been expected.

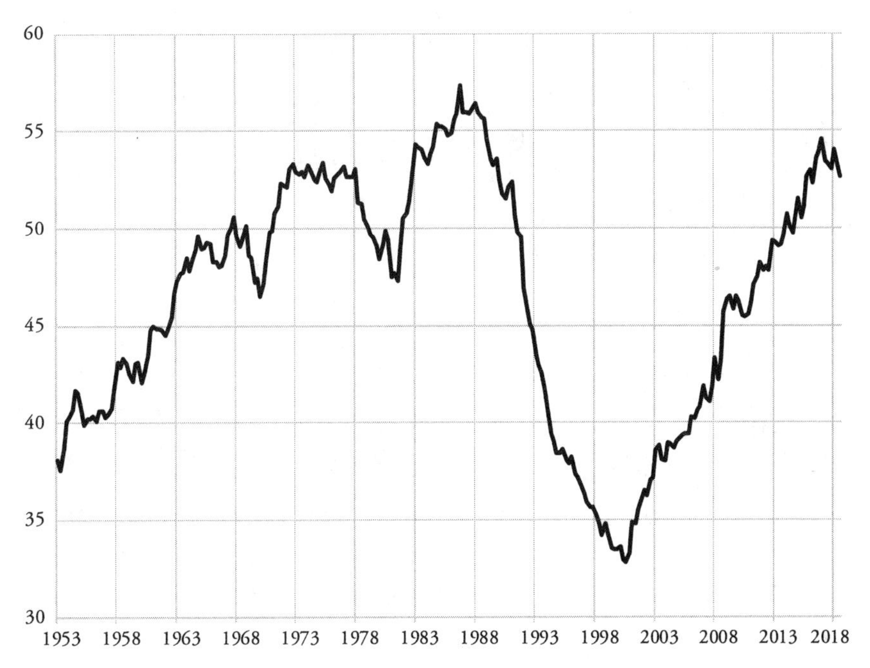

FIGURE 7.3 US household holdings of money as a percentage of GDP
Source of data: Federal Reserve Board, US Bureau of Economic Analysis

The picture changes when we look at Figure 7.4. In this chart, we have added to money by including household holdings of the range of fixed-income instruments—Treasuries, agencies, municipals, and corporate and foreign bonds—as proxies for financial assets that are traditionally the closest substitutes for money and within the carry regime have become progressively more money-like. When we make this addition, the total of more obviously money-like financial assets held by households has been higher relative to GDP over the past few years than in previous times.

FIGURE 7.4 Potentially money-like household financial assets as a percentage of GDP
Source of data: Federal Reserve Board, US Bureau of Economic Analysis

The argument here is not that this chart represents the true situation better than the previous chart. The true representation of the perception of money holders—if such a thing could be measured—would look more like the chart of money relative to GDP further back in history, but becoming more like this last chart the closer we get to the present, as the carry regime has broadened. As central banks have become more interventionist, the range of money-like assets has broadened progressively, and they have each become more like money.

In other words, over the long term the demand to hold money has risen much more than suggested by the simple charts of money relative to financial assets or relative to GDP. The public has wished to hold more money relative to total assets and relative to GDP, and that wish has been satisfied, in part, by a wider range of assets being perceived to fulfill the function of money.

This perspective can then help to explain more simply phenomena that were observable in the years leading up to the 2007–2009 financial crisis and subsequently. First, as should be expected in the wake of a huge financial crisis and with an underlying trend toward debt deflation, the demand to hold money actually did rise substantially. Second, that increased desire to hold money was at least partly satisfied by the perception of what constitutes a monetary asset being hugely broadened as a result of central bank actions. From a monetary perspective this is the essence of the carry regime. It meant that there was a very large effective increase in the money supply, which is why outright severe deflation did not occur, at least initially.

The carry regime, however, always contains weak links that are evidenced at the macro level, the aspects of the regime that eventually give rise to carry crashes. In Chapter 2 we touched on the weak links in the currency carry trade. From 2003 to 2007 a major weak link was the large credit carry trade in which high-risk mortgages were financed with low-cost funds, driving housing prices to bubble valuations. In the renewed, bigger, carry bubble that emerged from the monetary experiments of the 2007–2009 financial crisis, the US stock market—and by extension the US corporate sector—became the weak link.

Over the years since the financial crisis, the increased moneyness of a broad range of assets has continually driven up equity prices. Corporations—nonbank companies—have been able to issue debt that is perceived by the public as a good substitute for money, the proceeds of which they can use to buy back their own equity. Through that process the public swaps equity for "money," while equity prices are driven up. This means that nonbank companies seem to become more like banks—levered entities that have monetary liabilities—at least until the point of the carry crash.

The Carry Crash and the Deflation Shock

It was explained in previous chapters that carry crashes are a necessary part of a carry regime. A carry crash, in a way, is the means through which traditional market and economic forces manage to exert themselves in a system that is becoming progressively less of a market system, at least as it is conventionally understood. Each carry crash brings forth more central bank and government intervention that hastens the demise of the market economy. But the carry crash is when (traditional) market forces reassert themselves. It is in part because carry crashes occur that the prospective returns to carry trades are high.

Once we see that the carry regime is a regime that extends moneyness to nonmonetary assets, then we see that the carry crash has more profound economic implications. A carry crash is not the mirror opposite of a carry regime but rather a temporary and very violent reversal of the central features of the carry regime. Volatility suddenly spikes. The liquidity created during the carry regime's expansion evaporates. The asset prices or currency exchange rates that had been artificially supported by the carry regime collapse. There is a rush to delever. Many, or most, financial speculators face margin calls.

As explained in the previous chapter, in a global carry regime the VIX can be understood as the price of money. The spike in volatility thus represents a sudden jump in the price of money. Moneyness evaporates as the volatility of financial assets goes skyward. With much higher volatility, those financial assets—corporate debt, junk bond ETFs, etc.—that had come to seem almost as good as money suddenly look instead like merely highly risky financial assets. At that point the demand for true money will rise sharply. This means rapid deflation, because unless the central bank is able to expand the true money supply very quickly, the existing true money supply will be deficient—the definition of a severe monetary deflation. The real burden of debt will then further rise sharply, collapsing credit demand even more, in a rapid vicious circle.

A critically important implication of this dynamic is that the deflation associated with the carry crash occurs in the form of a shock. Conventional economists (basically all the economists that are ever seen or heard in the media) do their job by scrutinizing runs of data—for employment, production, spending, perhaps even money supply measures—and extrapolating from them. The assumption is that the economy develops in a smooth fashion. If jobs are being created, the money supply is growing, and inflation is at a comfortable level, then there is no risk of recession or deflation. But the carry regime does not develop in a smooth fashion; it is discontinuous.

The money supply may be growing, but once the carry crash occurs, the true money supply will be deficient. The inflation rate may have been at a comfortable level in the low single figures, but that can turn negative very quickly indeed in the carry crash. To repeat our statement from earlier in the book—a stock market crash does not signal recession; it is the recession. The cycle of carry bubble and carry crash and the economic cycle have become the same thing.

Our somewhat counterintuitive conclusion from this is that the carry regime ultimately weakens the power of central banks. The central bank appears powerful during the carry bubble. Hints from the central bank that it is supportive of the economy and the financial markets easily help to grow the carry bubble further, and further create the sense of an all-powerful central bank. But once the bubble bursts and the carry crash begins, then the central bank is left scrambling. If the central bank succeeds in resurrecting the carry bubble, and hence broadening the carry regime further—as central banks finally did in 2009—then the illusion of central bank power can be restored, probably to an even greater extent than before. But really, more than being in control of it, the central bank is merely a captive of the carry regime; it is the vehicle for the broadening and extension of the carry regime and the rent-seeking opportunities that the regime ultimately permits.

What this chapter has explained is that the carry regime is fundamentally deflationary in nature, but it has the effect of broadening the scope of money to encompass financial instruments that are not normally considered to be money, at least during the carry bubble phases. This process of expanding moneyness keeps deflationary forces at bay; even more than this, it can even appear inflationary for extended periods. From this perspective the carry regime can perhaps be seen as a market mechanism that enables an uneasy monetary equilibrium to be maintained in an otherwise unstable fiat money system. Without the carry regime's existence, the system would tip over into spiraling deflation and debt destruction.

The overall point is that the carry regime, in a sense, operates on a knife-edge, from which it can easily be tipped over into dislocation. Fundamentally, the monetary system is unstable—the consequence of a fiat money system, which has accommodated excessive debt and leverage. The carry crash in itself does not necessarily mean the end of the whole carry regime. Central bank action, in particular, could restore the carry regime and kick off the whole carry trade cycle again. For it to do this, central bank action must increase the money supply enough to accommodate the sharply increased demand to hold true money and also further increase the sense that debt and risk are socialized. Once market participants believe that it is more likely that the returns from carry will accrue to them, while losses will be protected or spread around the economy as a result of central bank and government action, then they will resume carry trade activity. A new carry bubble can begin.

8
Carry, Financial Bubbles, and the Business Cycle

The Business Cycle in the Carry Regime

There have always been different theories about the business cycle, the cycle of recovery, boom, and recession that economies typically experience. A conventional perspective would be that as an economic expansion matures, the economy's unused capacity is gradually diminished and the "output gap" narrows. Wage growth tends to pick up as unemployment falls. Gradually, inflationary pressures build and interest rates rise. At some point these pressures sap spending power; higher interest rates squeeze mortgage borrowers and other debtors, and the economy tips over into a downturn.

An old-fashioned monetarist perspective would put more emphasis on central bank policy and the growth of the money supply. From this perspective economic expansions tend to end when the economy begins to overheat. As the expansion runs on, the demand for credit, including bank credit, tends to pick up. The central bank needs to raise interest rates to keep money supply growth on an even keel. But usually the central bank is too slow to raise rates. With the economy stronger and short-term interest rates too low, the demand for bank credit increases. The money supply consequently begins to grow more rapidly. Asset prices are inflated, encouraging more growth of credit and money—given that the central bank is "behind the curve." Eventually, generalized inflation begins to appear. This forces the central bank to act more aggressively, but for a time inflation continues to increase because it is a lagging indicator. The net result is that spending power in the economy is squeezed, and the economy tips over into recession. Declining asset prices then exacerbate the downturn until the central bank loosens policy—and the cycle begins again.

Both of these perspectives, particularly the monetarist perspective, accord asset prices—especially financial asset prices—an important role. Asset prices respond to interest rates or the money supply and have an influence over spending behavior. In the economic expansion phase, when interest rates are "too low," money and credit growth and asset prices will tend to rise. This all goes to encourage greater spending in the economy and a further economic acceleration, leading eventually to economic overheating and inflation. In this model of the way things work, asset prices are still considered to be connected to the economy in a very direct way. When financial asset prices are rising, it must mean that the economy is doing well and will continue to do well. Economic commentators will say that a recession is nowhere in sight, albeit that they will be concerned about the possibility of inflation and rising interest rates in the future.

When we understand the economy from the perspective of carry, it looks very different. An economy in which the force of carry is strong is an economy in which debt burdens are heavy. The sense of liquidity comes less from high money supply growth and more from the use of leverage (carry trades) and the suppression of financial volatility that seems to liquefy nonmonetary assets. In the expansion, economic and financial liquidity seem high, and asset prices rise. But both rising financial asset prices and high liquidity are the direct result of carry. The growth in the economy—which is ultimately mostly reversible—is also the result of carry, which produces high profit share and tends to bring GDP from the future, as described in the previous chapter.

In the world of extreme carry, high financial asset prices do not guarantee that the economy is "good for now." The carry crash can occur suddenly—at the point when leverage has reached too great an extreme to be sustainable—and the carry crash means an economic crash and almost certainly a financial and economic crisis. The concept of the business cycle no longer describes a somewhat smooth pattern of oscillations in the economy over time; rather it is a progression of steady but unspectacular growth interrupted by violent shocks—exactly like the pattern of carry trade returns described in this book. Furthermore, attempting to predict the shocks requires a different forecasting approach from those used by conventional economists.

Carry Bubbles and Carry Crashes

Any attempt to predict economic crises in this world of carry-driven economies requires an understanding of the development of the carry regime. The economic crisis is the carry crash. The carry regime develops as a sequence of long carry bubbles interspersed with violent carry crashes. In global financial markets, strong carry bubbles developed over the periods 1993–1997, 1999–2000, 2003–2007, 2009–2011, and 2012 onward. Clearly identifiable carry crashes occurred in 1998, 2000, and 2008. Minor carry crashes, or corrections, also occurred in 2011, 2015, and 2018. The 2011 carry crash was probably limited by the impact of the US Federal Reserve, which was aggressively implementing quantitative easing policies at that time.

Global financial markets are extremely complex. Carry trades can be implemented in all the different financial markets and instruments—debt instruments including junk bonds, currencies (currency carry trades as discussed in Chapters 2 to 4), equity markets (selling volatility, including implementing dip-buying strategies as described in the following chapter), and commodities markets, such as the oil market. Although it should be likely in a major global carry crash, such as occurred in 2008, that there will be a period during which carry trades are unraveling across all the different financial markets (a simultaneous carry crash), it is not necessarily the case that carry bubbles and crashes in different markets will be perfectly correlated with each other all the time.

In Chapter 7 we explained how the carry crash is associated with the evaporation of both market and economic liquidity. This most applies when the spike in volatility is centered on financial instruments that are perceived as more money-like (for example, debt instruments and exchange-traded funds composed of debt instruments). If there is a carry crash in instruments that are less money-like, such as commodities, then the immediate result may be for speculative funds to be channeled into other carry trades. So as liquidity in the economy starts to evaporate, rather than all carry trades crashing at once, certain carry trades may crash while other carry bubbles become even larger. Liquidity is diminishing, but in some sense, the liquidity that remains chases the carry trades that still seem to work.

One good example of this phenomenon was the relationship between the bond and equity carry trade and the currency carry trade in the early stages of the 2007–2009 financial crisis. A second good example was the relationship between the oil carry trade and the volatility-selling bubble in the S&P 500 from mid-2014 into 2015.

At the beginning of the financial crisis in the summer of 2007, credit spreads had begun to widen and the VIX measure of implied volatility of the S&P 500 began to rise, as the carry trade began to come under pressure. However, the currency carry trade bubble—and also the carry trade in oil (see below)—grew further. As discussed in Chapter 2, the currency carry trade did not begin to collapse until July 2008, fully one year from the beginning of the carry crash viewed as a whole. It was as if, in the initial phases of tightening liquidity, there was still scope for speculation and all of that speculation was then channeled into currency and commodity carry trades.

In the case of the oil carry trade, this is perhaps even clearer. It can be seen from a very simple chart that compares the oil price with the S&P 500 (Figure 8.1).

What constitutes a carry trade in commodities—in terms of the definition used and in terms of equivalence with other carry trades—is different from what is often understood. Oil, in particular, is sometimes said to be a "carry trade" when there is contango in the oil market; further out futures prices are high in relation to spot and nearer futures prices. This encourages oil traders to store oil; increasing inventories of physical oil are being financed, or "car-

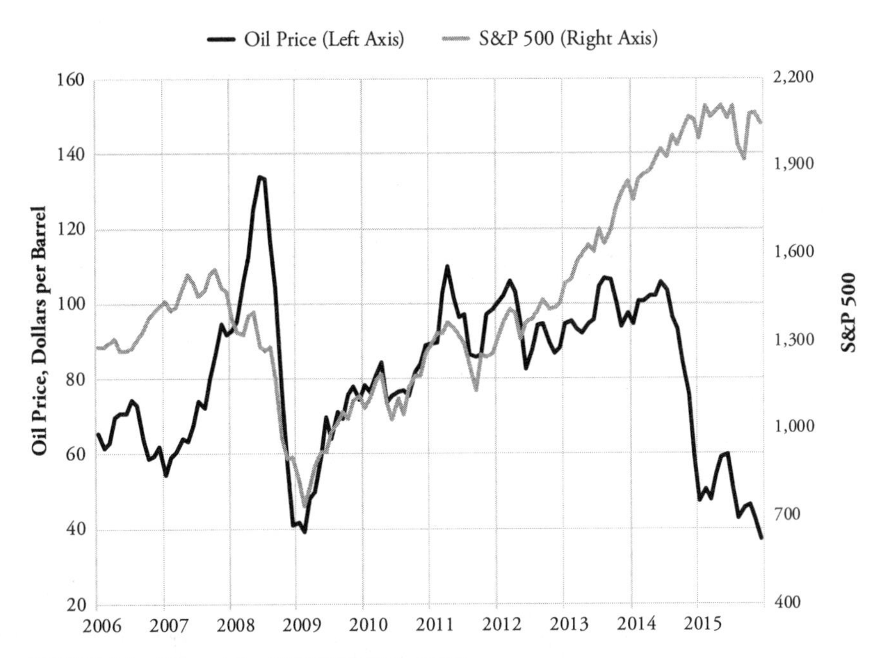

FIGURE 8.1 Oil and the S&P 500 (2006–2015)

Source of data: Federal Reserve Bank of St. Louis FRED Economic Data

ried," from this perspective. But really this is only an arbitrage that represents the market working as it should—transmitting the demand pressure down the curve and ensuring that future supply will be there to meet expected strong future demand. In contrast, carry, as we understand it, is the market "acting not as it should"—or more accurately not as it should from the very narrow perspective of a textbook classical model of equilibrium.

Consider the simple currency carry trade, in which the carry trader is borrowing in a low interest rate currency to invest in a higher interest rate currency. The forward curve is downward sloping—more distant forward prices for the higher interest rate currency in terms of the lower interest rate currency are cheaper. In the basic oil arbitrage trade described, the futures curve is upward sloping. The equivalent of the currency carry trade in the oil markets will occur when the oil futures curve is downward sloping (in backwardation) and futures traders buy oil forward, hoping to profit from the lower cost of oil in the future relative to the present.

The oil carry trader—in this sense of a carry trade, not an arbitrage—by buying oil forward in the face of a downward-sloping futures curve, is providing liquidity to oil producers who need to sell their production forward. If oil producers, for example, "frackers," are heavily indebted, they need to lock in prices for future production to ensure their ability to service their debt. If their consequent requirement for forward sales of oil depresses futures prices relative to the spot price—that is, turns the futures curve inverted, or in backwardation—then carry traders seeking to profit from relatively cheap futures prices for oil are there to take the other side of the producers' trades. We can think of them as providing finance to the producers in this case, almost equivalent to buying their debt.

So if speculators are engaging in carry trades, they will be buying futures further out, in anticipation of picking up the income represented by the discount between the future and the spot price. Going back to our very first characterization of carry trades as trades that make money if "nothing happens," we can see that if the oil price does not change, then carry traders will profit as lower longer-dated futures prices "roll up" to the higher spot price. This increase in price is often referred to as the roll yield. As long as carry trades such as this are increasing, they act to support the price structure—because they represent increasing long positions in the market.

In this case, oil carry trades can be perceived as supplying liquidity to the market that allows producers to hedge future production. This could be particularly important if producers are heavily indebted. But an underlying theme of this book is that there can be a fine line between an "appropriate" amount of liquidity provision through carry trades and an excessive amount that encourages an unsustainable buildup of debt and leverage. For example, say that the oil price has been too high given the prospective level of output and that this is encouraging the development of high-cost debt-financed production that is being hedged at the high futures prices. In the absence of carry traders, as forward hedging increases, backwardation in the oil market would increase to the point that inventories of oil would be run down. Those holding inventories of oil would be better to sell spot oil and buy forward at much lower forward prices. Selling pressure would thus be transmitted back along the forward curve, resulting in lower spot prices, which in turn would discourage new drilling or fracking operations and reduce future supply. But if carry traders are active in buying oil forward to pick up the roll yield, then this may not happen. The whole price structure is supported, and prospective supply and industry indebtedness continues to increase.

Further, it may be easy for this scenario to occur. Carry traders possessing the balance sheet and expertise to earn the premium for providing liquidity to commodity producers earn appropriate returns. As these returns become observable, they act to draw in other carry traders, and the familiar self-reinforcing dynamic begins to take hold in which expanding carry positions initially support the trades' profitability but ultimately destabilize the market. As we discussed in Chapter 5, "The Agents of Carry," we should not be surprised to have seen this dynamic happening more in the last 20 years than previously. The growth of hedge funds means that there are now very large pools of capital that can quickly be deployed in these trades when opportunities seem attractive. Appropriate liquidity provision can very rapidly turn into a carry bubble.

Nevertheless, unlike with currency carry trades or the stock market, there are no central banks that make it their business to support oil prices. There are governments—such as the Saudi government—that provide support, but the constraints under which they operate are much greater. Because of this we should expect an oil carry trade to be more vulnerable and short-lived, compared with a stock market or currency carry trade. Without the direct interference of central banks in the market, the oil carry trade merely delays somewhat the inevitable market price adjustment.

The evidence, from both price action and the structure of futures prices, suggests strongly that oil became a large carry trade from mid-2007 until mid-2008 and then again from early 2013 until mid-2014, following both of which periods the price collapsed in a carry crash. The price behavior alone—a ratcheting up and then collapse—is suggestive of a carry bubble followed by a carry crash. But the other facts fit this explanation also. Figure 8.2 shows the West Texas Intermediate front month contract and the spread between the fourth contract out and the front month contract. During the time when the price was ratcheting higher, from late 2007 through early 2008 and again from early 2013 through mid-2014, the spread between the

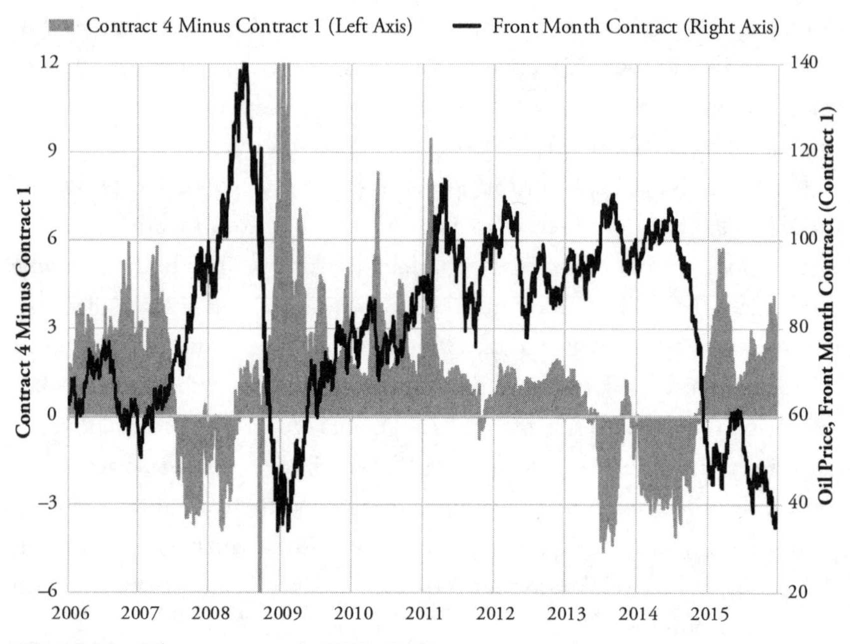

FIGURE 8.2 Oil as a carry trade (2006–2015)
Source of data: US Energy Information Administration

fourth contract and the first contract was negative—that is, the market was in backwardation—and it did not turn positive again (contango) until the price had fallen sharply.

In the financial markets and in the media, the rise in oil prices up to 2014 and the attendant boom in oil production in the United States were considered to be unequivocal positives for the US economy. Then, when oil prices collapsed in the second half of 2014, the majority view became that lower oil prices are similar to a tax cut for the consumer in the developed economies. This would boost effective real incomes, which must be good for economic growth in the developed world, including the United States. Some were concerned about possible bankruptcies in the oil industry and the problem of excessive debt in the industry, which would be difficult to service at much lower oil prices.

The truth is much more subtle. The mispricing of risk that is the consequence of carry bubbles results in misallocation of resources. During an extended carry bubble, it becomes no longer possible to know what the economy would have looked like in the absence of the bubble.

It may be useful here to consider an extreme hypothetical example of resource misallocation that helps to think about the consequences of asset bubbles for the economy. Imagine that the government and central bank announce that their most important economic objective is to ensure that the price of tulip bulbs rises continuously and rapidly and that they are prepared to print unlimited amounts of money and intervene in the tulip bulb market to achieve this result. As a result, there would be a big increase in tulip bulb production with farms converting to tulip production, many small tulip businesses and intermediaries appearing, and a huge accumulation of tulip bulb inventories, with rampant tulip bulb speculation. In the short run, measured GDP and private-sector profits would increase.

Imagine then that the tulip bulb bubble bursts and the government and central bank back away from supporting the market, reversing their previous policy. The tulip bulb industry would collapse, and tulip producers' debt would go into default. Some might argue that this would be good for consumers and gardeners because now tulips and bulbs are so much cheaper. Others might argue that it would be very bad for the economy because of defaulting debt and loss of GDP. Both would be true, but both miss the point.

The main point is that, as a result of the tulip bubble, GDP and wealth would end up lower than they would have been in the absence of the bubble. The bursting of the bubble in itself improves the long-run potential for GDP at that moment because it means no more wasting of the economy's resources in this area. But achievement of this improved potential requires no more interference from the authorities. In the very short run, measured GDP and measured wealth (and employment) will be lower. The fact that tulip bulbs are now much cheaper makes no difference to this short-run result.

The short-lived oil carry bubbles, of course, were not direct results of government intervention in this manner. However, they can be seen as one of the broad effects of the rise of carry, which we would argue has been substantially the result of central bank and government interference in markets. Therefore it is appropriate to see the consequences in the same light.

Most people would argue that oil is different from other commodities because oil is an important part of the economy's costs, it is an important part of consumer expenditure, and it is essential. This makes no difference. All that matters is whether the oil price was a bubble or not. Carry bubbles distort the allocation of resources in the economy and in the long run cause GDP to be lower than it would have been in their absence. In the shorter term they can actually increase measured GDP, but this increase in measured GDP (the output of things that are only being produced because of the bubble) is not indicative of rising standards of living properly defined. In the carry crash, the "phony GDP" associated with the bubble disappears. Therefore, the carry crash in itself improves long-run prospects for true living standards—in theory. Unfortunately, in the carry regime the carry crash is in reality only followed by another carry bubble.

Mispricing of Risk and Disguised Carry Bubbles

One of the characteristics of the existing carry regime is that each successive carry bubble has been different from the previous ones. All the asset bubbles can be identified as having their origin in carry, but no two bubbles have been identical. Furthermore, as the carry regime has progressed, each successive bubble is larger than the last. But this is certainly not apparent to most observers and participants, whether professional investors or financial commentators. As the carry regime develops through successive carry bubbles and carry crashes, it comes to encompass all aspects of the financial system and all sectors of the economy, undermining the yardsticks by which asset valuations are conventionally judged. Wall Street argues that equities are not in a bubble because price/earnings ratios are not unduly high, ignoring the reality that corporate profits themselves are a function of the carry bubble.

The carry regime thus acts to disguise the carry bubbles, making them harder to recognize from conventional metrics, paradoxically as they become larger than ever. More obscure measures—such as the measures of the currency carry trade included in Chapter 2—make the carry bubbles clear. But financial commentators focus on equity price/earnings ratios, equity dividend yields relative to interest rates, debt servicing relative to incomes, or an assortment of other measures that in reality only benchmark one aspect of the bubble against another. Much as an ant cannot see an elephant, the carry bubble is so big that the commentators cannot see it.

A defining feature of the carry regime is that risk is necessarily mispriced relative to a classic equilibrium model of the economy. It is important to note that risk may not necessarily be mispriced from the perspective of investors. An investor may, for example, buy a bond issued by a close-to-insolvent bank in an insolvent country because it has a yield higher than he can obtain elsewhere. He may be fully aware that the country is fundamentally insolvent and the bank may also be, but he may judge that creditors such as himself will be bailed out (by the IMF and/or other governments or central banks) if and when it comes to the crunch. Indeed, how to factor in the likelihood of government bailouts is an issue that credit rating agencies, such as Moody's, have had to grapple with in recent years. In this case, if investors generally take the view that a bailout for creditors is likely, then the yield on the bank's debt will be lower than it would be in a bailout-free world. Risk may not be mispriced from the perspective of investors, but it is mispriced relative to the free market counterfactual.

Risk mispricing can occur in more complex ways. Credit derivatives and structured finance played a large role in the 2003–2007 carry-credit bubble. Collateralized debt obligations (CDOs) that bundled high-yielding debt or credit default swaps (CDS) and divided the bundles into tranches, with higher-rated tranches having the first claims on the income streams from the bonds or CDS and the lowest-rated tranches—known as the equity tranches—having the residual claims on the income streams, obscured the nature of risks. This became even more so as structures became more complex as the bubble went on.

A basic problem with CDOs seemed to be the higher correlation of risk between the different components of the debt bundles than assumed. In simple terms, the principle of taking a bundle of junk debt and assuming that higher-ranked claims on the income stream deriving from the bundle must involve little or no risk assumed that the risks of default for the underlying bonds in the bundle were relatively uncorrelated. Unfortunately, once the US housing market crashed, and then the economy crashed, everything went down together, and the risks proved to be highly correlated.

Driving all this, though, was carry. As already described in Chapter 2, the currency carry trade was in full flow over 2006–2007. There was a desperation for yield together with enthusiasm for levered carry trades. Structured finance, in a sense, arose to fulfill that desire for carry and was the enabler of the mispricing of risk that carry entails.

Following the carry crash and financial crisis of 2007–2009, the carry bubble that emerged from 2009 was founded in the much more explicit support for financial markets provided by central banks and governments, both during the crisis and subsequently. This was mispricing of risk in the sense of socialization of risk: the famous "Heads I win; tails the taxpayer loses," from the perspective of the financial speculator.

The experimental monetary policies of central banks, their willingness to expand their balance sheets to support financial markets, from the Fed's quantitative easing policies to the European Central Bank's "whatever it takes" approach, sent a strong signal to speculators that central banks were standing behind them. As discussed in Chapter 6, the central bank's quantitative easing is itself a giant carry trade; the central bank buys higher-yielding debt instruments and finances these purchases by issuing its own low- or zero-yielding liabilities—the high-powered money, of which it is the monopoly supplier. If the central bank itself is implementing a giant carry trade, how can a financial speculator go wrong by following in the central bank's footsteps? At least that was the common notion. The mispricing of risk is then less to do with incorrect mathematical calculations about risk correlation and more, and much more simply, to do with the reality that the risks of loss are being borne by the public at large while the rewards accrue to financial speculators.

The near-total collapse of the world financial sector in 2008 was widely accepted at the time to be the worst-ever financial crisis. The rapidity with which it was turned, by government bailouts and extreme central bank measures, into a powerful new bull market in financial assets beginning in 2009, made it obvious that we were in a new carry bubble. But most did not see it as a bubble, and those who did lost credibility as the bubble went on. In hindsight, what skeptics did not see was that if central banks and governments were to succeed in creating a new carry bubble out of the ashes of the 2008 financial collapse, the bubble would necessarily need to be even bigger than that which preceded the crisis.

In a carry regime, successive carry bubbles must necessarily develop in a way that disguises their nature. For example, if after the internet bubble burst in 2000 there was immediately another, identical, internet bubble, it would have been difficult for the new bubble to surpass in scale the original. To put it bluntly, people are not that stupid. The driving force is carry, and carry will work to force the creation of new asset bubbles. But the bubble that emerges as the manifestation of carry must be believable at some level; the rise in asset prices must have a degree of plausibility.

In the bubble that emerged from 2009, the new feature was the more direct involvement of the corporate sector in the carry bubble, combined with the nonbank financial sector (sometimes called "shadow banks"). Given that the banking sector had faced a near-death experience in 2008, hugely increased regulation and the banks' own more cautious approaches prevented them from being at the center of the new carry bubble. But with the Federal Reserve cutting interest rates to close to zero and longer-term rates ratcheting down as global trend economic growth decayed further, other sectors of the US economy (and global economy) ramped up leverage in carry-type activities. Foremost in this development was the corporate sector. It was well known that corporates increased debt to finance share buybacks, thus raising earnings per share (see Chapter 5, Figure 5.2). But much less well understood is that it must have been also true that corporates were using financial engineering in ways that increased aggregate earnings; basically generating profits from carry trade activities.

Circumstantial evidence for this is the behavior of profit share in GDP for the United States (Figure 8.3). Profit share developed in a rather similar pattern to the S&P 500 itself, which, as was explained in Chapter 6, became a giant carry trade. Why should profit share have risen progressively through the cycles of carry bubbles and carry crashes as economic growth was decaying? As Figure 8.4 shows, US personal net worth, or wealth, showed roughly the same pattern of development relative to GDP. The fact that underlying economic growth has been decaying is indisputable. It is evidenced from data—for average rates of real GDP growth and productivity—and, more importantly, by the progressively lower level of real interest rates (long-term interest rates adjusted for underlying inflation). Very low real interest rates—which were roughly zero globally by 2015—must mean that the return to real investment is very low and trend economic growth is low.

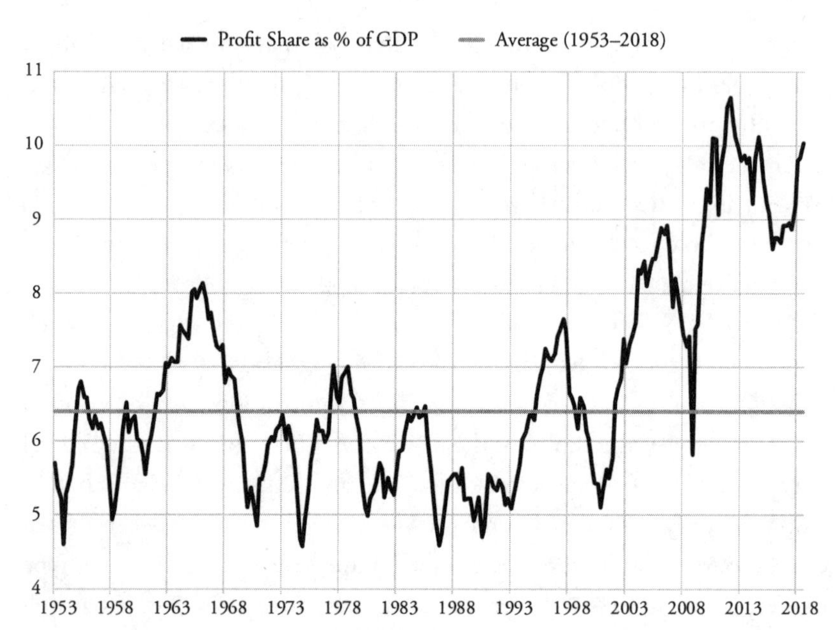

FIGURE 8.3 US (after-tax) profit share in GDP

Source of data: US Bureau of Economic Analysis

FIGURE 8.4 US personal-sector net worth relative to GDP

Source of data: Federal Reserve Board, US Bureau of Economic Analysis

Wall Street strategists and financial commentators looked at the level of share prices relative to earnings per share, or market capitalization relative to total profits, and argued that equity valuations were comfortable, particularly given super-low interest rates. But this was to overlook that profits were at an exceptionally high share in GDP. The historically very high level of wealth relative to GDP was the result of the very high level of financial asset prices, particularly equity prices. If Wall Street strategists were right, it meant that somehow, miraculously, historically poor performance of the economy had resulted in people in aggregate becoming enormously richer.

Very low real interest rates, meaning very low real returns on investment, should mean that earnings yields are low (and therefore price/earnings ratios will be high). But they must also mean that sustainable profit share is very low. As the carry bubble demonstrated, in the short term the profits can be high. If a company has access to the low financing costs that near-zero real interest rates and extremely low nominal interest rates give rise to, then the company management may well be tempted to issue debt and use the proceeds to invest in an asset that has a current earnings yield. This produces an immediate boost in profits. If that asset is a commercial property, for example, and many others are doing the same types of transaction, then commercial property prices will be driven up, and there could be a capital gain on the transaction as well.

In the long run, however, that current earnings yield cannot be sustainable indefinitely. If it were, it would have to mean that underlying growth was stronger, and so interest rates would be higher. The current earnings yield only holds up in the short term because, as previously explained in this book, the process of carry supports GDP in the short run. Once the carry crash occurs, the economy collapses and earnings evaporate. That is the point at which it becomes obvious that taking on debt to buy short-term earnings was unwise.

All conventional economic logic and common sense says that taking on debt in an economic environment of virtually zero underlying economic growth and very low inflation—with a high risk of deflation—is not sensible. The most sensible time to incur debt is when there is very high inflation, because very high inflation erodes the real value of the principal to the creditor and therefore reduces the real burden of the debt to the debtor. Yet during the carry bubble that began in 2009, companies, other entities, and individuals that took on more debt were generally rewarded for doing so. That is the nature of the carry bubble.

Of course, if the carry regime is sustained through the eventual carry crash, companies that have played the logic of carry and become more levered, if they have sufficient resources to survive the carry crash, can prosper anew. As long as it continues, the carry regime changes the economic logic to one in which the carry traders with the most resources win in the end.

Is There a Similarity Between Carry Bubbles and Ponzi Schemes?

There is a clear similarity between the dynamic described in our description of carry bubbles and that of a Ponzi scheme. For example, the idea that the new carry bubble, created out of the carry crash, tends to be larger than the preceding carry bubble, is similar to the case of a Ponzi scheme that suffers a run. If a Ponzi scheme is to recover from a run, then it will become even larger; the restoration of confidence following the successful test of confidence suggests this, as also does the requirement for the scheme to continue to grow larger because any outflows need to be financed with new inflows.

For example, imagine a hypothetical—admittedly completely unrealistic—alternative scenario for the notorious, and huge, Ponzi scheme run by Bernard ("Bernie") Madoff. Madoff's giant Ponzi scheme collapsed in December 2008, during the global carry crash associated with the collapse of Lehman Brothers. At the time of the Madoff scheme collapse, Madoff's clients had an illusory US$65 billion standing to their credit in the scheme.

Madoff's scheme was a classic Ponzi scheme, operated simply by marking up client accounts to reflect fabricated good and consistent returns, while financing any client withdrawals from the scheme with new client inflows. During the Lehman global crash, funds were being withdrawn from hedge funds, and Madoff's Ponzi scheme, which with its vast notional size had already been in difficulty for some time, was unable to attract the inflows necessary to meet the demand for withdrawals. But imagine that Madoff, who was once a pillar of the Wall Street community, had been able to go to the government and the

Federal Reserve and secure a bailout. Imagine that the Treasury had made a huge loan to his company—at a high interest rate—and the Fed had supplied liquidity and made an announcement that it was standing behind the Madoff fund and would supply whatever liquidity was required.

Of course, with such a cast-iron guarantee, funds would have been attracted back into the Madoff scheme. Clients would not be able to go wrong with the high and consistent returns offered and the availability of unlimited Fed "liquidity" support—or so they would have believed. Pretty soon, as markets recovered and the new carry bubble began to emerge, the notional amount outstanding in the scheme would have become larger than ever. New inflows would soon have been enough to pay back the government loan. Financial commentators would argue that the Madoff rescue had been a huge success and that taxpayers had made a profit on their loan.

Ultimately, there would come a point when the sheer size of the notional amount outstanding in the scheme would make another run inevitable. The Fed and the government would again have to make the decision on whether to bail out the scheme. This pattern of growth and collapse, or near collapse, calling forth government and central bank support in this hypothetical case—which then appears successful when the new cycle of scheme growth is triggered—is recognizably similar to the carry regime pattern of bubbles and crashes.

Ponzi schemes that are relatively large and long lasting usually have four main characteristics: (1) The funds supposedly standing to the credit of participants, or investors, are not backed by assets of equivalent value, when the value of assets is considered fundamentally in terms of the future flow of goods and services that they can lay claim to or produce. (2) The scheme will collapse once withdrawals exceed new inflows for any significant length of time. (3) The scheme is generally endorsed, or seemingly endorsed, by the government, or someone in authority, or someone who is highly respected. (4) The "fees" taken by the promoters, or insiders, are high relative to the funds committed.

As with the concept of carry, participation (as an "investor") in a Ponzi scheme can be rational from the perspective of the participant, even if not for the economy as a whole. Research on this notion has been produced by an economist formerly at Indiana University, Utpal Bhattacharya. In his paper, titled "The Optimal Design of Ponzi Schemes in Finite Economies," Bhattacharya shows that in a Ponzi scheme that is going to terminate, it can still be rational to participate in the final round (when contributions are considered as taking place in rounds) if the scheme is sufficiently large and a post-collapse bailout is anticipated that will, inevitably, impose costs on nonparticipants.[1] Extending this idea, an interpretation is that even if it is considered likely to be at a late stage in the viability of the scheme, it can be rational to be a participant. The calculation boils down to a consideration of the potential gain from the rest of the scheme's life less the expected cost of collapse to participants, relative to the expected cost of collapse to nonparticipants resulting from the government bailout.

The four characteristics of long-lasting Ponzi schemes echo characteristics of a carry bubble when applied to the economy as a whole, or at least the first three do. The first characteristic, which is basically stating that there is phony wealth, is also a characteristic of the carry bubble, as suggested by Figure 8.4. The second, the scheme collapsing when withdrawals exceed new inflows, calls to mind the carry crash. The third characteristic—that the scheme will likely only be long lasting if endorsed by someone in authority—has its reflection in the carry bubble in the support offered by the Fed and other central banks.

This all implies that carry bubbles and Ponzi schemes are in many ways analytically equivalent. But there are differences, which can be important in terms of considering the way that the economy would be expected to develop. A potentially important difference is that carry bubbles are more likely to misallocate the economy's resources in unproductive investment (although there will be excessive consumption and deficient savings as well), whereas a pure Ponzi bubble is likely to manifest almost entirely in excessive consumption and deficient savings.

From an economic perspective, a carry bubble can be characterized as a mispricing of risk, at least relative to a classical economic equilibrium. The Ponzi bubble, of course, is simple fraud—although the distinction is blurred

1. Utpal Bhattacharya, "The Optimal Design of Ponzi Schemes in Finite Economies," *Journal of Financial Intermediation*, January 2003.

in the case of the rational Ponzi bubble. The more fundamental difference between carry and Ponzi is that the carry regime is a more subtle manifestation of power imbalances in society, or indeed in the global economy. Because of that, it can ultimately be more dangerous.

9
The Foundation of Carry in the Structure of Volatility

Understanding the Carry Regime at a Deeper Level in Financial Terms

THE CARRY REGIME—THE PROGRESSION OF CARRY BUBbles and carry crashes in asset (and also commodity) markets—is not merely some abstract representation of financial market behavior. It has come to encompass the global economy, meaning that the global economy itself has come to demonstrate the same progression: fairly long periods of steady but unspectacular growth interrupted by terrifying economic crashes and crises that catch most unawares and struggling for explanations. It is a paradigm that affects everyone and has very broad consequences.

Even when we understand this, however, this knowledge raises several questions, which are difficult to answer definitively. Is the carry regime inevitable? Could the global markets and economy function in a different way?

If it is not inevitable or if it will not exist in perpetuity, what might replace it? In this case, how will we know if and when the carry regime is ending?

A starting point comes from understanding at a deeper level why the United States, and in particular the S&P 500 stock index, stands at the center of the global carry regime and the structure of market volatility that underlies this centrality of the S&P 500. This understanding may provide clues in the future about whether the nature of the carry regime is changing.

In this chapter we examine in more depth the structure of volatility, a topic that was introduced in Chapter 6. The material in this chapter may be quite abstract for those without an interest in derivatives markets. Conversely, those with expertise in derivatives markets will find some of the material familiar, and some of the material oversimplified. Our aim is to convey how the expected return from carry, or volatility-selling, trades is embedded in the structure of volatility and returns in the US stock market. As is a theme of this book, this can be interpreted as a requirement for the market to provide a return to carry traders to compensate them for being providers of market liquidity. A world in which there is more leverage—a condition that certainly applies to today's world—is a world in which the premium for selling volatility should be greater. This means high returns to carry trades, albeit punctuated by carry crashes. The interventions of central banks, in which the central banks take on the role of giant carry traders themselves, create a carry regime with much larger carry bubbles and carry crashes; during the carry bubbles, risks become seriously mispriced.

Volatility and Options

We have discussed, in Chapter 6, how in today's financial markets volatility is priced and traded. Trading with the market is buying optionality. Owning an option is valuable and therefore costly. If trading with the market is like buying an option, it too should be costly. How can we calibrate this cost? Of course, we can simply look directly at the premium on a particular option—but one way to gain a more intuitive sense of the cost of optionality is by thinking about the costs involved in replicating the payout to owning an option. In the case of an at-the-money call option, the payout profile is simple and familiar: at expiration, if the underlying asset price is above the option strike price, the call payout goes up one-for-one with the underlying asset price; if the asset price ends up at or below the strike price, the option is worthless.

Imagine a situation where the price of the asset starts off at 100. How would a speculator trade in order to replicate the payoff to a call option on the asset, with a strike price equal to 100, which expires in a month's time? The very simplest way would be for the speculator to resolve to own the asset whenever its price was above 100 and not to own it whenever its price was below. Since the current price equals the strike price and, if nothing changes over the next month, the call option would pay out zero at expiration, the speculator begins with no position. If the asset price remains below 100 during the next day, the speculator does nothing; but if instead the asset price rises above 100, the speculator needs to immediately buy the underlying asset. Over the course of the month, every time the price rises above the strike from at or below it, the speculator needs to buy; every time the price falls below the strike from above it, the speculator needs to sell. In other words, the act of replicating the payoff to a call option involves trading with the market. In this case, the number of times the speculator needs to trade is the number of times the asset price crosses the strike—the more the price moves up and down, the more trades are required.[1] Every time the speculator must trade, there is a cost—at a minimum, the cost of the bid-ask spread and any commissions or exchange fees—and the cost could be greater depending on the speed at which the market is moving and the availability of liquidity at the bid and ask when the speculator must trade.

More generally, instead of purchasing the full notional of the option every time it rises above the strike and selling the full notional every time it falls below, a useful rule of thumb for the effective replication of options might be for the speculator to purchase a proportion of notional that is equal to his estimated probability that the option will end in-the-money. Consider, for example, that the asset price is somewhat below the strike but there is

1. The option replication strategy outlined here is equivalent to the Black-Scholes replication of an option with arbitrarily low implied volatility.

still plenty of time before the option expires and the price is volatile enough to have a good chance of moving above the strike before then. And say the speculator believes the probability of the option expiring in-the-money is 40 percent. He might hold 40 shares of the asset in order to replicate an option on 100 shares of the asset.[2] In the same way, as the price moves up and down, his estimated probability that the option will end in-the-money will rise and fall. Therefore, he must trade with the market to maintain his replication strategy. When the price moves up, he must buy; when the price falls, he must sell.[3] It is easy to see that the cost of replicating an option by any strategy like this will be related to the volatility of the asset price.

Conversely, a speculator who wants to sell an option can replicate the payoff from writing a call by trading in the exact opposite way—by trading against the market. Trading against the market is selling optionality. In trading against the market, the speculator continually adds to losing positions: buying as the price falls, selling as it goes up. Historically, as explained in Chapter 6, volatility has been better to sell than to buy; it is systematically expensive. That is, there appears to be a risk premium—a positive expected return above the risk-free interest rate—to selling volatility. In particular, there has been an extremely pronounced and rich risk premium to selling US stock market volatility. This is important in understanding the nature of the global carry regime.

Selling Volatility by Receiving Implied and Paying Realized

The most straightforward ways of selling volatility on the S&P 500, such as shorting VIX futures, were covered in Chapter 6. But there are many ways of selling volatility, and understanding these various methods is important

2. This property—the estimated probability of an option expiring in the money—approximates the Greek delta.

3. Assuming, that is, that his expectation for the volatility of the asset is relatively unchanged, as his expectation for the volatility of the asset also affects his estimated probability that the option will expire in-the-money.

in order to understand how volatility selling translates into the stock market itself and by extension into other asset markets.

One very common, and very important, method is to construct a trade that profits directly if implied volatility in a certain period exceeds realized volatility. A way to do this is to sell options delta hedged. Delta hedging is a crucial idea.

Any option will change in price when its underlying changes in price. Take a very deep in-the-money option very close to expiration. The option will almost surely expire in-the-money, and its price will be very close to the current underlying price minus the option strike price. If the underlying price changes a little tomorrow, the option price will change almost one-to-one with the underlying price. Conversely, take a very far out-of-the-money option very close to expiration. The option will almost surely expire out-of-the-money, and its price will be very close to zero. If the underlying price changes a little tomorrow, the option will still be worth almost nothing; its price changes almost zero-to-one with the underlying price.

The extent to which the option price changes relative to the underlying price is called the option's delta. For small changes in the underlying's price, a trader can hedge the risk of being short or long a given option by being long or short the corresponding delta position in the underlying. More generally, if she had a portfolio dynamically trading the underlying so as always to have the same delta as a given option, she would be able to replicate that option; this replicating portfolio would have the same payoff as the option. This is exactly the idea we used above to explain the possibility of replicating options. This idea—that options can be replicated, and therefore hedged, by trading in the underlying asset—is (in theory) what allows options themselves to be easily traded.

The delta of an option itself changes when the underlying price changes. This change in delta with respect to price is called gamma. Gamma *is* optionality. If an option position has positive gamma, its delta increases as the underlying rises. This means the option position gains market exposure as the price rises—it provides levered upside exposure to the underlying asset—and as the underlying asset decreases in price, the option position's delta decreases. More exposure as the price rises and less exposure as the price falls is a desirable feature that therefore ought to be costly; this pattern of exposure is equivalent to trading with the market. In contrast, an option position with negative gamma has a pattern of exposure equivalent to trading against the market. This is risky, exposed to potentially explosive losses, and therefore ought to receive a return.

Selling options delta hedged means taking a short position in an option and taking a long position in the option's replicating portfolio. The option seller receives a fee for selling the option. The fee, which equals the expected cost of replicating the option over its remaining life, is driven by the option's implied volatility. Set against this income is the actual cost of managing the replicating portfolio. Since replicating the option means buying optionality—trading with the market—this cost will be given by the realized volatility of the asset. Thus, the profit from selling options delta hedged is determined by the difference between implied and realized volatility. Since implied volatilities systematically exceed realized volatilities, as shown in Figure 9.1, it is systematically profitable to sell options delta hedged.

What if a trader sells options unhedged? He receives a fee for selling the option, and he will pay out a random amount depending on where the underlying ends up when the option expires. On any single trade the profit or loss from an unhedged option is more random than from a delta-hedged option. But if a trader repeatedly sells options unhedged, then the long-run average payout will, in the same way, be given by the volatility of the underlying asset price. The difference is that it will be given by the volatility as measured over the tenor of the option, rather than the volatility as measured over the trader's hedging frequency. Say the trader is selling one-month options unhedged as opposed to one-month options daily hedged; the average amount he pays out will be given by the volatility of monthly returns rather than the volatility of daily returns.

Under the standard assumption of independent normally distributed returns, (annualized) monthly volatility should be the same as (annualized) daily volatility. Yet empirically, monthly and daily volatility systematically differ. This difference can be interpreted as another component of the volatility risk premium.

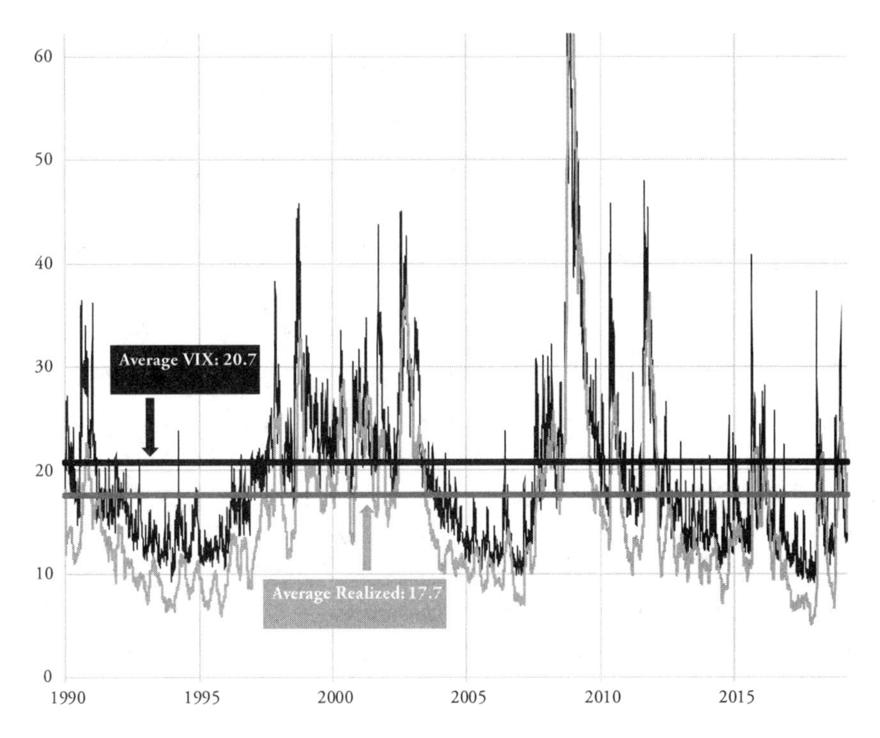

FIGURE 9.1 VIX and S&P 500 realized volatility
Chart shows VIX, in black, compared with trailing 60-day close-to-close S&P 500 realized volatility (annualized) in gray, from the first trading day of 1990 to March 29, 2019. Horizontal lines show the average VIX and average realized volatility over that period, where average is calculated as root mean square. The long-run implied-realized gap has been about 3 volatility points.
Source of data: Yahoo! Finance, authors' calculations

Selling Volatility by Receiving Realized (Near) and Paying Realized (Far)—or Buying the Dip

Let us return to the trader selling delta-hedged options. Why does she wish to hedge? As just described, the return to a delta-hedged position is more certain, less exposed to noise, than an unhedged position. Hedging allows her to transfer some of the risk of her short option position to another party. The counterparty who takes on this risk will demand a return as compensation.

We can understand the nature of this risk by considering specifically what positions the trader's counterparty must take. The trader delta-hedges by replicating a long option position. She trades with the market—she adjusts her hedges over some specific but usually short-term time horizon, perhaps daily or even intraday. Therefore, over that same short-term time frame, her counterparty does the opposite; he must replicate a short option position by trading against the market. The counterparty must earn a premium for taking on risk—and that risk comes from trading against the market over the specific time interval that the trader uses to adjust her hedging portfolio.

How can the structure of returns in the underlying market allow for a risk premium to those speculators who directly sell optionality by trading against underlying price movements? The answer is by having greater volatility as measured over short horizons than as measured over longer horizons. In particular, speculators who daily replicate a short one-month option position (that is, speculators who are the counterparties to daily delta hedgers of short one-month options) will be paid, on average, if the volatility of daily returns exceeds the volatility of monthly returns. This has clearly been the case for the past 25 to 30 years, as the chart, Figure 9.2, of the daily-to-monthly volatility ratio for the S&P 500 shows.

The observation that daily volatility exceeds monthly volatility implies that returns are mean reverting. Large short-term moves in one direction are likely to reverse partially over longer horizons. What is the most direct way to exploit this property?

Selling optionality involves trading against the market. Say a speculator follows a strategy of buying or selling, as a proportion of his equity, the exact opposite of market moves. For example, if he starts with $100 and the market rises by 1 percent, he sells $1 worth of shares. If the market falls by 2 percent, he buys $2 worth of shares. Let us call this strategy "selling one realized gamma." (Let us call the inverse strategy, buying or selling as a proportion of equity the exact same as market moves, "buying one realized gamma".) We need to define a frequency—a replication horizon—for this activity. If at the end of every day the speculator checks the daily price change and adjusts his position by that amount, then he is "selling one daily realized gamma."

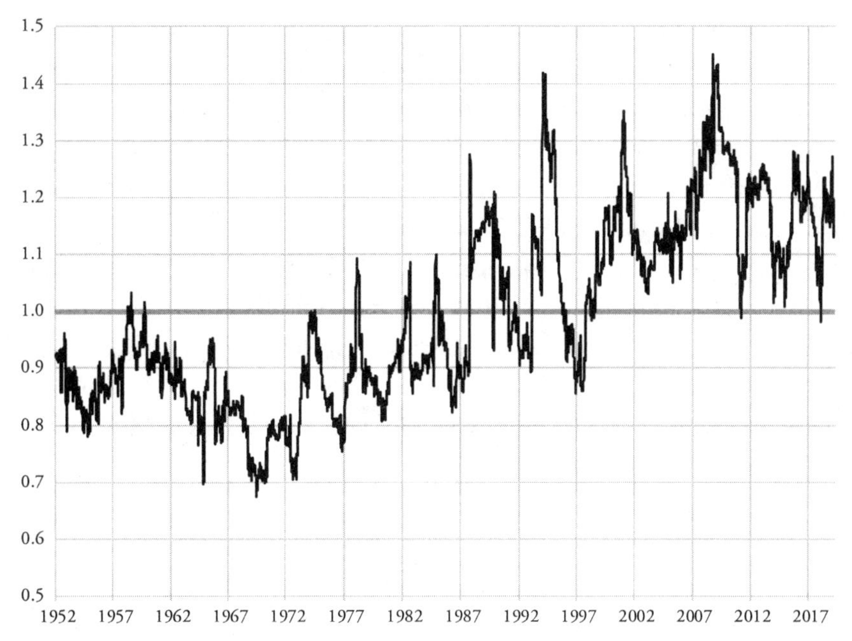

FIGURE 9.2 Ratio of daily to monthly volatility for the S&P 500
Chart shows trailing two-year volatility of daily returns divided by trailing two-year volatility of monthly (21 day) returns. Values above one mean that daily volatility was greater than monthly volatility over the trailing two years; values below one mean the opposite.
Source of data: Yahoo! Finance, authors' calculations

If instead he checks the price change and adjusts his position at the end of every month, then he is "selling one monthly realized gamma."

Selling optionality in this way creates significant risk. Because the speculator always sells as the market goes up, he is potentially exposed to exploding losses if the market continues to move higher—if it displays upside momentum. Similarly, the speculator buys as the market falls and is exposed to losing all his capital if the market keeps moving lower—if it displays downside momentum. Because this strategy involves risk, the speculator will need a premium to engage in this activity. However, if the price bounces around while eventually returning to near its starting point, then the speculator will have been able to buy low and sell high around the fluctuations in price—and so will receive a profit that will be greater the more volatile the price has been.

One consistent feature of the S&P 500 over the past 30 years is that the market's volatility has systematically differed between measurement, or replication, horizons. Specifically, volatility is higher at shorter horizons such as one day than at longer horizons such as one month. This means it is profitable to sell realized gamma at the higher volatility, shorter, horizon—and buy it back at the lower volatility, longer, horizon. Buying realized gamma back at the lower, longer-term volatility ensures that the risk of exploding losses is hedged at that horizon. The profit from a strategy that sells one daily realized gamma and buys one monthly realized gamma, as described above, is directly proportional to the difference between the daily variance and the monthly variance—that is, to daily volatility squared minus monthly volatility squared. Figure 9.3 shows the historical return path of this strategy for the S&P 500.

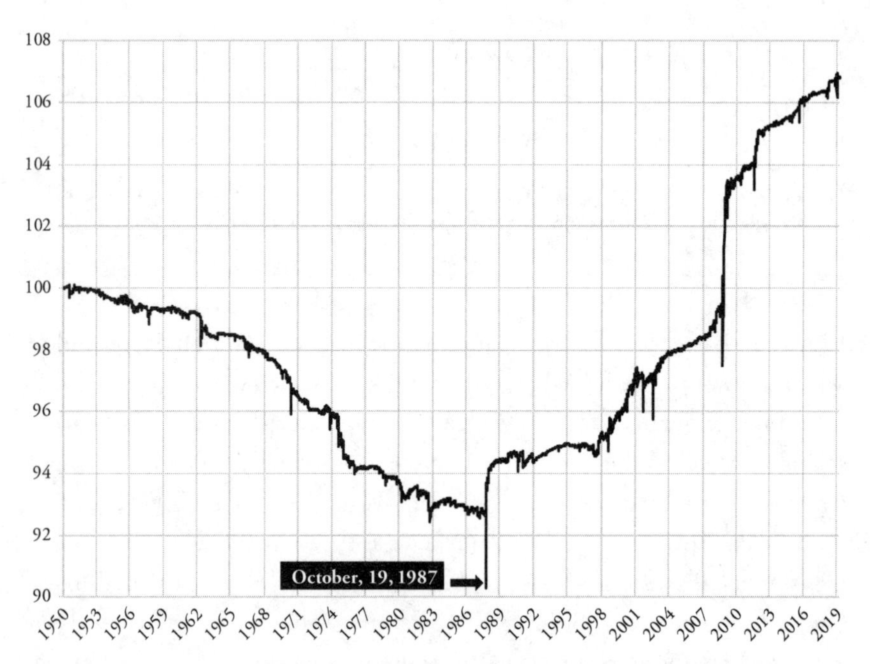

FIGURE 9.3 21-day realized gamma minus 1-day realized gamma for the S&P 500
Chart shows the return path of a strategy selling daily realized gamma (trading against the market every day) and buying back 21-day realized gamma (trading with the market every 21 days). The October 1987 stock market crash is clearly visible, as are smaller transient drawdowns in 2001, 2002, 2008 and 2011.
Source of data: Yahoo! Finance, authors' calculations

The evidence from Figure 9.3 suggests a persistent positive return for a strategy that bets on mean reversion of the S&P 500 since October 1987. It is unclear whether the modern mean-reverting behavior of the S&P 500 truly began in 1982 with the advent of index futures trading or in 1987 following the unprecedented stock market crash of that year. Of course, it was index futures that made possible portfolio insurance, which was widely understood to be the proximate cause of the 1987 crash—and portfolio insurance is simply the replication of long options. Prior to the advent of index futures, implementing a momentum strategy such as portfolio insurance on broad equity indexes—a strategy that requires frequently trading with the market—would have been rendered impractical by trading costs, and it seems likely that in the distant past the mean-reversion volatility premium described here was more than subsumed by the wide bid-ask spread for individual stocks. (The bid-ask spread can also be thought of as a form of volatility premium, as we will briefly explain below.)

Empirically we observe that all the profits from this kind of short-term mean-reversion strategy come on the long side (that is, from buying when the market has fallen). Strategies such as this, which replicate short optionality, work by *buying the dip*.

Every trader today has come to know that buying the dip is a profitable activity. Why should it be profitable? One perspective is that the dip buyer is providing needed liquidity. Because a falling market makes traders want to sell or need to sell. A falling market makes traders willing to pay in order to sell. ("Get me out" is the cry of some traders—sometimes with a swear word included to add some extra urgency.) This is consistent with the marginal trader holding a levered position and therefore needing to buy—being willing to pay a premium to buy—optionality.

What is the risk in buying the dip? The risk here is that there is a very large downside monthly return compared with the volatility of daily returns. The risk is that the market keeps falling, without bounces; that downside returns become serially correlated. The risk is that the market briefly enters a state in which, instead of declines being likely to reverse partially over longer horizons, declines now cause further declines. This, of course, is exactly what happens when leverage dries up in a carry crash.

As an aside, the volatility of the US equity market over longer horizons of greater than five years has always measured substantially below its volatility over one-year horizons. This gives a perspective on the effectiveness of the long-term valuation of indexes (Shiller P/E, Tobin's *q*, and so forth) without reference to supposed fundamentals.

The Equilibrium Structure of Volatility Premiums

Selling volatility is selling optionality. Trading against the market is equivalent to shorting measures of volatility. Different measures of volatility correspond to different tenors of implied or realized volatility; the second VIX future corresponds to two-month forward implied volatility, while the activity of delta-hedging an option position weekly corresponds to five-day realized volatility, and so forth. Selling volatility is using leverage because it is effectively a short position—because it is agreeing to provide an "asset," optionality, whose price can rise without bound.[4]

Being short volatility should offer a higher expected return for any given measure of risk than being long stocks. This is because being short volatility means being short, being levered, being exposed to unlimited losses. (As an example, a speculator who had been long stocks from May to November 2008 would have lost about 40 percent of her money; had she been short VIX futures instead, she would have lost her money about three times over. Another example: A speculator who was long stocks on February 5, 2018, would have lost about 5 percent of his money; had he been short VIX futures instead, he would have lost 95 percent of his money.) In a levered, skewed

4. It should be noted that there do exist natural unlevered short volatility trades—in particular, selling puts fully collateralized. Such trades do not sell a constant amount of volatility, because their gamma—their effective volatility position size—shrinks as losses mount. Imagine a speculator who sells a fully collateralized at-the-money put, only to see the market immediately plunge by an unprecedented amount, say 30 percent. Volatility will have soared, and this may be exactly the situation in which a volatility-selling speculator might wish to be most short volatility. But the sold put will be so far in the money that almost all of its gamma will have turned into delta: the speculator will find herself effectively very long the underlying with almost no exposure left to its volatility. In order to be short volatility again, she will have to sell new options here.

carry regime in which stocks can potentially fall much faster than rise, in which volatility could rise much more than fall, this should be truer still.

Figure 9.4 summarizes the structure of volatility premiums at equilibrium on a single asset. This chart depicts three critical features of volatility. First, the top line shows that implied volatilities are greater further forward. This seems intuitive—it expresses the requirement that shorting VIX futures be profitable at all points along the VIX term structure. (The horizontal axis for implied volatility is at the top of the chart and goes from spot VIX out to VIX futures five months forward.)

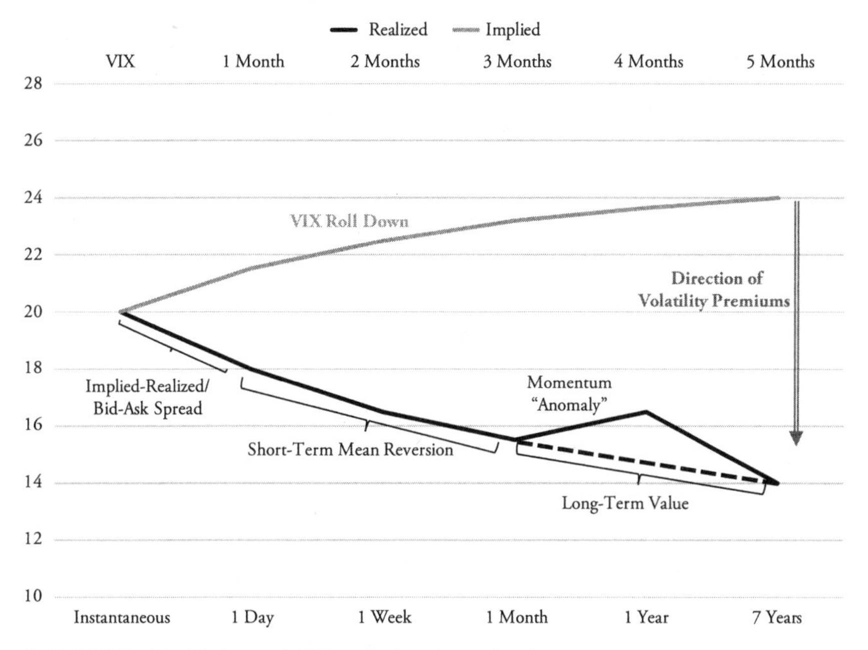

FIGURE 9.4 Equilibrium volatility premium term structure
Chart shows implied volatility spot and forward on the upper gray line, read off the top horizontal axis, and realized volatility across measuring horizons on the lower black line, read off the bottom horizontal axis. Data for implied volatility is a stylized version of the average VIX curve since 2009. Data for realized volatility is a stylized version of realized volatilities by horizon for the S&P 500 since 1988.

Second, the bottom line shows the results of computing realized annualized volatility—the fluctuation of the price that should be expected over a typical year—using data from different time intervals. When measured at short intervals, such as a day or week, volatility is greater than if it is computed using monthly or yearly observations. (The term structure of realized volatility is plotted over intervals from instantaneous to seven years, shown on the lower horizontal axis.)

The third feature is that implied volatilities are never below realized volatilities: even the lowest point on the implied volatility curve, the spot VIX, is not below the highest point on the realized volatility curve, which is instantaneous realized volatility.

A premium is extracted by selling a higher volatility and buying back a lower volatility. The graph visually summarizes all the examples of how this can be done that we have given in this chapter and in Chapter 6. A trader can sell volatility using longer-dated VIX futures and profit as they roll down the curve over time. Traders following this strategy exploit the first feature of the volatility curve and in doing so earn a premium for providing exposure to the implied price of liquidity and leverage in the future. Volatility can be sold in realized form (by trading against the market) at a short horizon such as one day, and then can be bought back (by trading with the market) at a longer horizon such as one month; this earns a premium by providing liquidity between short and long horizons, corresponding to the fact that realized volatilities decline with increasing time horizon. Lastly, volatility can be sold in the form of options at a specific tenor, and can be delta-hedged at some shorter frequency by replicating a long volatility position in the underlying. This exploits the last feature, of implied volatility being systematically higher than realized. The trader running this strategy is compensated for providing instantaneous liquidity to the market—in effect, behaving as a market maker.

There are a few other kinds of volatility premiums not described so far. There is skew, which is the fact that implied volatilities are excessively high for further out-of-the-money put options. That is, it is "expected" that volatility will rise if the market falls. Selling these out-of-the-money puts is excessively profitable; there is a greater premium for taking short volatility risk if the market falls. Skew seems interestingly parallel to short-term mean reversion. Both suggest the presence of a premium to dip buyers which grows as the size of the dip grows. Both visibly emerged after the October 1987 crash.

Market making—that is, collecting the bid-ask spread—is a volatility premium. Market makers suffer drawdowns when liquidity becomes one-sided and price moves violently. This is the same kind of event as when other volatility sellers suffer drawdowns, if perhaps on a different time scale. Our suggestion is that collecting the bid-ask spread should be equivalent to selling delta-hedged options. The intuition is that to delta-hedge almost continuously—which requires trading, and paying the spread, very frequently—should not be profitable; at some sufficiently high delta-hedging frequency, all the profit should be transferred to the market maker. Empirically, for the S&P 500 front e-mini future, realized volatility over horizons of less than three minutes somewhat exceeds implied volatility.

Finally, all the above refer to single assets. The volatility of portfolios of assets depends on both the volatilities of the assets and the correlations between assets. Portfolio volatility is higher with higher correlation and lower with lower correlation; so correlation changes affect the portfolio volatility. These correlations can embed risk premiums, in some cases richer than the volatility premiums on the underlying assets. Analogously to volatility, the full set of correlation premiums exists if (1) far forward implied correlations exceed nearer implied correlations, (2) short-term realized correlations exceed longer-term realized correlations, and (3) implied correlations exceed realized correlations. However, for rich correlation premiums to exist, it must be the case that portfolio volatility is more "important"—more demanded—than volatility on the underlying assets. In almost all such cases, the clear example being stock indexes, the portfolio is already known and thought about as an asset itself. Indeed, the evidence that the volatility premium on the S&P 500 index is richer than the volatility premium on individual large-cap US stocks suggests that the richest part of the S&P 500 volatility premium is in fact the correlation premium.

Not all assets display all these features through all history. On the contrary, it seems likely that the only short volatility premium that existed anywhere before 1987 was the market-maker's premium (and equivalently, the implied-realized gap). Other forms of volatility premium may have been negative—that is, volatility buyers got paid, as seen in the historical outperformance of momentum strategies across many asset classes.

Volatility is not charged for equally at all times and in all markets. Volatility premiums are more apparent on equity indexes than on single stocks or most nonequity assets. Since 1987, the single asset with the most prominent and richest volatility premiums is the S&P 500 itself. Other equity indexes followed it in gradually beginning to show all these features throughout the 1990s.

The S&P 500 Is Itself a Carry Trade

The expensiveness of S&P 500 volatility is the best empirical evidence (albeit still circumstantial) for the idea, introduced in Chapter 6, that the S&P 500 must be the sharp end of the world volatility trade and therefore that the VIX must be "global volatility." This idea places the S&P 500 at the center of the global carry regime. It explains why, even as other carry trades floundered somewhat over 2014–2017, the S&P 500 carry trade ballooned further in size, exemplified by dramatic returns over this period from short VIX instruments such as the XIV exchange-traded note (Figure 9.5).

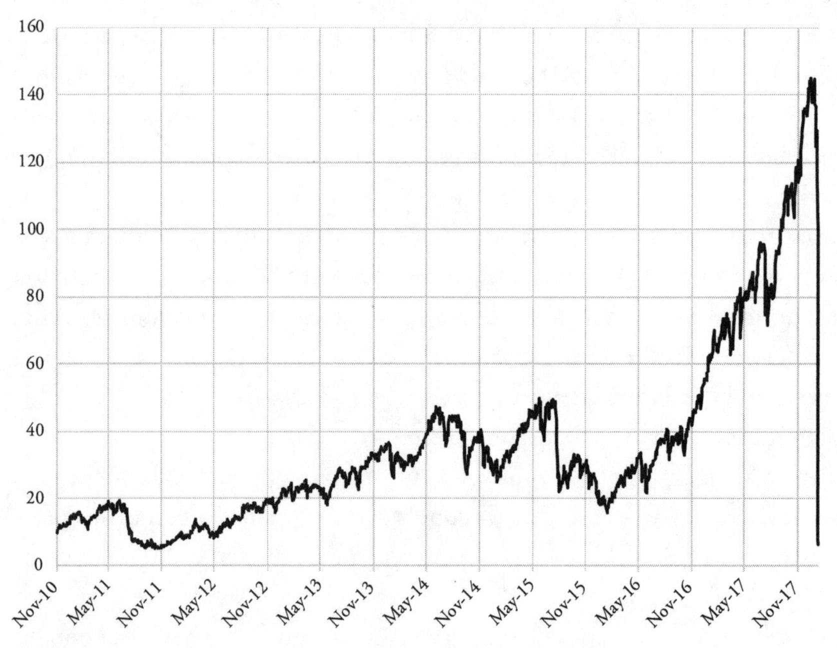

FIGURE 9.5 XIV price
Chart shows the (split-adjusted) price of the XIV short volatility futures ETN, from its inception in November 2010 until its failure in February 2018.
Source of data: Yahoo! Finance, authors' calculations

As Figure 9.5 shows, however, in February 2018 this instrument completely collapsed in price and was liquidated. This was the result of a "volatility shock"—a carry crash, now known as "Volmageddon"—that was associated with a rapid, but ultimately short-lived, decline in the S&P 500. But volatility selling in the S&P 500 resumed in the following months, and S&P 500 carry recovered—even as the Turkish lira experienced its own carry crash and currency carry generally contracted. This seems to be a further demonstration of the complexity of the dynamics among different types of carry trade, particularly late in a carry bubble. This phenomenon was also explained in the previous chapter in relation to the global financial crisis period and the later oil carry trade bubble.

We can conclude that in a highly levered world, there must be a return for providing liquidity. The S&P 500 is the world's premier hedging instrument, so providing liquidity to the S&P 500 must provide a particularly rich premium. The structure of volatility for the S&P 500 is such that volatility sellers—liquidity providers—will earn a rich risk premium in all the various ways that volatility-selling trades can be implemented.

What this means, as we approach the peak of the modern carry regime, is that the world increasingly behaves as if the ultimate source of financing for the entire global economy lies within the US equity index markets. Since the function of financial markets is to transfer risk—and the most liquid market must be where risk, transferred again and again, finally comes to rest—there may even be some real sense in which this is the case.

As an aside, the identification of the global liquidity risk premium with the equity index markets and especially the S&P 500 is plausibly related to the well-known negative correlation between equity indexes and sovereign bonds.[5] Apart from the S&P 500, the other most liquid markets in

5. This negative correlation emerged in October 1997; prior to that time, stocks and bonds were positively correlated. Depending on perspective, the shift from positive to negative correlation could have been caused by market recognition that the threat of deflation now outweighed the threat of inflation—or, alternatively, by market recognition that monetary policy would now react directly to changes in stock prices. The link between inflation/deflation and carry is explored further in the next chapter; either way, this correlation shift was seminal in the rise of the modern carry regime.

the world—in fact, more liquid than the S&P 500 markets—are the US dollar interest rate markets, including both Treasury bonds and interest rate futures. But volatility premiums in interest rate markets appear less rich. This makes sense considering the fundamental difference between bonds and equities: bonds are considered "safe assets," while equities are understood to embed the risk of ruin that is the root of the volatility premium.

In summary, carry trades must be profitable over time in a levered world. The problem occurs when central banks are volatility sellers on a large scale themselves. The expansion of carry trades by central banks makes them, for a time, excessively profitable, and more capital is drawn into them. At some point this depresses the prospective return to carry enough to bring about a severe carry crash. But the cycle of carry bubble and carry crash is associated with ever-greater leverage in the financial markets and in the economy. More leverage means a structure of volatility that further incentivizes carry—and the carry regime goes on.

This carry regime then determines the course of the economy: creating a pattern of economic growth driven by consumption and capital allocation driven by speculation, as opposed to a more healthy economy driven by the investment of the economy's savings in future growth potential. Given the accompanying background of excessive leverage and debt, this is something for which the world economy will be paying for a long time.

Can it be any other way? Can we envisage a world in which carry is not incentivized? And if not, why not? If not, the implication is that there is some more fundamental force that, at root, lies behind carry. We touch on these topics in the remainder of the book.

10
Does the Carry Regime Have to Exist?

Is the Carry Regime Inevitable?

GLOBAL FINANCIAL MARKETS HAVE COME TO BE DOMInated by carry; they exist in a carry regime. But as we have shown, in a levered world a long-run positive return to carry trades seems inevitable. Therefore, in practice, does it really mean anything to talk about the world existing in a carry regime? Is it possible to imagine anything different?

An obvious starting point, and one we believe can give us some insight into the nature of carry, is to consider the possibility of the exact opposite of a carry regime—a hypothetical "anti-carry" regime. What would be the characteristics and implications of such a regime?

First, to recap, the defining feature of the carry regime is that liquidity is positively priced. That is, "trading with the market" or taking liquidity—buying when the asset price rises, selling when the asset price falls—is systematically expensive. No matter how a speculator tries to do it, whether through trading strategies in the underlying over any time horizon or through any form of options strategy, she will pay away a risk premium on average. Conversely, "trading against the market"—providing liquidity—is systematically profitable or receives a risk premium on average.

The liquidity price for an asset can be expressed through a chart of volatility curves. For realized volatility the curve is of realized volatilities as measured over different time horizons; for liquidity to have a positive price, shorter-term realized volatilities need to exceed longer-term realized volatilities. For implied volatility the curve is of implied volatilities at different forward points; for liquidity to have a positive price, further forward implied volatilities need to exceed nearer forward implied volatilities—and all implied volatilities must exceed all realized volatilities.

The slope of realized volatility means that the asset displays mean-reverting behavior. While this mean reversion implies meaningful predictability of price movements, the perspective taken here is that this predictability is not an inefficiency. It is the simple result of liquidity having a positive price; it cannot be "arbitraged," because for a trader to attempt to arbitrage it, he would have to have liquidity and would have to provide that liquidity to the market. Many other apparent market inefficiencies can be viewed analogously.

The slope of implied volatility superficially appears to mean that the market expects price volatility to rise. Since volatility does not on average rise—it is empirically mean reverting to a stable level of long-run volatility—this cannot really be understood as an expectation. Instead this curvature is a risk premium paid to forward implied volatility sellers, that is, forward liquidity providers. In the same way, the gap between implied and realized volatilities makes selling spot implied volatility—selling contracts that pay out depending on realized volatility of the underlying starting immediately—profitable over time, as a risk premium to providers of instantaneous liquidity (which is parallel to the bid-ask spread, according to heuristic arguments outlined in Chapter 9).

This carry paradigm accurately describes the S&P 500 and its options markets over the past 30 or so years. It is an increasingly accurate description of other stock indexes, which have begun to display these behaviors, following the S&P 500. It is possible to imagine that eventually it should describe all financial assets.

Strategies providing liquidity are paid a high return per unit of apparent risk with relatively rare events in which liquidity disappears and liquidity providers are decimated. These events are short squeezes in liquidity. They seem to be inevitable given the nature of the premium—given that short rather than long is the naturally profitable side. They are self-reinforcing deleveraging cascades; their positive feedback nature makes them sudden and catastrophic. Insofar as the underlying asset provides a risk premium either long or short, they must always occur against that underlying premium—cause losses to receivers of the underlying asset premium—as the carry regime causes the underlying risk premium and its liquidity provision premium to become identified with each other. So in equity markets, liquidity short squeezes are to the downside. They form and cause the skew of both implied volatility and realized returns, this skew being another way in which the liquidity price manifests.

The high return-to-risk ratio of liquidity provision strategies is the natural complement of and compensation for the violence of the carry crashes in which these strategies are punished. We hypothesize that the equilibrium long-run expected return to liquidity provision can be at any level—the higher the expected return, the greater the corresponding risk of ruin brought about by these crashes. So liquidity can be fair value at any apparent price: its price has "multiple equilibria," or alternatively, it has no equilibrium.

The heart of this chapter lays out a series of thought experiments, from both volatility and monetary perspectives, which demonstrate that the carry regime is intimately linked to deflationary pressures and that an inflationary world would necessarily reverse many of its key features. These thought experiments are quite abstract and may be somewhat difficult to comprehend at first. They are not intended to forecast likely futures for the world, and in particular they are not intended to portray likely futures for the structure of volatility of the S&P 500. Indeed, it seems more likely that the end of the carry regime, or the birth of an anti-carry regime, would be associated with the receding importance of financial markets. Relatedly, it may be more likely still that, before its end, the carry regime will mutate into new forms not centered on the S&P 500. Plausible future focuses of the carry regime might include Chinese stock markets, global property markets, or, especially, equity-bond correlation. The point of the thought experiments is rather the insights they can provide into the nature of the present carry regime.

A Theoretical Alternative to the Carry Regime

If liquidity can be fair value at any price, a highly positive liquidity price cannot be the only possible state, at least theoretically. What would the world look like if liquidity were negatively priced, for example? If trading with the market were systematically profitable and trading against the market unprofitable? What would this mean? A first, necessarily speculative, attempt at characterizing this counterfactual world would be just to invert the features of the world as we know it.

In this counterfactual world, far forward implied volatility would be oversupplied. People would "want" to sell it—that is, they would on average be willing to pay for the privilege of selling it. Plausibly, as a result, options markets would "expect" volatility to fall into the future, with long-dated implied volatility below short-dated implied volatility.

Furthermore, it would cost more to trade with the market on longer horizons than on shorter horizons. Volatility would be greater over longer than shorter horizons. Markets would move more in the long term than the short term—for any long and short term, whether days, months, or years. This implies momentum; the price movements in either direction would be self-reinforcing.

Over the short to medium run, it seems reasonable that prices could have momentum. In fact, momentum at horizons of up to a year has been an empirical feature of returns in many markets. However, over the very long run, given that mean reversion is identified with the effectiveness of valuation as an idea, prices should be mean reverting. Because fundamentals are stable in the long run, and prices must be bounded relative to fundamentals, it seems hard to comprehend that extremely long-term momentum is possible. If we believe that fundamentals exist, the only plausible way for price volatility to be greatest over the longest horizons is if the denominator of the price—the value of the money in which price is measured—is unstable, presumably due to high and volatile inflation.

In this world, long-run average realized volatility would likely exceed long-run average implied volatility, so that buyers of spot options would on average earn money. At first glance, a negative implied-realized gap would seem to suggest a negative bid-ask spread, which is extremely implausible. But given finite trading volume, it just requires that prices move with such vigorous ultra-short-term momentum that volatility measured over intervals of minutes or more exceeds the instantaneous volatility, including the bid-ask bounce, which can be captured by even the most effective market-making strategy. In this world, specialized market makers would on average be unprofitable. This would have to be a world in which there was so much natural supply of liquidity that specialized market makers would not need to exist. Figure 10.1 is a chart summarizing this hypothetical inverted, or "mirror," regime.

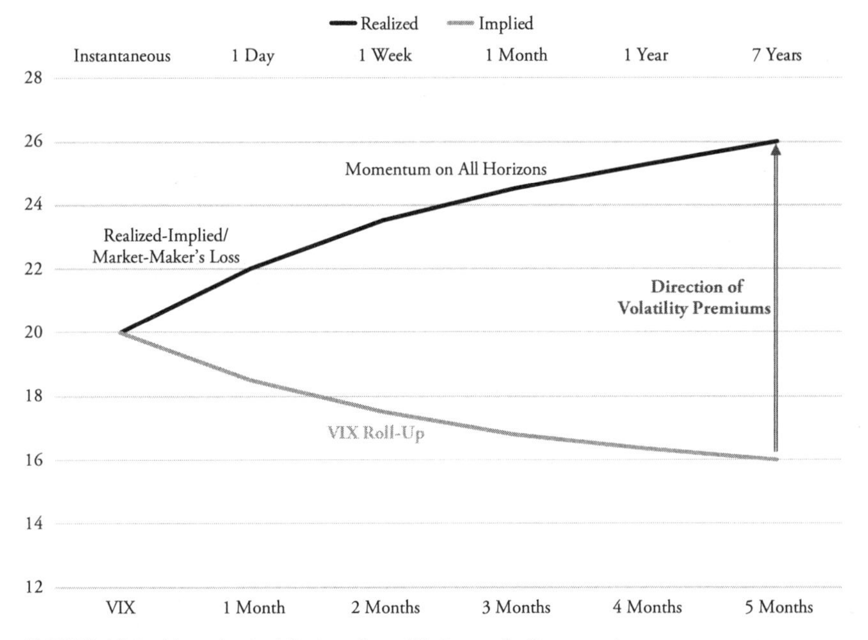

FIGURE 10.1 Hypothetical "mirror" equilibrium volatility premiums term structure
Chart shows implied volatility spot and forward on the lower gray line, read off the bottom horizontal axis, and realized volatility across measuring horizons on the upper black line, read off the top horizontal axis. Data is a mirrored version of the equilibrium volatility premiums chart for the carry regime shown in Chapter 9.

Very possibly, the skew seen in both implied and realized volatility would reverse direction. Calls would become more expensive than puts; the largest up weeks or months in the underlying would be bigger than the largest down weeks or months. This feature, as with long-run price momentum, would seem to be consistent with this hypothetical world being an extremely inflationary one.

Take the intuition that the carry regime is driven by the presence of enormous leverage that must on average be rebalanced by buying optionality. A speculator truly has no choice but to buy this optionality—she can either rebalance her leverage regularly or run the risk of buying all the optionality back at once if she is forcibly stopped out of a position following significant losses. Because she has no choice but to trade in this way, she can be made to pay a premium for optionality.

What is the inverse of this dynamic? A regime that is driven by underleverage, and enormous reserves of excess cash, that must on average be rebalanced by selling optionality. The positive liquidity price world is overlevered, resulting in immense demand for liquidity, and so the negative liquidity price world must be underlevered, resulting in immense supply of liquidity. So the sense in which we have used the word "liquidity" throughout—meaning capacity to trade and take on positions—is consistent with the traditional economic sense of "liquidity"—meaning monetary aggregates. After all, they are really the same thing. The overlevered world must be deflationary and the underlevered world inflationary.

A Monetary Perspective on Carry and Anti-carry

As might be expected, therefore, the idea that the carry regime in global financial markets is associated with pressure toward disinflation or even deflation—while the simple opposite of a carry regime, one in which speculators would be rewarded for being long volatility, would be associated with inflation or probably accelerating inflation—can also be viewed from a purely monetary perspective.

A carry regime will tend to feature high levels of indebtedness that will weigh on new bank credit growth—as we have been seeing over recent years.

Monetary growth will therefore tend to be fairly low over the long term, in the absence of offsetting actions by central banks.

This combination will also mean that the demand to hold money (in all its potential forms)—relative to income—will tend to be quite high. In itself, other things being equal, this will exert pressure toward deflation. If deflation is not to happen, money growth will need to be reasonably high, at least higher than average. Given that the demand for bank credit is likely to be fairly weak, there are two ways that higher-than-average money growth can be achieved. One way is via direct central bank actions. The second way is if nonmonetary financial assets come to be considered as good, or even perfect, substitutes for money. In practice, this second way is likely to require central banks to take responsibility (at least to some degree) for these nonmonetary assets—that is, practically, to treat them as contingent liabilities of the central bank.

This second way is what we have called increasing "moneyness," and as we have explained in Chapter 7, this is a direct result of the carry regime. Carry bubbles, which over time produce low volatility of financial asset prices, encourage risk assets—or at least certain risk assets—to become perceived as being as good as money. The carry regime in itself therefore enables the higher demand for money to be satisfied and therefore helps to prevent deflationary collapse. In a circular fashion this enables the carry regime to continue.

From this perspective the carry regime can perhaps be seen as a market mechanism that enables an uneasy monetary equilibrium to be maintained. Without the carry regime's existence, the system would tip over into spiraling deflation and debt destruction.

The mirror opposite of a carry regime would therefore be one in which debt tended to become less of a burden. This would encourage new credit creation to be stronger, meaning, other things being equal, higher demand for bank credit. Without offsetting actions by central banks, money supply growth would tend to be higher. Any consequent inflation would erode debt burdens further. The demand to hold money would be weak over time; money would be unattractive because inflation reduces the real value of money. To some extent this declining demand to hold money as an asset could be met by reduced moneyness. Financial assets that had previously been thought of as good substitutes for money, and therefore more or less part of money holdings, would gradually come to be considered as even worse to hold than traditional money. This will happen naturally if the volatility of the prices of those financial assets rises. This will therefore be the simple anti-carry regime—in which long volatility bets would pay off over time—and it would be consistent with pressures toward high inflation, although without inflation spiraling completely out of control.

A carry crash is a dislocation in the fragile equilibrium of a carry regime, which suddenly collapses the economy into a deflationary spiral. Moneyness evaporates as the volatility of financial assets goes skyward. Then the demand for true money rises sharply, forcing rapid deflation. The real burden of debt rises sharply, collapsing credit demand even more, in a vicious circle.

The hypothetical exact opposite, therefore, would be an anti-carry crash in an anti-carry regime. Inflation would spiral out of control. Demand to hold true money would collapse while the demand for (at least some) risky assets would rise relatively. During the dislocation these risky assets would appear better than money, presumably because they would have some inflation-hedge characteristics. The collapse in the demand for true money would accelerate inflation further.

The point here is that both regimes, in a sense, operate on a knife-edge, from which they can be tipped over into dislocation. The carry (or in an inverse world the anti-carry) regime can be seen as the way in which the market creates an uneasy stability out of this fundamentally unstable situation. Crashes occur when this uneasy stability can no longer be maintained—in a sense, when the house of cards tips over. Monetary instability increases enormously, and a huge dislocation occurs across financial markets. In a carry crash, the economy tips into a deflationary spiral; in a theoretical anti-carry crash, inflation spirals out of control. The end of the dislocation and the restoration of the regime occur as the result of action by central banks. In the carry crash the central banks expand the money supply enough to offset the loss of moneyness as financial assets collapse in price and volatility spirals higher.

A "True" Anti-carry Regime

The sketch of an anti-carry regime outlined so far, of a simple mirror image of the current regime, is naïve. Most notably, it is still a form of carry regime in the broadest sense in that it remains profitable to bet against market "expectations." It just becomes the case that the direction of "expectations" inverts.

A way of moving toward a model of a true anti-carry regime is to consider one curious feature of the current regime: that the most risk is closest to the present. Nearer forward implied volatilities are more volatile than far forward implied volatilities. While spot volatility whips around, far forward volatility barely moves. The distant future is considered to be relatively certain; the idea that "volatility is mean reverting to a stable long-run level" is fully accepted by the market. For the S&P 500, implied volatility five months forward has been barely a quarter as volatile as the spot VIX (Figure 10.2).

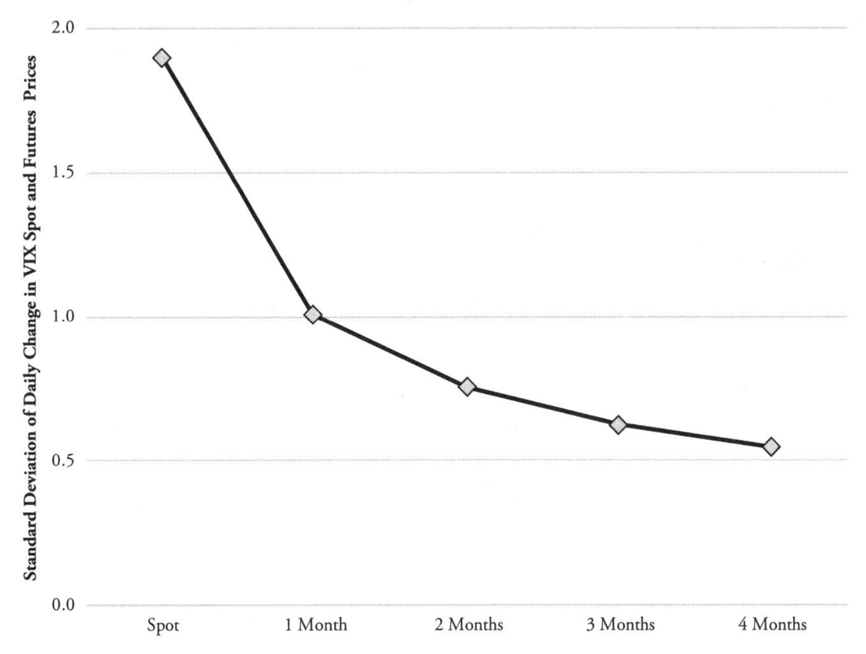

FIGURE 10.2 Volatility of VIX spot and futures
Chart shows daily volatility, in volatility points, for VIX spot, VIX 1m forward, 2m forward, etc., where forward points are interpolated from the futures curve, over the period from October 23, 2006 to March 29, 2019.
Source of data: CFE/Interactive Brokers, authors' calculations

The same is true on the realized spectrum. Realized volatilities are somewhat more stable measured over longer horizons than measured over shorter horizons, as mean reversion increases when volatility increases. This idea that volatility is itself mean reverting can, again, be associated with the long-run effectiveness of valuation. And similarly to the long-run effectiveness of valuation, it seems implausible that things could be any other way.

However, if the prices for which volatility is measured are themselves extremely unstable, in an accelerating inflationary spiral, this might be expected to break down. In such a world, uncertainty about volatility would increase, not decrease, further into the future, and the point of greatest uncertainty would be the point at infinity rather than the current instant. It seems highly unlikely that implied volatility could be in backwardation in such a world; distant future volatility must be both more volatile and higher than near future volatility. And the implied volatility curve would be flattest near the spot and steepest in the distant future, in order to keep ex-ante risk-reward ratios for trading volatility in approximate balance (given that distant future volatility is much more volatile). Presumably, extremely long-dated volatility would be unpriced and unpriceable.

If carry is to fail and volatility buyers are to be paid, then volatility must simply be rising over time faster than the upward slope of the implied volatility curve. This is the true anti-carry regime, where market "expectations" systematically underestimate future change. All of this would be consistent with a completely uncontrolled hyperinflationary spiral. This is the world in which money dies.

Figure 10.3 is a chart guessing at the shape of this anti-carry regime. The key feature of this world cannot be shown on an equilibrium chart, because it portrays a system not at equilibrium in the usual sense. That key feature is that volatility, along with inflation, is always accelerating higher.

The hypothetical worlds—both the mirror world and the anti-carry world—are, for the moment, imaginary, and it is unlikely we have covered all the possible ways in which a negative liquidity price could manifest. But any negative liquidity price world is likely to share some or many of the basic features outlined here. Above all, a negative liquidity price world is likely to be inflationary, or highly inflationary.

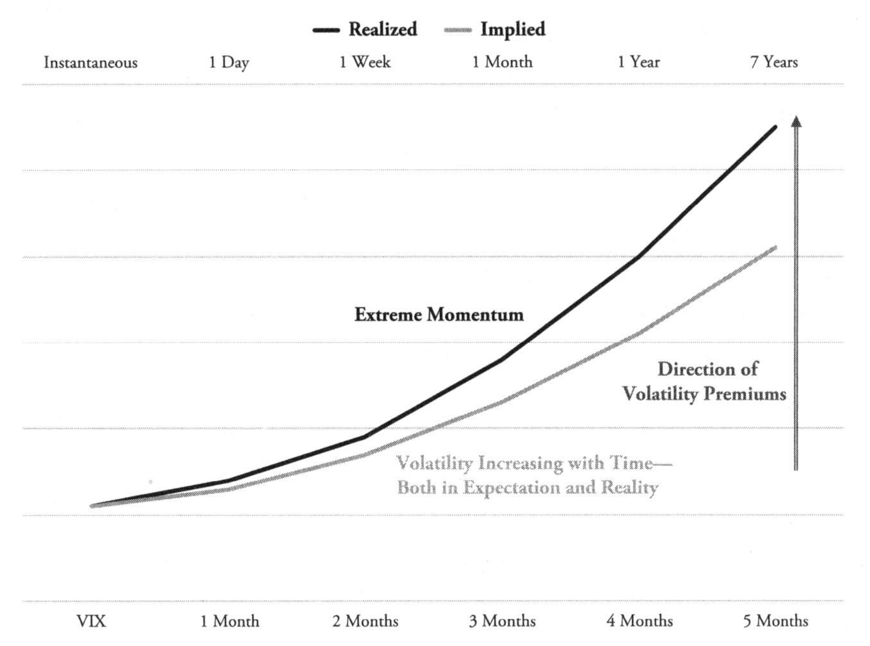

FIGURE 10.3 Hypothetical anti-carry volatility premiums term structure
Chart shows implied volatility spot and forward on the lower gray line, read off the bottom horizontal axis. Realized volatility across measuring horizons is plotted on the upper black line, which is read off the top horizontal axis. No vertical axis is shown because there is no long-run average level of volatility.

Carry and Anti-carry Are Two Sides of the Same Coin

From this, necessarily rather speculative, discussion emerges an important truth: a hypothetical anti-carry regime is, in crucial ways, fundamentally not so different from the carry regime. From the point of view of society as a whole, and not merely financial speculators, both the carry regime and the hypothetical anti-carry regime will have the feature that those with the greatest resources will be the winners.

Anyone can be a carry trader; many people are, most without knowing or understanding it. Because, in a carry regime, carry trades have a strongly positive long-run return, necessarily many "ordinary people" will be drawn into them, at least indirectly. These can be people who put their life savings into higher-yielding investment products without understanding the risks—which is not strictly a carry trade under our definition but would still be hurt as a by-product of a carry crash—or, for instance, take out low interest rate foreign currency mortgages to finance a house purchase or over-extend in buy-to-rent property investments, both of which are direct carry trades. Then there are all the broad indirect negative impacts of the carry crash: overlevered businesses going bust and jobs being lost, financial institutions bankrupted. In a discussion of carry crashes with the authors, a friend remarked that "only people in finance are wiped out in carry crashes; ordinary people are not wiped out." Sadly, that is not the case.

A certain level of carry is necessary for society. Economies need liquidity services, and only those with strong balance sheets—the wealthy—are in a position to provide them. Profits from carry do increase their wealth, but the liquidity provided also increases overall societal welfare. However, in a carry regime the economy is awash both with demand for liquidity and with liquidity supplied by carry traders, many of whom would not be able to survive a carry crash without the intervention of the central bank. Further, by cushioning the carry crash to some extent, central banks further increase the profits of those natural providers of liquidity—the very wealthy. Those who survive the carry crash are then in a position to prosper anew in the succeeding carry bubble, taking their wealth to even greater heights. The inequality of wealth across the economy accelerates.

A mirror opposite of the carry regime is unlikely to be different. The equivalent of the carry crash in a simple mirror-image anti-carry regime is a collapse in the value of money with inflation spiraling out of control. Would it be likely that a poor person would benefit from such an eventuality? Obviously, it would not. In general, whether in a carry regime or a simple anti-carry regime, it will be those with the greatest resources that will ultimately come out of the dislocations relatively better off.

This brings us to a simple truth. At the heart of the carry regime or the hypothetical anti-carry regime lies monetary instability. It is the fundamental instability of fiat money—the fact that the problem of money has not yet been solved—that leads to the emergence of the carry regime in financial markets. In any society some will have more power and command over resources, and some will have less. What fiat money does is allow this imbalance of power to manifest directly in the financial and economic world. The way it does this is through the development of the carry regime.

In a positively priced liquidity world—the carry regime—there is a positive return for being able to provide liquidity in all circumstances, which requires resources. Absent central bank intervention, those who only have sufficient resources to provide market liquidity in good times are wiped out in the carry crashes. But in the negatively priced liquidity world of the simple anti-carry regime—an inflationary world—there must be a positive return for demanding liquidity in all circumstances, for being able to be a taker of liquidity potentially at all times. This means, for example, being in a position to take advantage of the aftermath of the extreme inflationary spiral that would be the manifestation of dislocation in the simple mirror-image anti-carry regime. This also requires resources.

Fundamentally, therefore, in some sense carry is its own antithesis.

Carry as Rent-Seeking

The notion of carry as fundamentally being about power and control of resources calls to mind the economic concept of rent-seeking. Wikipedia defines rent-seeking as extracting an income "by manipulating the social or political environment in which economic activities occur, rather than by creating new wealth. Rent-seeking implies extraction of uncompensated value from others without making any contribution to productivity."

Rent-seeking is usually thought about in terms of an industry group or interest group lobbying politicians in order to secure monopoly power. The classic example is taxi drivers securing and defending a taxi licensing scheme. This is a good example, and very contemporary in these days of the "sharing economy." Taxi licensing is a good analogy for the carry regime to the extent that in a growing city the taxi owners benefiting from the monopoly power endowed by their license will benefit not only from higher incomes but also from the increasing market value of the license, the fundamental value of which depends on the discounted future income stream deriving from taxi fares. This is similar to the way that the carry trader benefits from the income from the carry trade—which is the primary motivation for the carry trade—but also benefits from asset price appreciation as the carry bubble grows.

The analogy is not perfect, though. Rent-seeking traditionally is about obtaining monopoly power through lobbying the government. Carry—in its financial and extreme sense—is about extracting an income from the authorities' own monopoly power, specifically the central bank's monopoly over the supply of money and the government's power to tax. In a subtle way this involves what is usually referred to as "regulatory capture." This is the situation in which the regulator—in this case the government or central bank—which is supposed to act in the public interest, ends up mostly acting in the interests of the regulated, in this case the financial industry, particularly speculative finance.

Furthermore, the carry regime is a process of evolution, in which the financial system and the whole investment industry gradually evolve, through successive carry bubbles and carry crashes, into a system that exists almost entirely to benefit from carry. In its extreme form carry is the same as rent-seeking in that it does not create new wealth; in fact, as it becomes more extreme, it destroys wealth relative to an alternative in which carry did not exist. If the financial system becomes entirely dominated by carry, then it will no longer be contributing to productivity growth. As resources in the economy are devoted increasingly to carry, then genuine investment in the economy—in productive assets other than the service of liquidity provision—will decay, ultimately to zero, as will genuine economic growth.

The carry regime—the process of carry bubbles and then crashes that wipe out carry traders with fewer resources—will be associated with a relentless increase in income and wealth inequality. It remains a subject for debate whether the blame for this can be laid at the doors of the leading central bankers of recent years or whether the fundamental nature of carry makes it inevitable that a fiat money system will evolve into a carry regime regardless of who is leading the central banks. But it is clear that central banks have been agents for the transmission of carry into the explosion of inequality that we have experienced. If we aspire to create economies in which all can participate and prosper, then the framework in which central banks operate, both legal and intellectual, will have to be greatly altered—and this likely applies also to other agencies of government and multilateral agencies (such as the IMF) that participate in bailouts and otherwise involve themselves in financial markets.

Ultimately, this means we need to prepare for potentially dramatic change in our monetary system, as society begins to understand the implications of carry and searches for ways to make the system more stable and equitable. In particular, if central banks come to be seen as agents of carry—and carry comes to be properly understood as reinforcing inequality—then we can expect continuing challenges to their independence and objectives.

11
Carry Is Synonymous with Power

Carry Flows from the Weak to the Strong

> The grave Sir Gilbert holds it for a rule
> That ev'ry man in want is knave or fool.
>
> —Alexander Pope

WHAT IS THE FUNDAMENTAL ORIGIN OF CARRY? WHY, THAT is, does carry exist? We have already explained, in Chapter 6, that in a highly levered world, the value of money is the price of volatility. Those with the means to provide liquidity have the advantage over those who need liquidity, and that advantage *must* be exploited. This is the moral or law of carry. It is summed up above as Sir Gilbert's rule: "Ev'ry man in want is knave or fool." (The couplet above, from the eighteenth-century English satirical poet Alexander Pope, refers to Sir Gilbert Heathcote—the only person to have had two separate terms as governor of the Bank of England, from 1709 to 1711 and from 1723 to 1725.)

Why are those in need "knaves or fools" who must be taken advantage of? At least in part, it is because they can be treated as if they are. If they have need and the speculator has the capacity to fill their need, then they are weak and the speculator is strong, and by the law of carry the speculator must exploit them; for those who exploit the needy will outcompete those who show charity to the needy, until the charitable are outcompeted to such an extent that they in turn become the needy. In short, the law of carry is the law of the jungle, "red in tooth and claw," and we are always in the jungle.

Carry trades leverage a difference in yields between a source and use of funds. What determines yields? Need determines yields. Less creditworthy means more needy. The wealthiest homeowners pay the lowest mortgage rates; the companies closest to bankruptcy have the highest bond yields. There are two ways to interpret this relationship. The first is to consider that the neediest borrowers are also the riskiest and have the highest probability of default. The more that borrowers need to scrimp and save to pay back their debt, the more likely that some shock or surprise befalling them will prevent them from making their payment. The second is to consider that the neediest borrowers can be squeezed the hardest.

Need, first of all, comes from threats to survival, and survival is a deeply felt impulse for all entities that survive—whether biological or corporate. The equivalence, for a levered entity, of rebalancing costs with the expected risk of ruin manifests the link between carry and ruin. More generally, need could arise wherever agents might suffer some irreversible negative consequence—in the language of random walks, if they might touch an absorbing barrier. A person might justifiably fear, for example, losing a limb, or, for another example, gaining a criminal record. And while a company or investor that loses assets could eventually regain them, unlike a limb, the well-known fact that if you have lost 50 percent you need to make 100 percent to get back to where you started means all losses contain some ghost of irreversibility.

This need is the source of the excess returns from carry strategies. From the perspective of need, uncovered interest parity fails because high interest rate developing countries need capital and therefore can be exploited. Historic normal backwardation in commodities did not reflect market expectations that commodity prices would fall, but market understanding that producers need to hedge and therefore can be exploited. Volatility carry works because levered traders need liquidity to rebalance their leverage and therefore can be exploited.

Carry, in short, is a flow from the weak to the strong; from the needy to the needless; from those who have no choice to those who do. Entities that have excess liquidity with which to take risk will lend it, receive carry, and so gain more excess liquidity. Entities that lack liquidity, need liquidity, and must borrow for it, will pay carry and so become more lacking and more needy. As in the Gospel of St. Matthew: "For unto every one that hath shall be given, and he shall have abundance: but from him that hath not shall be taken even that which he hath."

As stark as it appears, this is why capitalism progresses. It is the motive of Darwinism in the market and the driver of evolution in the economy. The evolutionarily unfit are punished with rising yields and thereby condemned to extinction; while the evolutionarily fit are blessed with excess liquidity with which to grow and prosper. (This is true only on average—in the particular, some who should be fit will face a run of bad luck and go extinct, while some who should be unfit will have a run of good luck and multiply.)

Carry Is Cumulative Advantage

A second idea is needed to explain why this is so important. This idea is called "cumulative advantage." A famous set of experiments to demonstrate its mechanism and effects, the Columbia MusicLab experiments, simulated a virtual pop music chart (in order, basically, to answer the eternal question of why so many huge pop hits are so poor musically).

These experiments, run in 2005, set up and publicized a website offering free downloads of songs by unknown bands. Participants came to the website to listen to, rate, and download the 48 songs it offered. (This was in the period after the fall of Napster and before the rise of modern music streaming services, when such a website might have had some appeal.) Visitors to the website were split into two conditions: one that was just given band and song names and one that could also see how many downloads other songs had—their popularity. The effect was predictable: if participants could see the popularity information, they were more likely to listen to songs that were already more popular, making the biggest hits bigger. As a result, final download numbers were far more unequal when participants could see popularity than when they could not.

Further, the participants who could see the download numbers were randomly assigned to eight independent parallel groups. The participants could only see popularity within their own group. And the songs that became the biggest hits within each of these groups were different. A song that ended as number 1 in one of the groups was number 40 out of 48 in another. In each of the groups, the songs that gained a lead at the very beginning of the experiment—for whatever reason—found that lead amplified and eventually locked in by the influence of the visible popularity numbers. This is the effect known as cumulative advantage.

As the experiments continued, the experimenters switched the menu of 48 songs from random placement in a grid to a list ranked by popularity. Of course, this further increased the size of the cumulative advantage effect. In the words of the experimenters: "Increasing the strength of social influence increased both inequality and unpredictability of success. Success was also only partly determined by quality: The best songs rarely did poorly, and the worst rarely did well, but any other result was possible."[1]

Cumulative advantage can be most clearly understood as a characteristic of many strategic games featuring chance or imperfect information, for example, card games such as most variants of poker. The core dynamic of these games is that once one player has gained an advantage—in poker, a bigger chip stack—it is incumbent on that player to use his advantage to strangle his opponent(s) out of the game. His opponents might be able to come back by outplaying him or "outlucking" him, but with equal luck and equal skill, a small advantage gained by chance will tend to turn into a runaway lead and victory. Just as in the Columbia MusicLab experiment, where a small advantage across the first few downloads and ratings would on

1. M. J. Salganik, P. S. Dodds, and D. J. Watts, "Experimental Study of Inequality and Unpredictability in an Artificial Cultural Market." *Science*, vol. 311, no. 5762, 854–856 (2006).

average lead—through chaotic random processes—to dominant final market share, the larger the advantage, the greater the outplay or outluck necessary to overcome it.

Cumulative advantage is what allows games to be won or lost, rather than going on forever. (Most athletic competitions—races over a set course, soccer, basketball, etc.—do not require the cumulative advantage mechanism, although all games played by humans can display a form of it through mechanisms of confidence and team trust.)

Financial markets are of course a strategic game featuring chance and imperfect information. Carry is the mechanism of cumulative advantage in financial markets. For a company (or country with foreign currency debt) in financial distress, increases in the yield that the markets require it to pay cause decreases in the chance it will survive just as much as the other way around. And for a levered entity, losses result in increases in leverage that increase the cost of volatility hedging.

Most games have structures that affect the degree to which cumulative advantage takes effect. For example, in poker played with blinds or antes, the larger the blind or ante size relative to the total quantity of chips on the table, the more rapidly the game will end—which is the same as saying, the more rapidly chips will on average gravitate toward the biggest stack. In other games it may be harder to see what levers can be pulled, what rules could be changed, to increase or decrease the effect of cumulative advantage. Fortunately, in financial markets it is easy to isolate this effect: in every financial transaction, carry flows from the party with less liquidity to the party with more liquidity. Insofar as spreads on different assets are correlated, a systemic increase in spreads is an increase in the cumulative advantage effect. It is in recessions or crises, when spreads widen, that the weak or unlucky companies and holders of capital are culled, and their assets flow into the hands of the strong. In the modern economy these are the carry crashes.

In this way carry drives the phenomenon of "multiple equilibria" in financial markets. An entity that is dependent on capital infusions—whether an economy with chronic current account deficits, or a sovereign with chronic budget deficits, or a tech "unicorn" racing to outspend its competitors to monopoly—might find its debt quite sustainable at a low enough interest rate. Then as long as the rate is low, the entity will be creditworthy and therefore will warrant a low rate. But if some shock causes the rate to rise, so that it has to borrow more to meet its ballooning payments and so finds its need for capital exploding—then the entity will now be risky, no longer creditworthy, and therefore will warrant a high rate. The lower a borrower's yield is, the safer that borrower is and therefore the lower the yield that the borrower deserves. The higher a borrower's yield is, the riskier that borrower is and therefore the higher the yield that the borrower deserves.

Cumulative Advantage Is Luck Compounded

Cumulative advantage might be thought of as that which crystallizes randomness. In the MusicLab experiment, the random chance of which songs happened to get clicked on first became the social reality of "these songs have the most downloads already—and therefore must be better." And this social reality perpetuates itself.

Phenomena like this are not isolated to academic experiments but are common throughout the world. The most famous and easily explained example, an example that everybody understands, is the long odds of becoming a movie star. As we all know, to become a movie star, an aspiring actor needs beauty, charisma, determination, acting talent, and more—plus, most importantly, the "big break." This is because a film that casts a star will sell more tickets than it would if it cast an otherwise identical, but not famous, actor. Stars bring their fans, and as known quantities they bring wider audiences comfort; they fill the theaters. So the most important qualification for a potentially star-making role is to already be a star. This model of stardom is so well known as to be part of our popular culture.

Big breaks are arbitrary. Harrison Ford, according to legend, had turned to doing carpentry on the side in order to make money as a struggling actor. He was installing a door in the offices of a regular client—who happened to be a movie producer—on the day that an up-and-coming director named George Lucas was in the building, doing casting calls for a new science fiction film. Johnny Depp was picked for his first acting role, over the director's original choice, on the advice of the director's teenage daughter, who had a crush on him. Charlize Theron was arguing with a bank teller when the man behind intervened; he turned out to be a talent agent. Such stories may be part or wholly myth, but they are illuminating. Is there anyone who thinks that the most natural movie star in the world—the person with the single most winning combination of good looks, charm, desire for fame, work ethic, etc.—is not at this moment waiting tables somewhere in greater L.A.? This is not to take anything away from the movie stars we have, who are (mostly) extremely good. They have to be; otherwise they never would have made it. But being good, on its own, is not enough to make it.

The other side of this is that already-established stars do not need to be as good as they were. They can become lazier, harder to work with, less good-looking, and for some time they will still be offered roles. Of course, this cannot be sustained forever. If they continue to lose their looks and skills, fans and the industry will eventually desert them. But for a period, these established stars can be objectively worse—less attractive, less motivated, delivering a less good performance—than the talented nobodies who are next in line behind them, and yet it will still be rational for the director and producer to prefer to hire the stars. This is what celebrity means. That is what cumulative advantage means.

Another example is that of network effects and lock-in in business, economics, and technology: the competition between VHS and Betamax, or between Facebook and Myspace and Friendster, or between Uber and Lyft. Betamax is often considered to have been a better technology, but it lost. Today, a direct competitor to Facebook could never succeed, no matter how much better its technology or design or business plan—because the appeal of a social network is the users who are already there, and those users are on Facebook. If Facebook is ever dethroned (and in time it will be), it will not be by another social network of the same kind, but by something entirely new that makes social networks of that kind irrelevant—which is to say, it will be disrupted.

Network effects, and therefore cumulative advantage, are especially prominent in communications technologies and technological standards. Microsoft Office may be possible (just about) to dethrone—but only ever by a competitor that also could manipulate the .xls file format, which dominates global business. Financial instruments, too, can be viewed as communications standards that have network effects. As mentioned in Chapter 10, while the centrality of the S&P 500 to global markets today is quite reasonable, it was not predestined and may not be eternal. So, ultimately, even today's convergence of the financial carry trade onto the S&P 500 and the VIX is an example of cumulative advantage at work.

In business generally, regular old-fashioned economies of scale are an attenuated form of the cumulative advantage effect. However, if an industry is a "natural monopoly," then business success is driven almost entirely by cumulative advantage. Considering that cumulative advantage—social proof, positive word of mouth from the right people, success in getting products into the hands of influencers and early adopters—may be more important for new firms today, especially in the software sector, might help illuminate why persistence of returns is widely observed among venture capital firms but not among public market investors. The cumulative advantage of the most respected venture firms means that the companies they back gain favorable publicity and become more credible to potential employees, customers, and other investors—and thus have a major head start in the race to dominate their niche. Cumulative advantage is the best kind of skill.

Cumulative Advantage Is What Perpetuates Itself

Cumulative advantage is implicated in all forms of fads, fashions, crazes, trends—even market bubbles. As illustrated by the example of movie stardom, cumulative advantage is behind "superstar effects" across all cultural products: music, books, success as a "public intellectual," and more. Cumulative advantage is likely behind the virulence of modern social media—Twitter mobs, disinformation, polarization—where visible numbers of likes, shares, and retweets show us collectively what is right (or safe) to say (or think), and thereby produce powerful feedback effects. Plausibly, cumulative advantage could be related to the persistence of social class, structural racism, and wealth inequality.

Another example, the murkiest but likely the most significant in our daily lives, is the natural formation of social hierarchies in animals: a big dog will slink away fearfully from a small dog who outranks it, and the fact that it could easily take the small dog in a fight does not even occur to it. As with celebrity, or network effects, social hierarchies in animals are not imaginary but are perpetuated by genuine social realities. Namely, the fact that the hierarchy is stable at all implies that all its members will act together to support it. The big dog slinks away not because it fears the small dog but because it fears the wrath of the whole pack (although surely it is unconscious of this). A solipsist might point out that such examples of cumulative advantage exist only in our heads. But it is not that they exist in our own heads that matters so much as that they exist in everybody else's.

Accordingly, it seems likely that an innate appreciation for—and blindness to—cumulative advantage is hardwired into the structure of our brains. (While scientists who study the behavior of other animals are free to describe these phenomena explicitly, humans are rarely fond of acknowledging to what extent we ourselves are affected by animal considerations of hierarchy. If anything, people who acknowledge such considerations are usually, and perhaps understandably, seen as attempting to manipulate them to "unjustly" gain rank.) Like the philosophical joke about the fish who asks "What is water?" the very invisibility of cumulative advantage is the strongest argument for its importance.

The rise of technology and the increasing interconnectedness of the world today may make cumulative advantage effects more significant than ever before. Today's great companies and market darlings—Amazon, Microsoft, all social networks as illustrated above, and even to a lesser extent Apple and Google—are principally dependent on cumulative advantage in a way that companies of the old world, such as Exxon or Toyota, are not. For many of today's most interesting companies, their cumulative advantage—not their technology or superior products (let alone oil reserves or car factories)—is their greatest asset, and even more tellingly, their cumulative advantage is often explicitly invoked as being at the heart of their bull case. Outside the business world, franchises and sequels seem to be spreading unstoppably across all entertainment markets; recent years have seen the invention of the "Instagram influencer" and the rise of new forms of celebrity on YouTube, Twitch, TikTok, and more. And today the youngest self-made billionaire in history built her empire off the back of a reality TV show that was primarily popularized by a leaked sex tape. The central thesis of this book is that cumulative advantage effects in financial markets are more pronounced today than at any other point in the postwar period: the *carry regime*. But financial markets reflect the world, and it may be that the carry regime extends beyond them.

In short, in games with strong cumulative advantage effects, just as in our original example of the MusicLab experiment, it is not particularly likely that the best player will win. (Plausibly, the converse of this is that strong cumulative advantage effects may make it possible, at least, for one of the better players to win when otherwise players are too closely matched for the game to distinguish accurately among them.) Analogously, we believe that financial markets with strong cumulative advantage effects are not particularly likely to allocate resources optimally. At the highest level, this is the thrust of our argument against the growing carry regime in modern financial markets.

Throughout this book, we have invoked classical economic equilibrium as something like an opposite to carry, as something that appears to be violated by carry bubbles, by carry trades, by the carry regime. This is not a coincidence. As we hope these examples have made clear, carry—cumulative advantage—is that which is out of equilibrium; it is that which has no equilibrium. Carry is that which creates its own equilibrium.

Cumulative Advantage Is Why We Exist

So far we have emphasized the neutral or negative aspects of cumulative advantage. We have portrayed it as the reason we watch the most famous actors rather than the most talented; as why we use the technologies that came first, or were seeded among the right influential crowd, rather than the best; as why we bow to the mob over our own judgment. This may all be true, but it is only one perspective.

There is another extremely well-known example of cumulative advantage, of random variation perpetuating itself and becoming permanent. It is called evolution. Consider the origin of life: organic chemicals bubbling in the primordial soup, stirred by the turbulence of the early solar system.

By chance—a lightning strike, a meteorite impact, or simply quantum randomness—a few of these chemicals momentarily enter a configuration that causes reactions with its surroundings that then make more copies of that configuration. And as these configurations are jostled again and again, most of them break apart, and a few by chance find themselves in new and maybe more complex shapes that allow them to replicate faster and more perfectly. And then, over billions of years, these simple configurations become amino acids and proteins: RNA, DNA, cells, multicellular organisms . . .

It was cumulative advantage that allowed the first self-replicating molecule in the primordial ocean to spread—or more likely, the *n*th self-replicating molecule in that ocean to spread faster than, and thus wipe out, those that came before it. It was cumulative advantage that propagated random mutations in certain lucky African primates that gave them larger brains and improved communications skills, allowing them to invent tools, fire, agriculture, and writing; allowing them to cooperate to spread over and ultimately conquer the earth. We are made of cumulative advantage.

Evolution, too, displays all the flaws of cumulative advantage described above. As much as we admire its results, which are systems of biochemical nanotechnology far exceeding the understanding of scientists and engineers today—as much, that is, as we are enamored with ourselves—it is hopelessly path dependent. The famous example is the enzyme rubisco, the most abundant enzyme on earth, which drives photosynthesis by catalyzing the capture of carbon dioxide from the atmosphere. However, rubisco evolved before oxygen was abundant in the atmosphere, and in today's oxygenated atmosphere rubisco can and does "mistake" oxygen for carbon dioxide—capturing oxygen instead of carbon dioxide, producing toxic by-products, and wasting metabolic energy. Because of this feature of rubisco, photosynthesis is about a quarter less efficient than it otherwise would be. But rubisco is too interlocked with the rest of the intricate biochemistry of plants to be replaced now with an enzyme suitable for an oxygenated atmosphere. Instead, plant biology has over time evolved an increasingly complex patchwork of mechanisms to work around and minimize the cost of this inefficiency, and ecosystems have sprung up around existing plants that pollinate them, propagate their seeds, and provide their nutrients. Any novel mutation to reinvent photosynthesis without rubisco would need extraordinary luck to overcome these entrenched advantages.

The processes that govern neurons in the brain, too, are governed by cumulative advantage. The more frequently a synapse is activated, the stronger it becomes and the greater the effect it has. Synapses that are rarely activated are pruned over time. (In the brain, the flaws of cumulative advantage take the form of depression, addiction, and more.) And of course, this book is about carry in financial markets, which allocate goods and services across the economy and so form the nervous system of human civilization—which, imperfect though it may be, has accomplished remarkable things. Wherever there is life, wherever there is intelligence, there is cumulative advantage. It does not seem plausible this could be a coincidence.

Carry Is Everywhere

According to today's understanding of physics, uncertainty or randomness is a fundamental property of the universe. We have described cumulative advantage as that which crystallizes randomness—that which harnesses randomness, makes transitory chance permanent, shapes chaos into order. And as we have attempted to explain throughout the book, the perspective through financial markets (and especially volatility)—by reducing all the uncertainty of the world to the single dimension of price—clarifies this link between carry and uncertainty.

The root of carry is (excess) liquidity. Liquidity means the ability of a portfolio or entity to absorb shocks, negative realizations of uncertainty, and keep going unimpaired. Liquidity means the ability of a portfolio or entity to promise to bear shocks on behalf of others, for a price, which in turn means the ability to profit and grow from nonnegative realizations of uncertainty. *Liquidity means that which faces uncertainty.* Liquidity is best defined as distance from ruin. The inevitability of uncertainty in the universe means ruin is always only finitely far away; it is through carry that this inevitability of final ruin for every single individual or entity becomes the inevitability of adaptation, and something like progress, across the entire ensemble of individuals or entities.

Because risk, ruin, and liquidity are not merely financial—they have real analogs—the characteristics we have described of financial carry trades apply to the real analogs of carry trades too. These visible characteristics include short volatility exposure—"that which pays if nothing changes"—and a sawtooth return path. To be at the head of any hierarchy, whether alpha of a pack of dogs or CEO of a major corporation, is to receive carry—the best pieces of meat and mating opportunities, the big bonuses, and the use of the corporate jet—but in exchange the leader must be ever vigilant, for there are so many challengers to the throne. The more vicious the internal politics of a company, government, crime family, or simply social group—which is to say, the more willing agents within the organization are to use ruin against each other—the faster and steadier will be the ascent of skilled carry traders, and the faster yet and more terrifying will be their eventual fall. The analogs to financial carry crashes are boardroom coups, political purges, and sudden executions.

Indeed, the strongest and most fearsome carry regimes in history can be easily identified as nonfinancial: Stalin's Great Purge, Mao's Cultural Revolution, and more, with the clearest examples of all being the Reign of Terror during the French Revolution and the killing fields of the Khmer Rouge. Each of these cases occurred where violence, torture, murder—in other words, ruin and carry in their purest and most terrible forms—were not merely allowed as inevitable but were actively embraced in the service of some supposed greater good. In each of these cases, the carry that the revolutionaries unleashed escaped their control and took on a life of its own; the means became the end. It is almost too obvious to point out that in each of these cases the original project of the revolutionaries was to overthrow an existing and opposing carry regime. If a simple, stylized lesson can be taken from these examples, it may be that the invocation of carry against carry is the most dangerous thing of all.

Carry Is Power

The point is this: "Carry" is the euphemism used in financial markets for power. The mechanism of power is cumulative advantage, and power in its true form is cumulative advantage with no referent—that is, advantage measured along some dimension that is unanchored from any reality other than itself. (Beauty is not wholly unanchored, nor is singing or acting talent; "famous for being famous," however, is.) Power must exist as long as risk exists: it is the capacity to withstand risk (and survive), and it is the capacity to take risk (and prosper). In other words, it *is* optionality. It is inevitable, it is necessary, and it is the motor for the emergence of complexity—life, consciousness, civilization—in the universe.

However, the rise of what we have called the carry regime necessarily means a progressive de-anchoring of the structure of market prices from fundamental economic reality (since self-sustaining de-anchoring from fundamentals is what pure power is). Over the very long run, this de-anchoring weakens growth and increases economic risk. Monetary policy has—likely at first inadvertently—promoted this de-anchoring and finally is being captured by it. This de-anchoring, invisible though it may be, is having increasingly corrosive effects on the political environment and social fabric across the developed world. In short, power, inevitable though it may be, should not be encouraged to grow too strong.

12
The Globalization of Carry

What Do (Financial) Markets "Want"?

From the perspective of a standard textbook of financial economics, the question "What do financial markets want?" would seem nonsensical. A financial market is supposed to be little different from any other type of market, the farmers' market in the center of town, for instance. It is either a physical place or a virtual place, where buyers and sellers meet to conduct transactions that are mutually beneficial. The shoppers get the vegetables for dinner, and the farmers make their living. It does not make any sense to talk or think about what the farmers' market "wants," so why should it make any sense to talk about what the financial markets "want"?

Yet in the financial world, it is fairly commonplace to consider what the market wants, or expects. Financial journalists might often write of "the market" wanting the government to implement a certain policy or wanting the Fed to cut interest rates, for example. Most people would probably say that this is simply shorthand for talking about what investors want. But when we think about financial markets as dominated by carry, and in turn carry as being a phenomenon of cumulative advantage and power, in what amounts to a type of evolutionary process, then we can see these notions in a different light. In the context of evolution, a species "wants" to survive and reproduce. It develops a set of physical and behavioral traits that aim to maximize its fitness for a certain environment, but that environment itself changes—mostly gradually but occasionally abruptly. Thus, there is a continual feedback loop of local adaptation and environmental change. When we think of a financial market not merely as a neutral hub for the effecting of transactions but as an evolving network that has its own structure, then it might also be reasonable to think about what the market wants.

In Chapter 5 we took this perspective when examining how the balance sheets and incentives of financial institutions have helped drive the evolution of the carry regime. This helps us understand how markets have arrived at their current state. Of course, the current structure will change too—the incentives and constraints facing these institutions will change. And the institutions themselves will change. Hedge funds were bit players 25 years ago and now are the key price setters in many markets. There are almost certainly bit players today that will grow to be central to markets 25 years hence. This institutional change in turn will interact with the developments in the functional nature of the market—of market making, with technology or with regulatory decisions.

Our strong belief, therefore, is that the market will continue to evolve, and it will tend to evolve to promote carry. Regulatory developments—importantly in the realm of monetary policy—and changes in the nature of institutions themselves will tend to be in the direction that makes the force of carry stronger. What the market wants is stronger carry—greater concentration of power and wealth. What the market wants is financial corporatism—large corporations with monopolies or quasi-monopolies and governments and regulatory agencies that are sympathetic to them and implement policy accordingly and with a central banking system that acts to support their share prices. This is the combination that encourages the further growth of carry.

Of course, the arguments are rarely made in these terms. Instead, investors are told they need more liquidity, more access to credit, and less volatile markets. These are all things that carry traders provide. Thus pressure rises for new products, new institutions, and new regulations to provide society with these features of carry. The force of carry, in some sense, is then able to capture the political system. But more than this, what has developed in more recent years is the full globalization of carry. Left-wing political activists think of this as "global capitalism." It really is not global capitalism. "Capitalism" means different things to different people, different on the political spectrum. But the essential elements of capitalism surely include free markets—including free financial markets—businesses operating in a very competitive environment, private and transferable ownership of businesses, and governments that provide a framework of the rule of law and ensure a stable medium of exchange. What we have today is quite far removed from this concept and much closer to something that could be described as financial corporatism.

At the world level, cooperation between governments, the influence of multilateral agencies, and, in particular, cooperation between central banks have been crucial elements in encouraging the globalization of carry. The currency carry trade, discussed at length in the earlier chapters, has been an important transmission mechanism for this globalization.

The Globalization of Moral Hazard

In Chapter 7 we discussed how the carry regime in global financial markets is ultimately associated with a convergence of economic growth and interest rates toward zero—a "vanishing point," as we termed it. In Chapter 9 we argued that the S&P 500, because of its great liquidity and depth of derivatives markets, must be a carry trade that stands at the center of the global carry regime. It is a small step from those insights to recognize that as the convergence toward the vanishing point takes place, there will be a simultaneous convergence of the carry trade on one carry instrument—the S&P 500 itself.

In the background of this convergence under the global carry regime is the globalization of central bank-created moral hazard. We have stressed in this book that the moral hazard created by central bank policies has played a fundamental role in the rise of carry in financial markets. Low or zero interest rates in the major developed economies, bailouts, central banks' quantitative easing policies, and their implicit promise to intervene in the event of market "instability" have all encouraged investment or speculative strategies that seek to extract a return from expectations of low market volatility.

Given the increasing dominance of the dollar as the carry funding currency of choice, along with its role as the world's major reserve currency, a further, crucial, element of the picture has been the US Federal Reserve's liquidity swap arrangements with other central banks and the Fed's willingness to enter into liquidity swaps on a large scale when there is stress in the dollar funding markets. Central bank liquidity swap arrangements can also be perceived as underwriting the "circular flow of dollars" in the global economy (a topic of the discussion of the currency carry trade in Chapter 2). When we think of the global carry regime as being a fundamentally deflationary regime composed of trillions of dollars of potentially interconnected currency carry trades, credit carry trades, and volatility selling trades in general, then it would be unlikely that this regime could exist with the dollar as the predominant funding and reserve currency without the Fed's underwriting of it via liquidity swaps.

To illustrate, we can return to an example used earlier in the book, of a hypothetical Brazilian company that has borrowed dollars to finance a domestic investment. Imagine that at the time the funding matures and has to be refinanced, there is a global carry crash; carry trades are being unwound, and the Brazilian currency, the real, plunges against the dollar. In these circumstances it is likely to be difficult for the Brazilian company to refinance its dollar borrowing on terms that are not punitive. This is where liquidity swaps come in. The Brazilian central bank gives access to dollar funding to a Brazilian bank to refinance the company's debt, and the central bank in turn acquires these dollars via a liquidity swap with the Fed.

Figure 12.1 shows the outstanding balance of Fed liquidity swaps in billions of dollars. A careful comparison with Figure 2.2 in Chapter 2 (for indicators of the dollar carry trade) suggests that Fed liquidity swaps are inversely correlated with the outstanding dollar-funded carry trade. When the currency carry trade contracts, the Fed increases its provision of liquidity swaps, and when the carry trade is growing, the Fed reduces liquidity swaps.

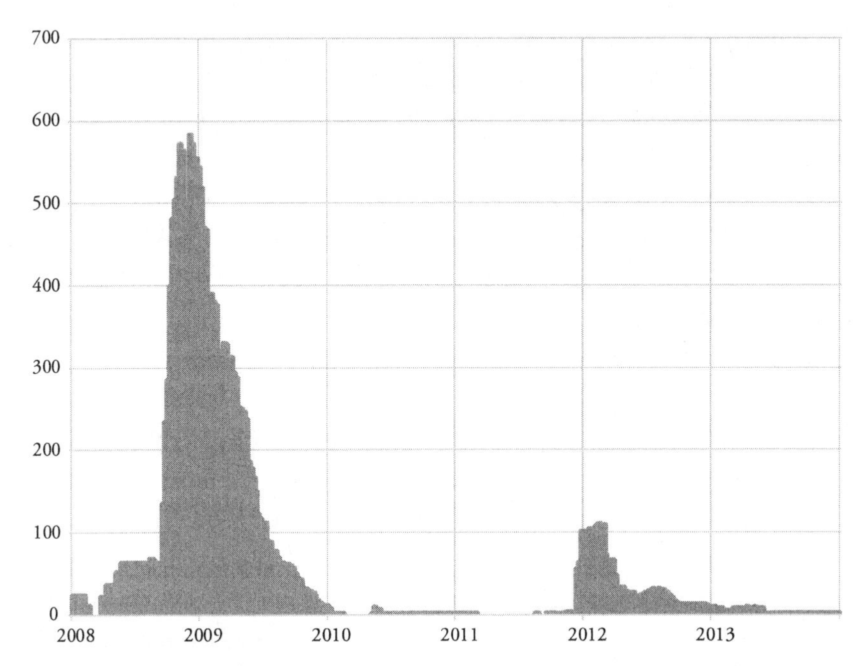

FIGURE 12.1 Federal Reserve liquidity swaps outstanding, 2008–2013 (US$ billion)
Source of data: Federal Reserve Board

This is because when the carry trade contracts sharply, as it did before and after the Lehman bankruptcy in 2008, dollar borrowers are unable to roll over financing. Once this process starts, it can be very difficult to stop, even for countries with ample dollar foreign exchange reserves. For example, in October 2008 Korea's currency fell sharply against the dollar, and its stock market plummeted by over 30 percent. This happened even though the country had built up the world's sixth largest holding of foreign exchange reserves—about US$250 billion—and had strong macroeconomic fundamentals. Despite this it was only when the Fed swap line was in place that the Bank of Korea was able to stabilize its currency.[1] Why would a US$30 billion swap line from the Fed stabilize the market when the Bank of Korea had already spent US$60 billion of its own dollar reserves in vain? The reason is that the Fed ultimately has unlimited amounts of dollar liquidity at its

1. J. Aizenman, Y. Jinjarak, and D. Park, "International Reserves and Swap Lines: Substitutes or Complements?," National Bureau of Economic Research, March 2010.

disposal, and the swap line was a signal that it saw stabilizing dollar markets outside the United States as part of its remit.

The Fed signaling that it saw stabilizing—that is, suppressing volatility in—global dollar funding markets to be important is critical. Indeed, the announcement of a Fed swap line alone was enough to compress credit default swap spreads in other emerging markets that received US currency swaps (Brazil, Mexico, and Singapore). In the end these countries did not need to draw meaningfully on these facilities. The signal from the Fed was enough.

The Fed was not the only central bank that felt compelled to bail out carry trade creditors. The Swiss central bank entered into swap agreements with the Hungarian central bank and the Polish central bank in October 2008. This can be seen as having been part of a wider bailout of the Eastern Europe carry trade. In the case of Hungary, the European Central Bank entered into a credit line, and there was also a fully fledged US$25 billion rescue package from the IMF, EU, and World Bank. But the Fed entered into swap arrangements with many central banks. In October 2013 the Fed announced that what had been temporary swap arrangements with a number of other central banks had been made permanent.

When central banks make these types of announcements, they are usually greeted with approval by the media and the financial industry generally. The swap agreements are clever "new tools" that the central banks have come up with that will "rein in market volatility." No one, at least no "sensible person," likes market volatility, so what could be bad about that? As noted with the Korea example, the potential contagion aspects of, for example, a squeeze in global funding markets—which may not always seem based in fundamentals—makes a particularly compelling case for central bank actions to underwrite the markets in circumstances of financial stress, via liquidity swaps or other tools.

The problem is that these bailout mechanisms remove market discipline from the lending side of the currency carry trade. Consider a country with high interest rates. If interest rates are particularly high, it must be for a reason, and that reason would usually involve a comparatively high rate of inflation. If the inflation rate is high, then, in general, property prices and other prices in the economy will tend to rise. If people are able to take out mortgages, for example, in a low interest rate currency, then that will be very tempting—particularly if it is believed that the central bank will not allow the exchange rate for the domestic currency to fall much or to fall rapidly. A property investor or speculator can then buy a property with a high rate of price appreciation while financing the purchase at a low interest rate.

A bank or other lender ought to be wary of entering into such a transaction with a mortgage borrower. The bank will have to fund the loan by borrowing the foreign currency in the interbank market or other funding markets. There might be a risk of losing access to foreign currency funding. If the low interest rate foreign currency does appreciate sharply in the foreign exchange markets, then the property buyer may be unable to service the mortgage and may fall into negative equity.

What would happen if this latter eventuality did come to pass? Ordinarily, if the bank had made many such mortgage loans, its solvency might be threatened. It may find it difficult to roll over its foreign currency funding. Banks or institutions in the home country of the foreign currency, which would be the natural providers of the funding, may well be reluctant to extend credit if they fear a widespread insolvency problem. But if central banks have arranged a network of foreign exchange swaps, then that problem is eliminated. The bank simply refinances its foreign currency borrowing by borrowing from its own central bank, which in turn borrows from the foreign central bank.

This then makes easier an "extend and pretend" situation. Rather than foreclose on the mortgage borrower, the bank can just let things be and hope that the situation resolves itself—without writing off any of the loan. If, as indeed happened following the financial crisis, the currency carry trade builds up again—more borrowers are tempted to borrow the low interest rate foreign currency—then the domestic currency exchange rate might recover, reducing or eliminating the insolvency problem, at least for a period. There is a clear "Ponzi" aspect to this; as long as more "participants" can be encouraged into this carry trade, then everyone can seem to be a winner again, at least for somewhat longer.

So market discipline is severely weakened. The risk of bankruptcy is reduced, from the point of view of both the borrower and the lender. Any market constraint on the growth of the carry trade is left mostly to operate on the borrower (would-be carry trader) side—the risk that the borrower faces that currencies will move unexpectedly against her. However, this risk is perceived to be limited if central banks are believed to be very interventionist—as they have been. The "margin call" risk is sharply reduced by the willingness of the global network of central banks to provide liquidity in any currency.

Very few financial market commentators question the direct involvement of central banks in funding for foreign currency borrowing or the cooperation between central banks globally; it all seems very reasonable if it reduces market stresses and prevents crisis. Except that it is not. Free market economies work to produce rising living standards over time through a process in which the millions of people who make up an economy make decisions on working, spending, and saving (and investing), guided by prices and their assessment of risk and potential return. Certainly, the rise in living standards that this process produces over time does not usually occur in a straight line; it can be three steps forward and two steps back at times. But eliminating the discipline of the markets is likely to result in cumulative misallocation of resources and ultimately poorer living standards over the very long run.

In the specific case mentioned, of mortgage borrowers in a high interest rate country taking out low interest rate foreign currency mortgages, the distorted assessment of risk involved in this decision will mean that the cost of mortgage credit appears cheaper than it really is. There will therefore be too much mortgage credit extended, and real estate prices will consequently rise more than genuinely justified. So there will be a real estate bubble; too much property will likely be built, ultimately leading to a waste of resources, the true cost of which is revealed when the property market finally crashes.

Because carry trades create imbalances such as this, in the end the carry crash must still occur. Central bank and government interference in markets has the effect of greatly prolonging the carry bubble, leading to a cumulatively larger waste of resources. Over time this will seriously destroy growth.

The Insidious Structural Aspects of Carry

As the global carry regime has advanced, the centrality of the US economy and its financial markets has become ever more obvious. The dollar, the world's reserve currency, has become the dominant funding currency for the global currency carry trade, its role entrenched further by the willingness of the US Federal Reserve to provide backstop funding through liquidity swaps with other central banks. The S&P 500 has become central to the overall volatility-selling trade in financial markets and by extension has come to stand at the center of the global carry regime. This combination has effectively seen the Fed slipping into the role of being the world's central bank. The almost magical way in which carry seems to transform risky nonmonetary financial instruments into "near money" is then transmitted from the United States to the rest of the world. Wealth appears to increase dramatically, not merely in the United States, but across the world, along with ever-larger carry trade capital flows.

At the same time, the carry regime outside the United States is inevitably more fragile. Carry crashes in specific emerging economies or in other vulnerable countries can occur more readily than in the United States. The carry regime creates economic imbalances, and emerging economies, for example, do not have the luxury that the United States has, of being able to create the world's reserve and major funding currency. The vulnerabilities and imbalances include imbalances between income and spending, changes in the financial structure of economies, and even changes in the employment structure and the skill sets of populations. Some of these issues have been touched on in this book, such as the rise of private equity and hedge funds and their role (Chapter 5), the imbalances created by currency carry trades (Chapters 2 and 3), and even the changes in the nature of money itself (Chapter 7). But the consequences of the growth of carry can go beyond even these, to something much deeper and more philosophical: an adaptation of the intellectual context to the rise of carry.

On Wall Street a whole generation of investors and professionals, and possibly more than one generation, has "grown up"—learned their trade and their trading—in the carry regime. They have no real understanding of anything different. The carry regime is not some abstract idea; it becomes the way that people think. Interventionist central bank and government policies have been crucial to the development of the carry regime; they seem to "work" in the carry regime. So interventionism then becomes mainstream thinking in economics. It has become conventional wisdom, for instance, to believe that it is the job of central banks to respond to volatility in the financial markets. So the longer the carry regime lasts, the more that the intellectual—and policy—climate adapts to accommodate it.

Economics is crucially about expectations and how they are formed. In the example of Turkey, used earlier in the book, the country's high inflation rate, high interest rates, uncompetitive currency, and large current account deficit financed substantially by capital inflows into short-term debt should have discouraged investors from investing in Turkish domestic currency debt. They should have expected that the overvalued currency would fall substantially and that currency decline would outweigh any yield premium from the Turkish debt. Because of this thinking, in theory the current account deficit would not be readily financed until depreciation of the Turkish currency had reached a point that would entice investors back into purchasing debt instruments (or other Turkish assets). That point would occur when the currency is cheap enough, and therefore the country is competitive enough, to allow the current account deficit to narrow along a path consistent with outstanding debt growing in a more sustainable way.

In a carry regime, however, individuals' expectations are formed in conjunction with the expectations of others and are highly influenced by an understanding of the likely actions of the authorities. So an investor or speculator will likely look at Turkish debt and see a high interest rate, higher than on most other debt available in world markets. He will know that other investors and speculators are attracted by the high yields on offer. He will consider the credit ratings assigned by the rating agencies and consider Turkish government, central bank, and international government and agency policies. If he believes the Turkish central bank is likely to defend the currency, he will invest in the debt to pick up the extra yield. After all, he can always sell it later if the downward pressure on the currency looks to be growing too great.

In the carry regime, therefore, there is no quick return to equilibrium in the traditional sense. Imbalances in the economy, and associated debt, persist or become larger. For as long as the carry bubble goes on, capital flows to the imbalances, so everything appears all right. This ends when the carry crash hits, and liquidity evaporates. In the currency carry trade case of countries such as Turkey in the past, those countries that have large outstanding foreign currency debt will see the yields on that debt soar, and debt will be unable to be refinanced. In a country that experiences a crisis such as this, what may well happen, as discussed earlier, is that the central bank steps in to accommodate the refinancing of foreign currency debtors via liquidity swap arrangements. If the country itself is insolvent, then there may be a global rescue, led by the IMF.

In the carry crash, large investors and speculators who made these—what should, in any normal world, be highly risky—carry trades should by rights lose most or all of their money. In reality their losses usually end up limited by the various central bank, government, and IMF bailouts. When carry trades are considered as a whole—including the yield and capital gain they have already previously picked up—they likely still come out ahead. This has probably been the case for most carry trades implemented since the carry regime began. The net gains of carry traders over time, within the carry regime, to some extent come from losses that are made, or ultimately will be made and taken, by those governments and central banks (that is, taxpayers), as well as latecomers, that have insufficient resources to survive the carry crashes.

So imbalances are larger and persist for longer. The carry regime is necessarily associated with high levels of systemic leverage and related debt and an underlying tendency to deflation. Deflationary tendency, high indebtedness, and persistent imbalances inevitably mean low trend economic growth and by extension low interest rates. All these elements interact with each other and with the interventions of the authorities progressively to strengthen the carry regime. Gradually, the financial markets and the economic structure evolve to become a structure that accommodates and promotes carry. New financial instruments are developed to allow investors to profit from carry trades. Nonfinancial businesses are drawn into what are essentially carry transactions of various types to support or increase current profits.

In this world even those who recognize the dangers of the carry regime find it difficult to hedge against. Since a carry crash necessarily involves a huge spike in volatility, a natural hedge against this event would be a long volatility position. However, as we have shown in Chapter 6, an investor with a structural long volatility position would have lost virtually all her capital since 2009. Could those worried about a carry crash instead try to "tactically time" long volatility positions? In other words, can a carry crash be detected ahead of time and a hedge initiated just prior to the event?

There is some evidence that once the implied volatility curve inverts—that is, once the spot VIX starts to increase above further forward levels—short-term volatility continues to trend higher. However, the timing here has to be exquisite. A trader must shift from a neutral or short holding position to a long volatility position in a matter of days. In addition, this is not a fail-safe strategy; there is always the risk of false signals. And as with any tactical strategy, the question becomes, when should the long volatility position be closed? If the carry regime starts anew, which it has repeatedly in the last two decades, volatility can quickly fall back and the long volatility profits are wiped out. Thus, rapid tactical volatility trading may be an answer for some very sophisticated players, but it is not a realistic option for most investors.

Not only is it difficult to hedge against a carry crash; it is actually very challenging for investors to avoid becoming active participants in the carry regime itself, even if they recognize the dangers of the situation. As carry expands, asset prices rise as well, especially in markets such as the S&P 500 that are central to the carry regime. This does not go unnoticed by value investors. Valuation metrics that attempt to gauge the absolute return prospects to US equities—such as Shiller's cyclically adjusted price/earnings ratio or Tobin's q—have indicated the market to be expensive for years. Yet avoiding the S&P 500 based on these tools has been a consistently bad investment decision.[2]

The carry regime contributes to the S&P 500 looking expensive, but it also contributes to low real interest rates. Many market participants look at zero or negative real yields on bonds and conclude that equities are at least attractive in relative terms. Cash suffers from the same comparison. Real cash yields have been zero or negative for most of the decade since the 2008 crisis, making equities superficially seem attractive on a relative basis. In addition, for professional money managers whose pay and employment are a function

2. The authors have some personal experience with this.

of the money managers' performance relative to the market, holding cash is profoundly risky. Thus it becomes exceptionally difficult for them not to participate in the asset bubbles created by a carry regime. Indeed, it may be quite rational for most investors to keep buying into the bubble; it is version 2.0 of the old (and now almost quaint-sounding) Wall Street saying that "no one gets fired for buying IBM." No one gets fired for being long the S&P 500. After all, in a crash not only is there an expectation that the central bank will intervene, but also virtually all investors will be suffering as well, and so no institution is likely to be singled out as having made poor decisions.

Furthermore, if the carry regime ultimately continues, and if the carry crash is followed by a new carry bubble, those carry traders with enough resources to survive the carry crash will prosper anew, accumulating even greater wealth. The general pattern is that the carry crash will wipe out latecomers to the carry bubble— those who jumped on the bandwagon too late or those with insufficient resources to survive the carry crash. Those who are left—those with sufficient resources—will go on to take an even larger share of wealth and income in the next phase of the regime.

13
Beyond the Vanishing Point

Turning Junk into Gold

THE CARRY REGIME DESCRIBES THE WAY THE FINANCIAL markets and economy work, a way that is different from the understanding of more conventional thinking in economics and finance. It is because of the carry regime that economists using standard models have not been able to explain satisfactorily economic developments and financial market phenomena that have occurred over the past 20 years, including most notably the global financial crisis of 2007–2009.

We have argued in this book that carry is a naturally occurring phenomenon, but we have suggested that it has been turbocharged by the regime of fiat money and central bank policies. It is quite obvious, as we hope we have convincingly demonstrated, that financial markets and the financial system as a whole have been operating in a powerful carry regime at least since the early 1990s. Certain statistical analyses, including the data for the currency carry trade presented in Chapter 4, suggest that this clearly defined carry regime may have had its origins in 1987, immediately after the historic stock market crash of that year. That would tend to pin the blame on central banks, the Federal Reserve in particular. A defining moment was the Federal Reserve's explicit statement of support for financial markets and the financial system immediately following the stock market crash. The apparent efficacy of the Fed's actions in 1987 arguably could have laid the foundation for the carry regime to develop subsequently.

Monetary policy has become ever more a source of moral hazard, the tool for the further extension of the carry regime, rather than being about setting interest rates at a level consistent with long-run monetary stability. Very few observers of or participants in financial markets have understood this properly. In 2015, with the Fed having kept the funds rate at close to zero for more than six years, financial commentary and debate was obsessed with the timing of an expected Fed rate increase. Many market participants questioned why interest rates were still at zero given that the financial crisis was long since over—in their opinion. On the other side of the debate, others argued that the US inflation rate was still low and labor force participation levels still weak, so there was no rush to raise interest rates. This type of discussion continues to be couched in the context of a traditional monetary framework; higher short-term interest rates would slow credit demand (and money supply growth), except to the extent that the economy was picking up, and would put downward pressure on inflation unless the economy was strong enough. So in 2015 the question in economists' minds revolved around whether economic growth was strong and sustainable enough to merit an interest rate increase.

In reality, in the very extended carry bubble that already existed in 2015, these types of debates were rather similar to apocryphal medieval debates about the number of angels that can sit on the head of a pin. Both the financial markets and the economy had become a function of carry rather than interest rates per se. Short-term interest rates were only important to the extent that they sent a signal about the central bank's willingness to support financial markets. If an interest rate increase appears to be part of a process in which the central bank is withdrawing its support for financial markets, and by extension the carry regime, then it is possible that an interest rate increase could trigger a carry crash; the carry crash means the evaporation of liquidity and economic collapse. In this paradigm, whether the economy is strong enough to merit an interest rate increase therefore is a question that misses the point. The right question to ask is whether an interest rate increase could provoke a carry crash. Quantitative easing was even more important in this respect; QE was a giant carry trade in itself.

Furthermore, the carry regime means that underlying economic growth is diminishing. When much of the economy's resources become devoted to an activity (carry) that is, in the extreme, similar to a form of rent-seeking, it must be that the underlying or trend economic growth rate is declining, whatever GDP data show in the short term.

Most people cannot understand this because the carry regime creates the sense that central banks are all powerful even as, in a fundamental sense, they are becoming weak. Huge attention is paid to every utterance of a central banker. How could the central bank's main policy interest rate not be that important? It must be incredibly important, at least in the eyes of financial market participants.

The carry regime suppresses volatility and drives up the market values of financial assets and at least some real assets (such as real estate). Nonmonetary financial assets seem to acquire monetary qualities. Debt that was formerly considered junk appears to be safer; the application of structured finance seems magically to turn doubtful credits or credit derivatives into triple A–rated securities. Financial products such as ETFs appear to offer investors the best of all worlds: access to exotic assets such as frontier market equities and local currency emerging market bonds alongside the ability to trade them daily. The central bankers appear almost as the fabled King Midas, who was granted his wish for everything he touched to be turned to gold. Only, of course, in one version of the fable he touches his beloved daughter and tragically realizes the error of his ways. We might wish that policy makers may experience the same kind of epiphany—only, then, we too must be careful what we wish for.

What Lies Beyond the Vanishing Point?

If there is no will to change, where will this end? In Chapter 7 we discussed the concept of the carry regime progressing to a vanishing point. At that point the carry regime has resulted in GDP being borrowed from the future to such an extent that trend economic growth is zero, real interest rates are zero, and nominal interest rates are zero or possibly even negative. The big questions—particularly for investors—are these: (1) Is it possible that the carry regime can end before that point? (2) How can we tell the difference between the complete end of the carry regime and merely a carry crash that will be followed by a new bubble? And (3) what will follow the carry regime if it does end?

These are big questions and impossible to answer definitively. The second question highlights the need to distinguish between the actual end of the carry regime and what is merely a severe carry crash, such as the financial crisis of 2008. The 2008 global financial crisis might have felt like the end of the world at the time, but ultimately asset price recovery was quick, and equity prices marched on to new all-time highs. In the end, 2008 led to the further strengthening of the carry regime.

Of the various features of the carry regime that have been discussed in this book, possibly the two most important in this context—the most important for investors to understand and consider—are that the carry regime is associated with underlying pressure toward deflation and that the carry regime (in its financial expression) significantly owes its existence to central banks and the way that they have managed the modern fiat money system. These features, which are crucial, suggest that the absolute end of the carry regime is likely to be marked by either systemic collapse that ends the dominant role of central banks or galloping inflation—or both. If a crash results in neither of these two things happening, then the likelihood is that the carry regime continues and there will be a new carry bubble.

In Chapter 10 we discussed the abstract possibility of an anti-carry regime, which would be the mirror image of the carry regime, featuring high inflation, with inflation spiraling out of control during anti-carry crashes. But we also noted that such a mirror carry regime would not really be a true opposite. In some fundamental senses—an associated trend to rising inequality, concentration of political and economic power, etc.—the anti-carry regime would be very similar to the carry regime. In such an anti-carry regime, there would still be fiat money, and presumably there would still be central banks, or at least some arm of government with monopoly power over the creation of money.

Spiraling inflation, however, could lead to the further development of alternative monies, which would ultimately replace fiat money. The emergence of cryptocurrencies has been an early sign that the fundamental, long-run monetary instability that lies behind the financial carry regime is already undermining trust in fiat money. Classically, the three functions that money fulfills are as a medium of exchange, a store of value, and a unit of account, the store of value being the crucial attribute in this respect. But these functions are related to each other; if money's utility as a store of value becomes critically undermined, it is then likely to become less viable as a medium of exchange. That is traditionally what has been experienced in hyperinflations, which is when other, competing, forms of money are most likely to appear. In hyperinflations historically these have famously been things such as cigarettes.

To be a sustainable form of money, the case is usually made that it must have certain physical and other attributes; some make the case that gold is the only substance that has these attributes. But we would suggest that these physical properties—things such as durability and divisibility—are not the critical aspects of money. We would argue that viable money in a modern economy should have at least one of two attributes: the monetary base must correspond to a claim on the asset base of the economy and therefore be linked to the economy's cumulative savings; or alternatively it must have a significant cost of production.

These points are debatable, and have been debated by economists. But if the monetary base does not correspond to a claim on the economy's real asset base—for example, hypothetically, if a central bank creates high-powered money (such as cash currency) but holds no assets of any worth—then money and wealth (meaning "genuine wealth") would become completely detached from each other. The claim that this should not be allowed to happen is rooted in the idea that there is no such thing as a free lunch, but it could be said to be also tied up with the notion that money is, at core, based on trust. Existing cryptocurrencies do not have the property of being linked to the economy's asset base in any way. The provenance of a holding of cryptocurrencies is instead achieved through the distributed ledger rather than as a financial claim. But cryptocurrencies do have a significant cost of production, meaning that the contention that they will develop into an alternative or even a superior form of money cannot be dismissed out of hand.

The ultimate solution to the problem of money could be technology that allows the use of assets—whether shares, bonds, property, or otherwise — directly as a medium of exchange. That is, the "currency" would be secured on the currency holder's assets, and a transfer of currency would be a transfer of a claim on some proportion of those assets. This would address the requirement that viable money should correspond to a claim on the real economy. It would eliminate the possibility of bank runs, in exchange for each currency holder accepting a small amount of day-to-day variability in purchasing power depending on the performance of the particular assets that the currency holder owns. With modern, liquid, electronic financial markets, such a solution may now be technologically possible. It could be implemented through a distributed ledger like cryptocurrencies, or through competing centralized private "banks" (which would be something between mutual funds and banks as understood today), or even through a service provided by a government monopoly.

At the moment such a solution seems unlikely to be widely accepted, as both the status quo and revealed preferences of the public seem to favor taking the risk of runs and crises over accepting floating purchasing power in normal conditions. But an extremely inflationary anti-carry regime, should it appear, could conceivably change opinions.

Developments such as these could eventually take us out of a carry regime, or even anti-carry regime, into a sort of nirvana in which money, and the control over money, is no longer a dominant force in societies. As implied here, such a development would most likely come about as part of a two-stage process: the carry regime destroyed first by inflation and then the inflationary anti-carry regime destroyed by the emergence of competing alternative monies.

However, it is not a certainty that the end of the carry regime accords to this pattern. It is possible to imagine a deflationary implosion of the carry bubble, somewhat similar to what already nearly occurred in 2008, from which central banks are unable to engineer a recovery. In terms of the vanishing point, this would basically entail convergence going much further than the vanishing point, with equilibrium interest rates falling far below zero. This, of course, is what some economists and observers have all along feared: interest rates below the lower bound. Given that, at the time of this writing, a fairly large total value of financial assets trade at negative yields to maturity, and several important economies have lived with negative short-term rates, this idea is not at all far-fetched.

An uncontrolled deflationary collapse at this stage of the carry regime would certainly end the regime and upend the current social, political, and economic order. The problem, as is obvious, is that what could follow could be much worse. Therefore, it would be more likely that central banks and governments together would implement extreme measures that would be outside the bounds of current law but would be deemed imperative to "save the world."

In this case one extreme measure would likely be direct monetization of government spending: sending checks to every family or individual—possibly in the form of "tax refunds" that are "paid for" by the direct printing of money. If implemented on a large enough scale, this would be sure to be highly inflationary and potentially ultimately hyperinflationary, causing loss of confidence in money.

However, if the extraordinary measures of dubious legality only involve the central bank balance sheet in a direct way (not the government balance sheet), then it may be more likely that the carry regime gets a new lease on life. For example, say, in the case of the United States, that the Federal Reserve begins to buy equities on a large scale, with the express purpose of supporting the equity market at some level. In theory this ought to be inflationary—in normal times—and it could be if it translates directly into equivalent expansion of the Fed balance sheet. But if the equity purchases are financed at least partly by Fed sales of Treasury bonds, then this would be presented as "extending along the risk curve." In this case the Fed would be very directly selling equity volatility. If this approach were to prove successful, it would likely mean an extension of the carry regime in the form of a new carry bubble.

Therefore, it has to be considered most likely that the carry regime will be ended finally by high inflation, which could come about via several possible routes. From a macro perspective, therefore, an important sign that the carry regime is ending would be the emergence of inflation itself, or it might be measures taken by the authorities that are so extreme that very high inflation becomes an inevitability.

What Are the Signs from the Volatility Perspective of the Carry Regime Ending?

It seems likely that we are still some way away from the end of the current carry regime, and when it ends, there will be considerable confusion for some time before the market settles into a new steady state.

From a volatility perspective (as explained in Chapters 9 and 10), it seems inevitable that an inflationary anti-carry regime must be associated with the direction of the volatility premium changing from short to long; it will become profitable to buy, rather than sell, volatility. There will be three major visible parts to this transition. First, implied volatility forward curves will settle into consistent backwardation. Second, prices will begin to behave with momentum over all time horizons: realized volatility measured weekly or monthly will consistently be above daily volatility. Third, skew will reverse, and calls will become more expensive than puts for risky assets. And ultimately, market participants will eventually come to believe that these conditions are normal.

It is unlikely that all three of these will occur simultaneously or even that they will occur in a predictable, irreversible manner. It is more likely that they will occur gradually as part of a process that will involve severe market dislocations, as the perception that these are now normal conditions will take a long time to emerge. In short, the transition into an inflationary anti-carry regime is unlikely to be smooth and may be traumatic. The most frightening and most final transition in the structure of volatility would be the inversion of the volatility-of-volatility curve—so that the volatility of long-dated volatility would become greater than the volatility of short-dated volatility. If this last were to occur, it would signify that money is dying.

From a currency carry perspective, the circumstances that would make currency carry trades unprofitable and appear dangerous would be extreme volatility in the carry recipient currencies (the currencies with the higher interest rates) or the major funding currencies. Potential exchange rate volatility would be so great as to make the yield pickup from borrowing in a low interest rate currency to lend in a high-rate currency seem an unattractive proposition. In turn this would occur if central banks were not expected to, or more likely were unable to, intervene to stabilize currencies. This would also be more likely in an environment of high and volatile inflation in which the demand to hold money would be unstable. Central banks in the carry recipient countries would be more protective of their foreign reserves and therefore would be unable to conduct large-scale foreign exchange intervention to defend their currencies. The Fed, possibly under political pressure not to bail out foreign countries, would be unable to provide assistance via liquidity swaps. We perhaps saw a glimmer of this world in 2008 when Korea tried unsuccessfully to stabilize its currency but only succeeded after Fed intervention.

In Chapter 10 it was suggested that an anti-carry regime could exist if the fall in the demand to hold money that is a consequence of inflation is satisfied, at least in part, by the loss of moneyness of other financial assets. For example, to put it in practical terms, people may hold various types of money funds, exchange-traded funds, or other financial instruments that they have come to regard as being as good as money. With the advent of high and unstable inflation, they need to reduce their holdings of "money." But in the first instance, they may seek to reduce these holdings of "near money," which, in this much more unstable economic environment, they may now view as being even less safe than "true money." This loss of confidence in near money could act as a stabilizing force, which means that true money continues to attract some demand for as long as inflation is not completely out of control—thereby preventing a total collapse in the demand to hold true money and consequent hyperinflation.

From all this it could be concluded that the total end of a carry or an anti-carry regime could only occur when there was so much monetary instability that neither increasing nor decreasing moneyness would act as a stabilizing force. This would be a state of affairs in which central banks had lost all control and price levels in the economy had become basically indeterminate. Again, in this state, other new forms of money would have already begun to emerge. If these new forms of money were to gain an increasing foothold and become the de facto monies of the economy, then inversion of the volatility-of-volatility curve could become apparent, at least for options contracts denominated in the old fiat money. But it is more likely that, by that point, financial markets would already have been re-standardized around contracts denominated in the new monies.

With all this discussion, the difficulty is knowing which has to come first: loss of central bank policy efficacy, high financial volatility, or inflation itself. Once there is one, then it could lead to the others, creating a vicious circle of interaction between inflation and monetary conditions. A sensible view would be to believe that the gradual emergence of higher inflation and greater financial volatility would probably occur together in this case. A necessary but not sufficient condition for a market crash to be the beginning of the complete end of the regime, rather than merely a carry crash to be followed by another carry bubble, would be inflation becoming entrenched. If this does not happen—and it did not happen over 2007–2009—then the market crash is more likely to be another in the sequence of carry crashes and carry bubbles. If, on the other hand, stubborn inflation emerges, it is more likely to be a precursor to the end of the carry regime entirely. Once high inflation is entrenched, central banks have lost policy flexibility, and ultimately new monies, not reliant on central banks, will be likely to appear.

A further factor to consider is that central bank balance sheets are themselves a giant carry trade. Central banks' balance sheets have a very low funding cost, negative to some extent for the European Central Bank and the Bank of Japan over the years following the financial crisis. But under quantitative easing policies, central banks have been huge acquirers of bonds, including government bonds, mortgage-backed securities, and corporate bonds (depending on the central bank). The interest rate spread that central banks earn is therefore potentially quite large, producing large profits (generally transferred to the government). However, as with any other carry trade, nothing comes for free, and a central bank carry trade is also subject to the risk of capital loss. Specifically, the risk is that the yields on the bonds that the central bank has acquired will spiral higher, reducing their value. This would be particularly likely in an environment of stagflation, when the economy is weak but inflation is high and rising. Even if the central bank holds all its bonds to maturity, high inflation will severely erode their real value, while the central bank's funding cost is likely to rise somewhat in the end if inflation is very high.

Central banks, uniquely, have control over their own funding costs, and it might seem unlikely that they would allow their own carry—the spread between the yields of the assets they hold and their funding cost that they set—to go negative. If an inflationary spiral were to inflict capital losses on them, they could counteract those capital losses by doubling down on their carry trades—buying more, now higher-yielding, bonds—as long as they kept the yield curve positively sloped, that is, kept their policy rate below the rising yields on long bonds. But it seems likely that, in such a spiral, keeping the yield curve positively sloped would exacerbate instead of arrest the spiral. Ultimately, they would then have to choose between restraining the inflation and maintaining their own solvency.

The collapse of the central bank carry trade, which could also include carry trades associated with central bank liquidity swaps, could then render central banks insolvent. In fact this has to be viewed as quite likely. We have implied that the profitability of the central bank carry trade is part of the reason for the existence of the carry regime. If the carry regime blows up, the implication must be that the huge central bank carry trade becomes severely loss making. If we take the view, propounded earlier, that viable money, or at least a viable monetary base, has to be rooted ultimately in a claim on the economy's real assets, then an insolvent central bank could mean worthless money.

To conclude, all this points to the idea that monetary inflation is the single most important element to consider when thinking about the end of the carry regime. As long as inflation remains under control, the central bank carry trade remains intact and the central bank has policy flexibility. Once inflation is no longer under control, then not only does financial volatility increase, but the solvency of the central bank itself may be undermined. The present monetary and financial system would begin to collapse as new monies would emerge. It goes without saying that this would be occurring in an atmosphere of crisis and extreme political instability.

History Tells Us to Expect Change

This notion that the carry regime's end will also be associated with the end of our current monetary system might, at first reading, seem extreme. Yet monetary systems in democracies are ultimately created by political decisions, which in turn reflect, albeit imperfectly, society's priorities with respect to economic outcomes. The Federal Reserve was created in the years following the Panic of 1907 in an effort to bring stability to a domestic banking system that was beset with recurring financial panics and bank runs. The international monetary system—the use of gold as a single global currency—was also changed around the same time by political choices made in response to the economic necessities of World War I. Neither the domestic banking system nor the gold standard worked for society, and so they were themselves changed.

This process of change was neither discrete, nor uncontroversial, nor even initially successful. The Federal Reserve System did not end bank runs; that required more political decisions, specifically the establishment of deposit insurance and effective bank supervision in 1933. The international system continued to adjust as well, first with failed attempts to return to gold, followed by the managed dollar-centric system of Bretton Woods, and followed eventually by the mostly open system of global capital flows we have today. Change in monetary arrangements, therefore, is not unprecedented, and the political nature of the process means that the resulting system ends up being a somewhat lagged reflection of society's key economic concerns.

In the last two decades, those concerns have been low inflation, financial market stability, and as much growth as possible without sacrificing the first two goals. Our monetary system has been altered in an attempt to meet those objectives; central banks have been freed from direct government control, and most now have specific inflation targets. The system has also evolved organically in response to changes in the financial markets they attempt to manage. For example, quantitative easing would once have been heretical, but now it is widespread and accepted. Taking this perspective, we can expect the current monetary system to change if it fails to meet its implied objectives of achieving low inflation, market stability, and growth—or if another objective, such as ameliorating wealth inequality, becomes paramount. Change can also be forced on the system, as it must react to changes in markets themselves, such as the emergence of the carry regime.

The emergence of the carry regime presents a specific existential challenge to the current system because it engenders both instability, in the form of carry crashes, and growing inequality. We have explained in this book how the two are inextricably linked: interventions to stabilize markets after a carry crash support the emergence of a new carry bubble and reinforce existing wealth imbalances. This places the Fed in an unenviable and, in our view, ultimately unwinnable bind. The Fed was born out of a desire to stop financial panics from infecting the real economy, so it must act in the wake of a carry crash. Yet those actions increasingly are seen as putting it on the side of the elite and as reinforcing unfair economic outcomes.

Thomas Piketty's 2014 book, *Capital in the Twenty-First Century*, is often described as a "surprise" bestseller. The term "surprise" is revealing on several dimensions. First, there was the surprise generated by his data showing that capitalism naturally gravitates toward very unequal wealth distributions over time. A more balanced distribution, which had been thought to be normal especially in the United States, was actually an exception due to the effects of World War II's massive capital destruction.

A second surprise was how deeply and broadly his work resonated. Clearly, the outcomes and processes Piketty described were of great concern to a wide range of people. Ameliorating wealth and income inequality is now discussed as an important political objective, appearing in various guises across the platforms of Democratic presidential candidates. We expect this trend to accelerate and intensify in the coming years. When it is seen in this light—inequality intensifying as a political concern, while the carry regime and the current monetary system reinforce it—history tells us that we must expect change.

The Opportunity to Lean Against Carry Was Lost

We have stressed in this book that carry is a naturally occurring phenomenon and is not in itself wholly bad. The return that carry traders earn is, at least in part, compensation for providing liquidity to markets and for assuming risk. This is a natural part of capitalism. But the management of the monetary system over the last few decades has helped carry returns become supernormal returns—to the detriment of the real economy and society broadly. Central banks must lean against this tendency, not encourage it as they unfortunately have done.

Realistically, 2007–2009 was the last opportunity for the authorities to lean against carry by allowing carry traders to suffer catastrophic losses, thereby helping to unwind some of the economically damaging structural effects of carry that we have discussed in this book. That opportunity was lost, and the carry regime has been strengthened further. The consequences for the United States and other countries—financial corporatism, growing inequality, an economy that no longer benefits a large proportion of the population, voters voting for nationalist or populist parties or movements—are becoming evident.

The result is that the next 20 years are guaranteed to be tumultuous. The financial markets stand at the epicenter of developments and will provide important clues to broader trends. These clues include the behavior of financial market volatility and the presence or otherwise of inflationary pressures in the economy. Forewarnings of inflation may be apparent in central bank or other government responses to crisis.

Ultimately, the verdict of history will likely be that the post–Bretton Woods experiment with fiat money failed. But technologies that have emerged could potentially provide the basis for future, workable monetary systems. Whatever it is that eventually arises from the ashes of the present monetary system, we have to hope it will be more effective in restraining the rise of carry.

Index

Page numbers followed by *f* indicate figures; *t* indicate tables.

About the Authors

Tim Lee is the founder of the independent economics consultancy pi Economics, serving financial institutions from hedge funds to traditional asset managers. Prior to setting up pi Economics in Greenwich, Connecticut, in 2003, he worked in London as a European economist and global economic strategist for asset management companies including GT Management and Invesco. Before London, he spent nine years in Hong Kong as an Asian economist for GT Management.

He is the author of the highly regarded *Economics for Professional Investors* (2nd edition, 1998) along with many articles in newspapers and journals. His commentaries and analyses have been widely quoted.

Tim was educated at Magdalene College, Cambridge University.

Jamie Lee works for renowned investment guru and philanthropist Jeremy Grantham, focusing on environmental research and volatility trading. He also specializes in quantitative modeling of financial markets. He previously worked as a macro analyst for asset management companies GMO in Boston and Ruffer Asset Management in London.

Jamie holds BA degrees in mathematics and in English from Dartmouth College, New Hampshire.

Kevin Coldiron is a lecturer in the Masters in Financial Engineering Program at the Haas School of Business, University of California, Berkeley.

From 2002 to 2014 he was the co-chief investment officer at San Francisco–based hedge fund Algert Coldiron Investors, which he cofounded. Prior to this he was managing director at Barclays Global Investors in London where he worked for eight years. At BGI he held positions as head of hedge fund strategies and head of European research. He began his career as a researcher for the Federal Reserve Bank of New York.

Kevin holds a BSc in finance from the Pennsylvania State University and an MBA from London Business School.